IMAGES
of America

ARROW ROCK

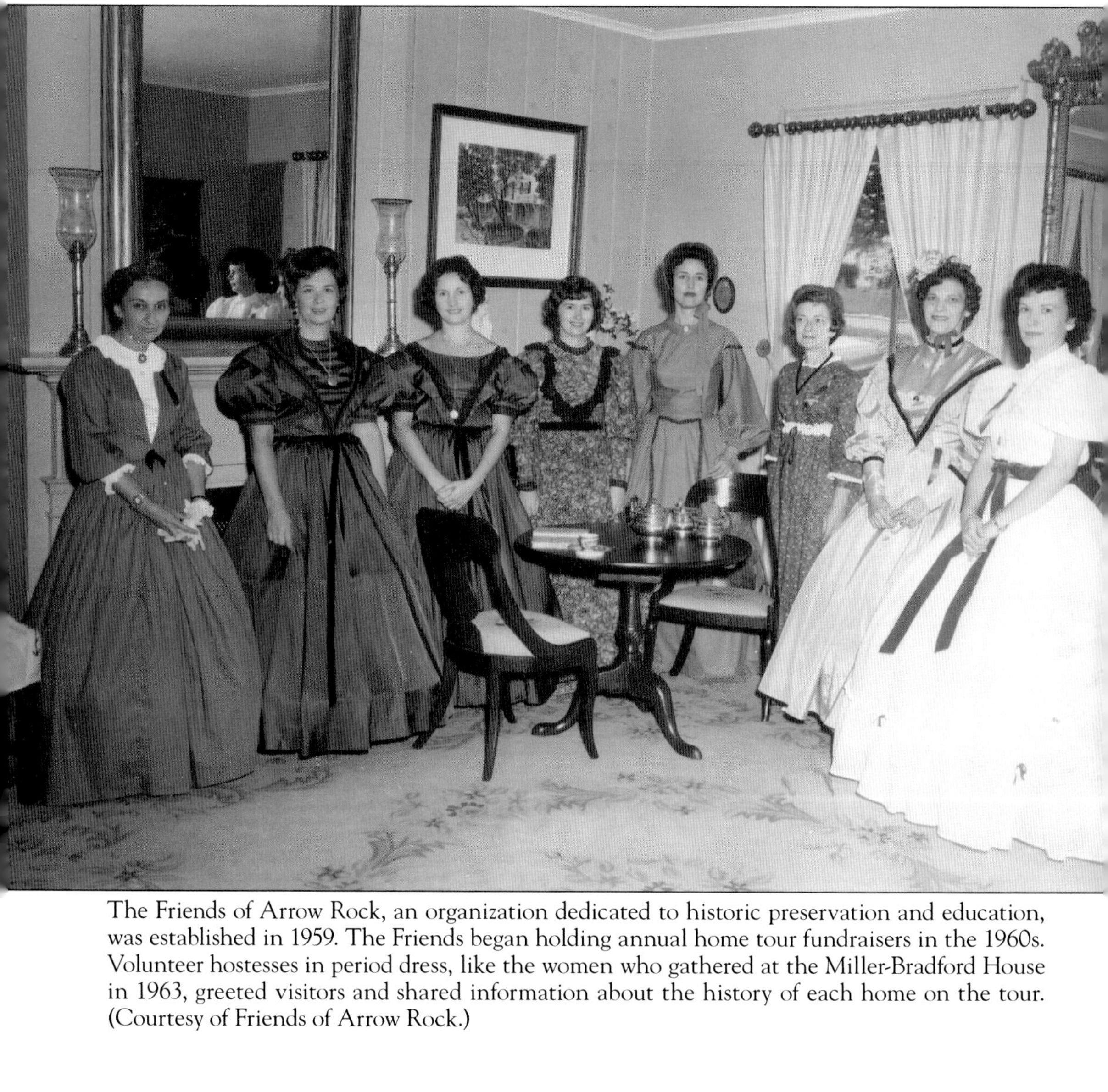

The Friends of Arrow Rock, an organization dedicated to historic preservation and education, was established in 1959. The Friends began holding annual home tour fundraisers in the 1960s. Volunteer hostesses in period dress, like the women who gathered at the Miller-Bradford House in 1963, greeted visitors and shared information about the history of each home on the tour. (Courtesy of Friends of Arrow Rock.)

On the Cover: The Daughters of the American Revolution, who were entrusted by the State of Missouri with maintenance and management of the Arrow Rock Tavern, celebrated the Tavern's centennial with a weekend of festivities in 1930. A Main Street parade, featuring floats that traced the town's history, was led by a woman who offered a stylish homage to Arrow Rock's early fur traders. (Courtesy of Arrow Rock Chapter, DAR.)

IMAGES
of America

ARROW ROCK

Sandy Selby
Foreword by Thomas B. Hall III

ARCADIA
PUBLISHING

ISBN 978-0-7385-9154-4

Published by Arcadia Publishing
Charleston, South Carolina

Printed in the United States of America

Library of Congress Control Number: 2011940527

For all general information, please contact Arcadia Publishing:
Telephone 843-853-2070
Fax 843-853-0044
E-mail sales@arcadiapublishing.com
For customer service and orders:
Toll-Free 1-888-313-2665

Visit us on the Internet at www.arcadiapublishing.com

To the people of Arrow Rock who have invested in the town's future by preserving its stories, artifacts, and architectural treasures

Contents

FOREWORD

Founded in 1829, the Missouri River town of Arrow Rock has been called "the most historic spot in Missouri." Its current population is only 56, but more than 100,000 people visit our town each year to enjoy its history, scenic beauty, and a wide variety of attractions. Antique shops, educational programs, art and craft festivals, museums, outdoor camping, history tours, the professional Lyceum Theatre, good places to eat and to spend the night, and many special events keep our town lively and interesting. There are also times for peaceful relaxation, away from the anxieties of modern life. Visitors to Arrow Rock often say they feel as if they have "stepped back in time" or that they are "living in the past."

Arrow Rock's often dramatic and remarkably significant 19th-century history has been well documented, most completely in Michael Dickey's 2004 book, *Arrow Rock: Crossroads of the Missouri Frontier.* The history of our town and its neighborhood is crowded with colorful characters; the Osage and Missouria Indian tribes, French fur trappers and traders, Lewis and Clark, Daniel Boone, Kit Carson, intrepid pioneers, travelers on the Santa Fe Trail, wealthy plantation owners, three Missouri governors, famed artist George Caleb Bingham, John "Quinine Doctor" Sappington, steamboat captains, canny merchants, leading jurists, red-hot rebels, staunch Unionists, Confederate bushwhackers, and ill-fated lovers all were here.

After the Civil War, history passed by Arrow Rock, and the town entered a period of suspended animation. Having gone into the war on what turned out to be the losing side and with no money to attract a railroad or build a bridge across the Missouri River, Arrow Rock entered a long slumber, a period of genteel poverty and gradual decline. By the beginning of the 20th century, some called it a ghost town. However, starting 100 years ago in 1912 with the formation of the Arrow Rock chapter of the National Old Trails Road Association, there began a remarkable period of historic preservation, restoration, and promotion of heritage tourism. This was largely the work of Arrow Rock's own citizens, who, mindful of its history, were determined not to allow our town to die. Photography is the perfect medium to record that recovery; hence, this book was created. We hope that it will inspire you to visit our much-loved little town.

—Thomas B. Hall III, MD
President, Friends of Arrow Rock

ACKNOWLEDGMENTS

Arrow Rock is known for its sense of history, but it is the sense of community that binds its citizens together. That community rallied in support of this book, which would not have been complete without the generosity of friends and neighbors who shared their precious family photographs. Heartfelt thanks go to Anna Mae Hodge, Elaine Breshears, Mary Duncan, Tempe McGlaughlin, Joyce Vinson, Thomas B. Hall III, Mary Kathryn Feuers, Missy Backer, and Mary Burge.

I am especially thankful to the Arrow Rock Chapter of the Daughters of the American Revolution, who entrusted me with their priceless scrapbooks, and to Arrow Rock Lyceum Theatre artistic director Quin Gresham for taking time to hunt for photographs during a busy week of performances.

The majority of photographs for this book were obtained from the archives of the Friends of Arrow Rock and the Arrow Rock State Historic Site. I am indebted to those organizations and their knowledgeable staff members.

Friends of Arrow Rock executive director Kathy Borgman met a barrage of questions with an endless supply of patience, and education director Pam Parsons checked facts and excised unnecessary commas in the manuscript. These women are a gift to the Arrow Rock community, and I am grateful for their assistance.

No one knows more about this town than Arrow Rock State Historic Site administrator Michael Dickey. He literally wrote the book on the subject and was beyond generous in his assistance with this project, especially in his meticulous review of the manuscript. Thanks, Mike. Let me know when you need a dog sitter.

I offer my love and appreciation to my husband, Marty Selby, who ably assisted with image selection, dish washing, and cheerleading, and who endured weeks of pizza and frozen dinners.

And finally, thanks to everyone who has ever labeled the back of a photograph. You are my heroes and will be regarded fondly by historians for generations to come.

Introduction

Native Americans found it first. They did not give the place a name or make a town out of it, but they used the flint rock they found on the river bluff to make their arrows. In 1732, a French cartographer made a note of that place on his map. He called it Pierre à Fleche, which translates as "Rock of Arrows."

On September 1, 1821, William Becknell and his four companions crossed the Missouri River and camped in the place that would become Arrow Rock. It was the very first trip on what would become known as the Santa Fe Trail.

The town was born in 1829, but it would be another four years before it took the name Arrow Rock. It was chartered as Philadelphia, but those who had identified the area as "the Arrow Rock" for years refused to adopt the citified name. In 1834, Philadelphia was out and Arrow Rock was in.

The town of Arrow Rock was sandwiched between the "Big Muddy" Missouri River and fertile farmland and intersected by the Santa Fe Trail. In the mid-1800s, that location practically guaranteed prosperity, and prosperity came quickly.

Pioneering families put down roots. They built homes and shops. Entrepreneurs constructed warehouses on the waterfront to cash in on the river trade. They established mills, built boats, and operated ferry services. A man named Joseph Huston converted his home to a tavern and made a good living serving the travelers who passed through the village.

The first generation of Arrow Rock residents included two men destined to be remembered by history: Dr. John Sappington, who defied current medical thinking and popularized the use of quinine as a malaria treatment, and George Caleb Bingham, one of America's most revered artists. However, the town was built through the labor and ingenuity of many, and names such as Lawless, Pearson, Stith, Hall, Turley, and Hogge still resonate in the community.

The community's financial fortunes resulted in increased political influence. Three Missouri governors called Arrow Rock home: Meredith Miles Marmaduke, Claiborne Fox Jackson, who served an abbreviated term as Missouri's only Confederate governor, and John Sappington Marmaduke.

As the United States began to struggle with the issue of states' rights and fracture into Union and Confederacy, Arrow Rock chose a side. Its economy relied heavily on a trade relationship with the South, specifically the Natchez region of Mississippi, and it followed that most in Arrow Rock supported the Confederacy. That was a costly mistake. When the war ended and Southern trade relationships dried up, Arrow Rock reeled from the economic blow. Two devastating fires, the first in 1879 and another in 1901, wiped out much of the business district. The Missouri River, which had been the town's lifeline, shifted to the east and left the town high and dry. The railroads built their tracks elsewhere. Arrow Rock had neither the money nor the political muscle to get a bridge built across the Missouri River.

People moved away. Crumbling, vacant buildings blighted the town. Arrow Rock's glory days were over.

If it is always darkest before the dawn, then the first glimmer of light came in 1912. The newly formed National Old Trails Road Association began to promote the idea of a coast-to-coast highway that would link New York to California using old pioneer and Indian trails. The notion gained enthusiastic support across the country. An Arrow Rock chapter formed that year and went to work developing a tourist attraction interesting enough to lure travelers down the long, muddy road to Arrow Rock. The group set up a museum room in the Arrow Rock Tavern. The National Old Trails museum room included an odd assortment of artifacts, not all of them authentic to Arrow Rock, but it was enough to revive interest in the old tavern.

In 1921, a second group of Arrow Rock preservation heroes emerged with the founding of the Arrow Rock Chapter of the Daughters of the American Revolution (DAR). The local chapter decided to start big when choosing a service project. It set out to restore the Arrow Rock Tavern. Despite the presence of the National Old Trails Road Association's museum room, the building suffered from neglect and was in jeopardy of being torn down.

The DAR recognized that the building that had hosted so many Santa Fe Trail travelers held a significant place in Missouri and American history. The women lobbied the Missouri Legislature for assistance, and in 1923, the state allotted $5,000 to purchase the building. The legislature appointed the DAR as permanent custodian for the business. As promised, the organization operated the restaurant and lodging businesses and interpreted the building's history through tours and display rooms decorated with period furnishings. In 1985, the DAR turned over control of the Arrow Rock Tavern to the Missouri Department of Natural Resources.

The State of Missouri was impressed with the DAR's successful restoration of the tavern. In 1926, the state established Arrow Rock State Park. At first, the park included only the land around the tavern, but it grew over time to take in other Arrow Rock attractions, including the calaboose, Big Spring, and the Academy Boarding House. Picnickers and campers flocked to the park to enjoy the peaceful, natural surroundings.

The town was experiencing a revival, but its rejuvenation was limited to a small area on Arrow Rock's east side. The people who were coming to visit the Arrow Rock State Park and dine at the Arrow Rock Tavern weren't buying homes in the village. Residential property values were low, held down by the unkempt appearance of so many of the houses in town. One house, the Miller-Bradford House, appeared to be on the verge of collapsing, but somehow, Bill and Cora Lee Miller saw its potential. The couple ignored the advice of friends and purchased the home in 1957. They restored the home almost entirely on their own. Their success piqued the interest of others, who began to recognize the importance of historic preservation.

Arrow Rock's preservation movement was gaining momentum, and it reached another milestone in 1959 with the founding of the Friends of Arrow Rock. The organization was, and is, committed to the protection of Arrow Rock's history through the preservation of its historic buildings. Its first project, the restoration of the Saline County Courthouse in Arrow Rock, was so successful, the organization continued to seek out other properties to save. The young organization gave the restored courthouse to the State of Missouri, but it has since purchased and preserved 12 historic properties and constructed one modern museum facility.

The Friends of Arrow Rock's fundraisers became tourist attractions all by themselves. The organization hosted annual auctions, beginning in 1960, that drew hundreds of bidders to the village. Those auctions, along with historic home tours, funded many of the organization's early restoration efforts.

The town was looking better, but it was not postcard perfect in 1961 when artistic director Henry Swanson opened the Arrow Rock Lyceum Theatre in an old church building on a budget of $3,500.

Years later, Swanson shared his impressions of 1961 Arrow Rock. "Living conditions were terrible, half the town was in shanty-town shape, our water came from the Santa Fe Spring (now condemned) in gallon jugs with bugs swimming in the water. Kansas City Power and Light had to rewire the town from the highway just to get 100 ampere service to the theatre. It was hard, desperate work, but still we opened on schedule with twenty-six dollars and change remaining from the initial capitalization."

It was a gutsy move to open a theater in a place as remote as Arrow Rock, but the curious came and bought tickets. A single admission ticket during the 1961 season was $2.20; a season ticket was $5. At those prices, the theater did not see an immediate windfall, but as the theater's reputation grew, so did ticket sales. Other artistic directors followed Swanson, and each left his distinctive mark on the theater, advancing it to new levels of success and professionalism. The Arrow Rock Lyceum, Missouri's oldest professional regional theater, celebrated its 50th anniversary in 2010.

The Lyceum shared its golden anniversary with the Arrow Rock Craft Club, which also opened in 1961. The craft club, the Heritage Craft Festival, annual artist workshops, and the Arrow Rock Lyceum Theatre have made Arrow Rock a popular destination for artists.

It is hard to imagine Arrow Rock as anything other than the picturesque village it is today. Historic homes reflect the care of their owners, eclectic shops line the boardwalk, and restaurants, such as the Arrow Rock Tavern, now known as the J. Huston Tavern, keep the tourists well fed. The Arrow Rock State Park, now the Arrow Rock State Historic Site, offers camping facilities and maintains a first-class museum that traces the town's history. The Friends of Arrow Rock keeps an office on the boardwalk and offers guided tours of its restored properties. The Arrow Rock Lyceum Theatre continues to impress new patrons who are amazed to discover such high-caliber productions in a tiny town.

Arrow Rock has come a long way from its darkest days in the early 1900s, but there is still work to be done. The Friends of Arrow Rock recently completed a million-dollar capital campaign to advance their preservation and education efforts. Preservation is an ongoing project, and even the most carefully restored buildings require vigilant maintenance.

Arrow Rock is not one of those historical villages where people dress in period costumes and pretend to live in the 1800s. Arrow Rock is home to 56 residents. It is infused with the personality of its people. It is quirky and charming. It is smart and self-aware.

It is a wonderful place to visit and a lovely place to call home.

One

A Place Worth Preserving

The people who built the town destined for National Historic Landmark status did not have that legacy in mind at the time. They simply were looking to carve out their piece of the American dream in a place that seemed situated for success.

In the 1800s, riverfront property was premier real estate, and Arrow Rock capitalized on its location beside the Missouri River. Waterfront businesses sprung up quickly. The river trade business was supported by area agriculture, and in turn, the river brought in merchandise that supported the efforts of local merchants. Travelers stocked up on supplies in Arrow Rock while on their way to find opportunity at the end of the Santa Fe Trail.

Artist George Caleb Bingham was here and so was "Quinine Doctor" John Sappington. For a time, it looked like nothing could come between Arrow Rock and long-term prosperity. The Civil War changed everything.

Arrow Rock cast its economic lot with the losing side in the Civil War, and its Confederate leanings cost it dearly. As relationships with trading partners in the Deep South dried up, so did Arrow Rock's waterfront. The Missouri River was inching away, heading toward a new channel a mile away from Arrow Rock.

The town was bypassed by the railroads, devastated by fires, and abandoned by hundreds of citizens. But in the midst of despair, a sense of community pride remained and, ultimately, it was that pride of place that saved Arrow Rock from the fate of many other long-forgotten towns.

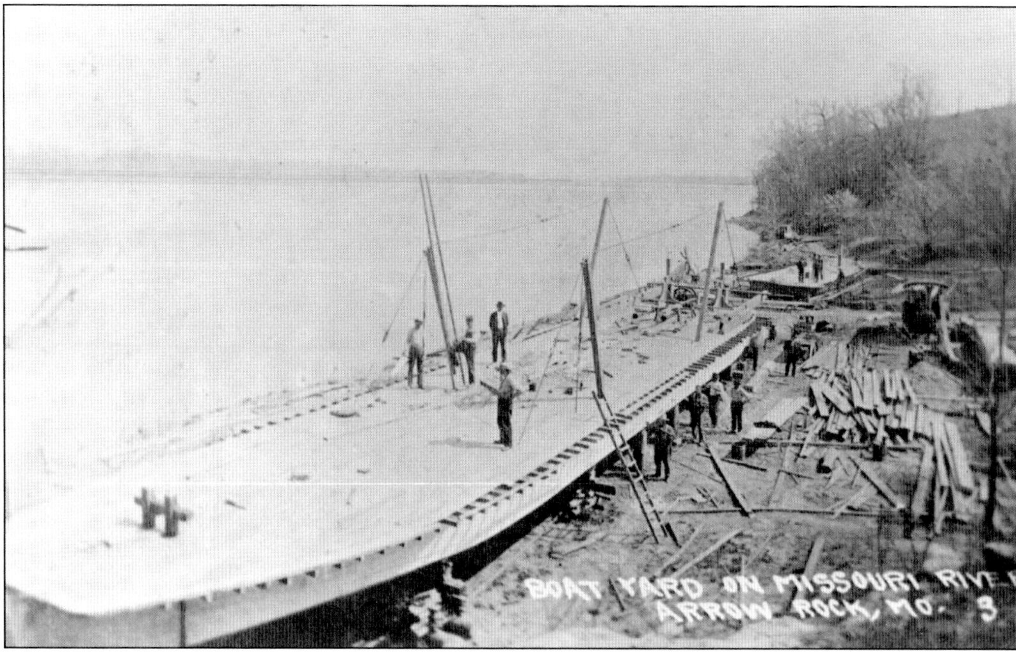

The Missouri River was the economic lifeline for Arrow Rock during its early years. As the town grew, so did its waterfront. Some of Arrow Rock's leading citizens built warehouses to take advantage of the prosperous shipping business. Gustav Moehle and his son established a boat-building business in 1890 and operated this boatyard for 19 years. (Courtesy of Friends of Arrow Rock.)

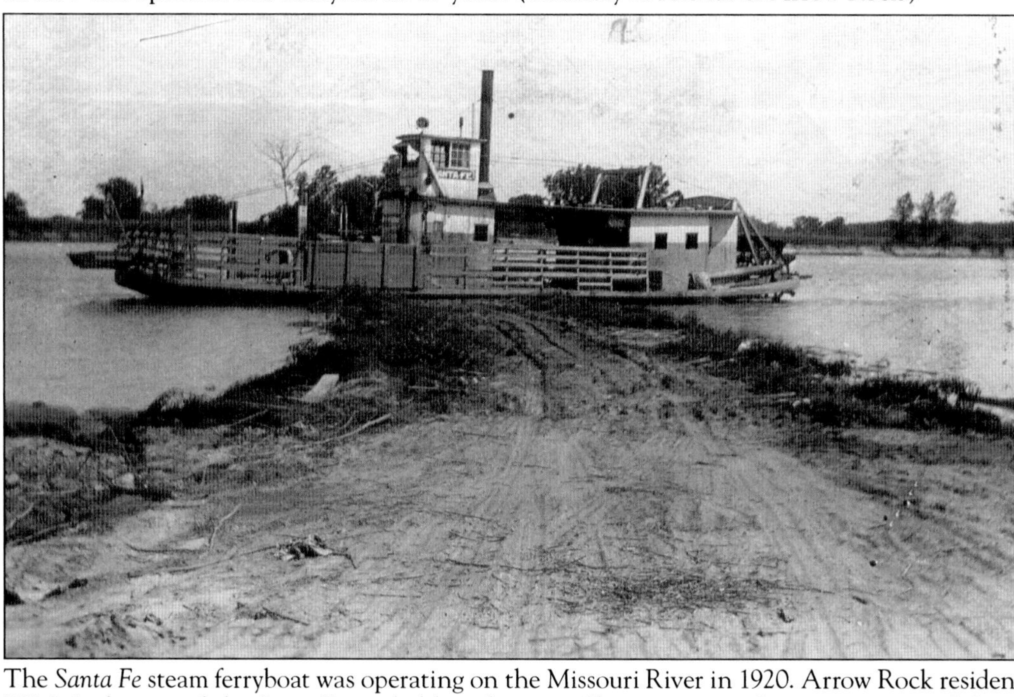

The *Santa Fe* steam ferryboat was operating on the Missouri River in 1920. Arrow Rock resident W.M. Leslie owned the *Santa Fe*, and although most of her trips were short jaunts up and down the river, one notable voyage took her from Lexington, Missouri, to Yankton, South Dakota, and back. She sank near Kansas City in 1931. (Courtesy of Friends of Arrow Rock.)

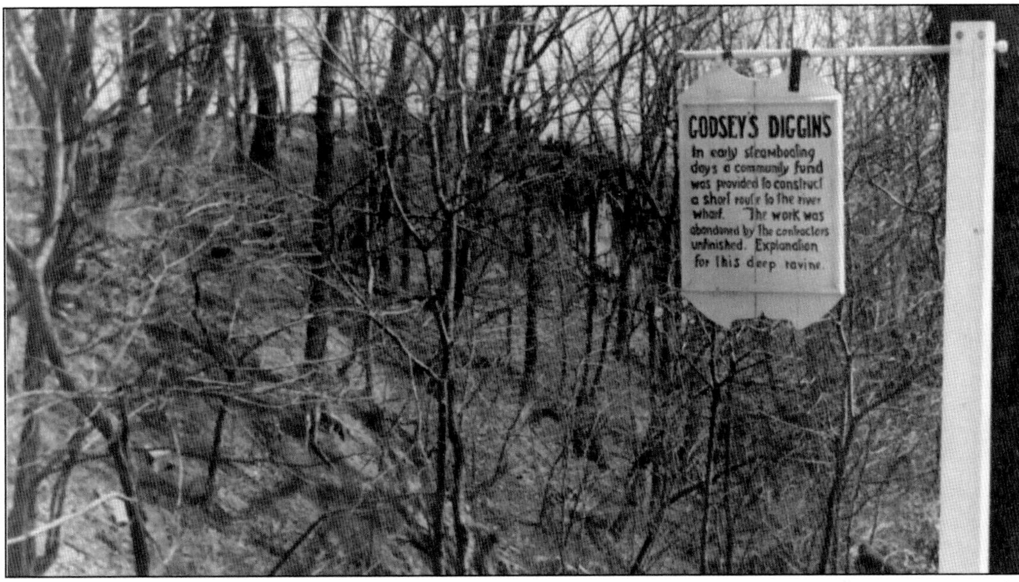

In the mid-1800s, the town contracted Burton Godsey to create a shortcut from Arrow Rock's business district to the riverfront by digging a ravine from the east end of Main Street to the banks of the Missouri River. The overly ambitious project was never completed, but an overgrown ravine remains as evidence of the attempt. (Courtesy of Friends of Arrow Rock.)

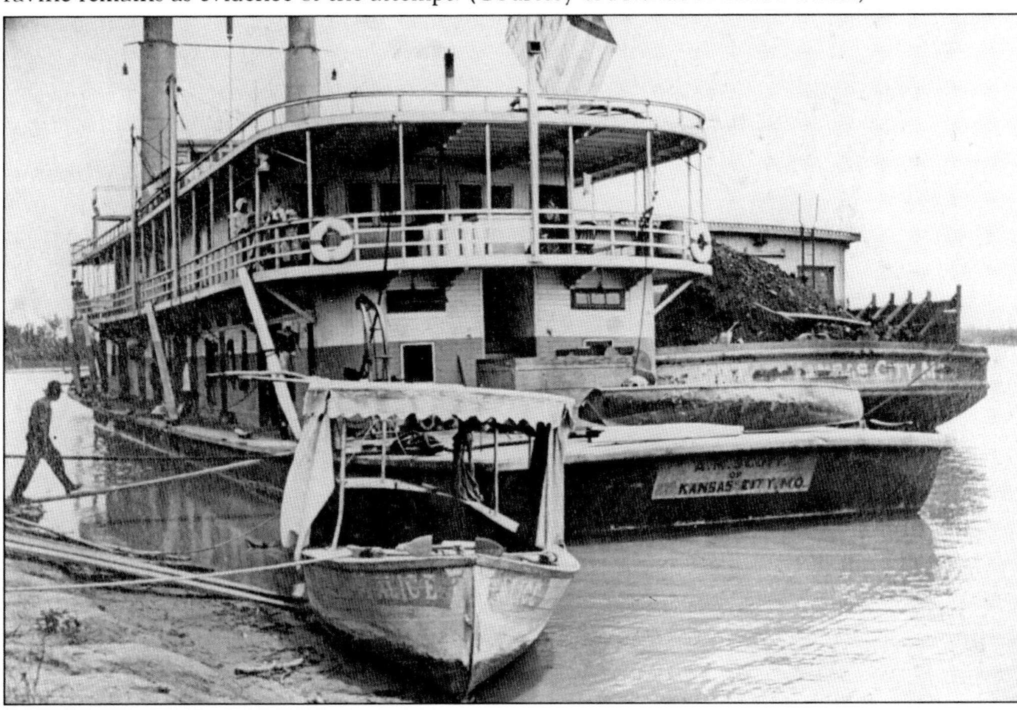

Boats of every size frequented the Arrow Rock landing in 1915, from large passenger steamboats like the A.M. *Scott* to the tiny *Alice*, which local resident Robert Lee Stith named after his deceased daughter. But Arrow Rock's glory days as a river port would soon come to an end. Gradual shifts in the river channel and the emergence of the railroads decimated the town's river-based economy. (Courtesy of Elaine Breshears.)

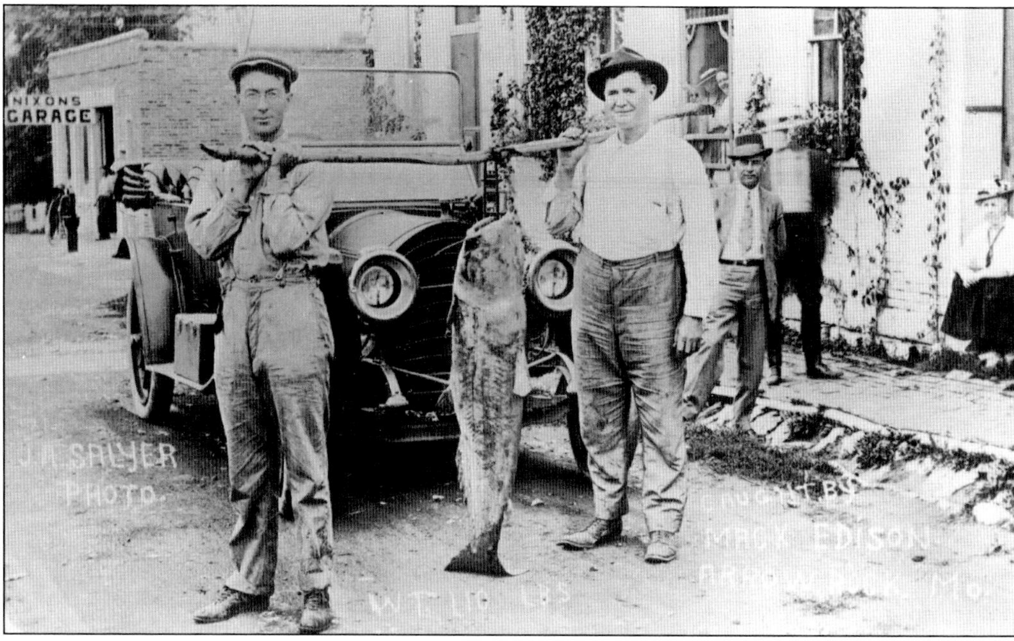

The Missouri River provided townspeople with a plentiful supply of fish, including some that would be the topic of wildly embellished fish stories for years to come. One whopper, the 110-pound catfish hauled in by local angler Mack Edison, required no exaggeration; however, in the early 20th century, 100-pound catfish were not are rare as they are today. (Courtesy of Friends of Arrow Rock.)

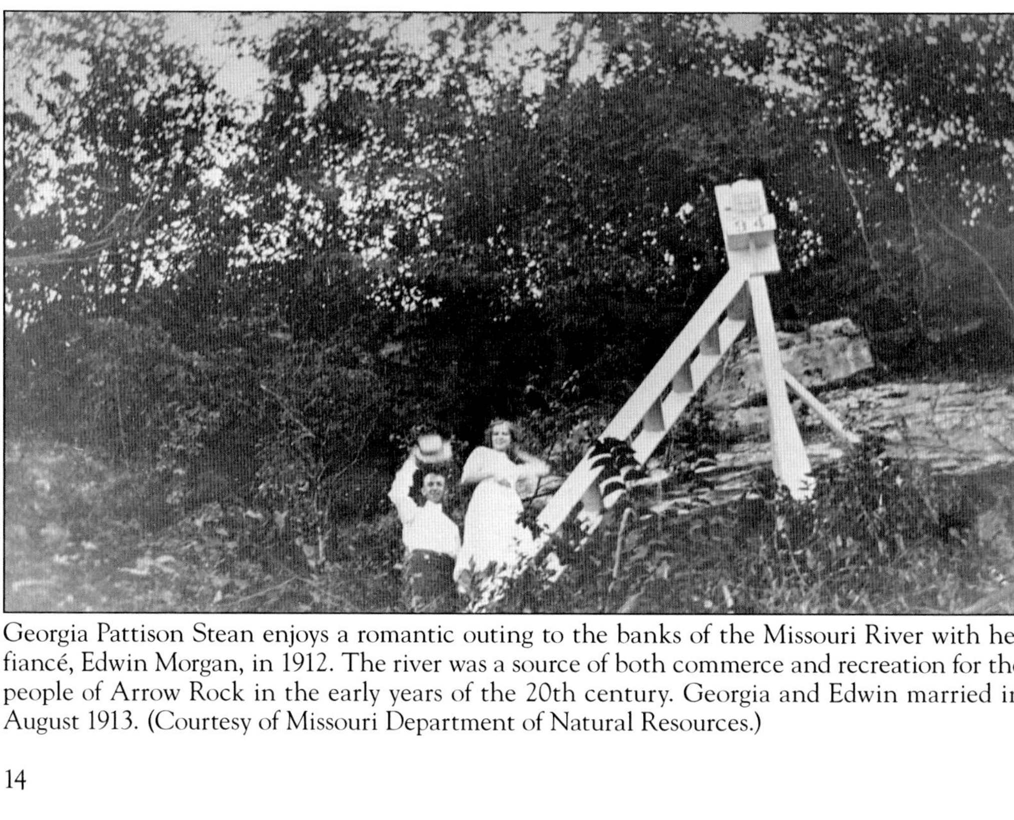

Georgia Pattison Stean enjoys a romantic outing to the banks of the Missouri River with her fiancé, Edwin Morgan, in 1912. The river was a source of both commerce and recreation for the people of Arrow Rock in the early years of the 20th century. Georgia and Edwin married in August 1913. (Courtesy of Missouri Department of Natural Resources.)

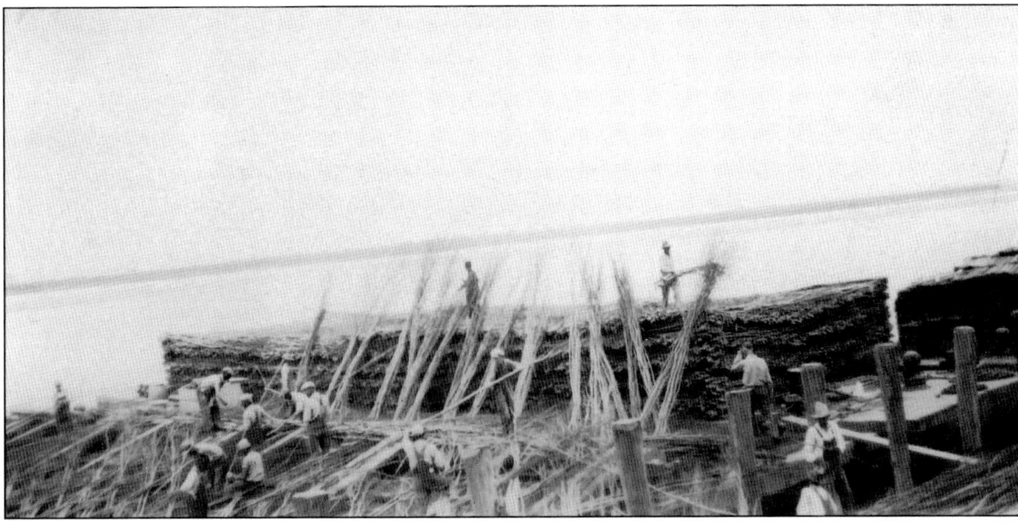

The US Army Corps of Engineers made its first attempts at taming the wild Missouri River in the mid-19th century. One method for managing bank erosion was through the use of large, woven, willow mats that conformed to the shape of the bank. Despite the labor-intensive undertaking, the river continued to shift. By 1927, it had settled into its current channel and left Arrow Rock behind. (Courtesy of Elaine Breshears.)

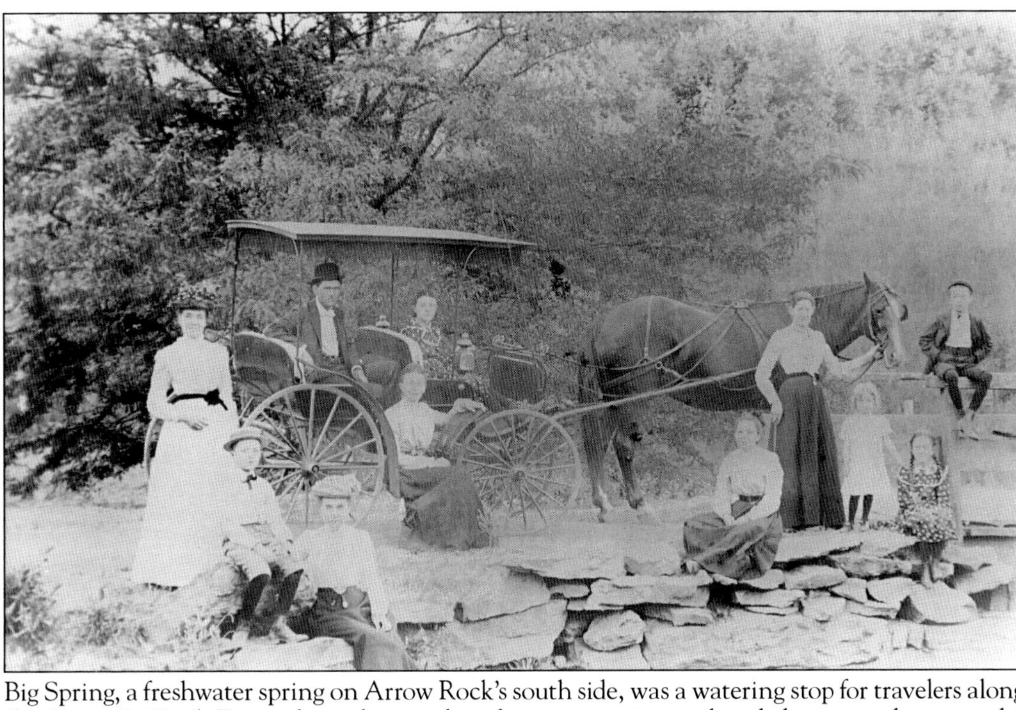

Big Spring, a freshwater spring on Arrow Rock's south side, was a watering stop for travelers along the Santa Fe Trail. Even after other modes of transportation replaced the covered wagon, the spring remained a popular destination for local residents, like these who visited the spring for a family outing in the late 1800s. (Courtesy of Missouri Department of Natural Resources.)

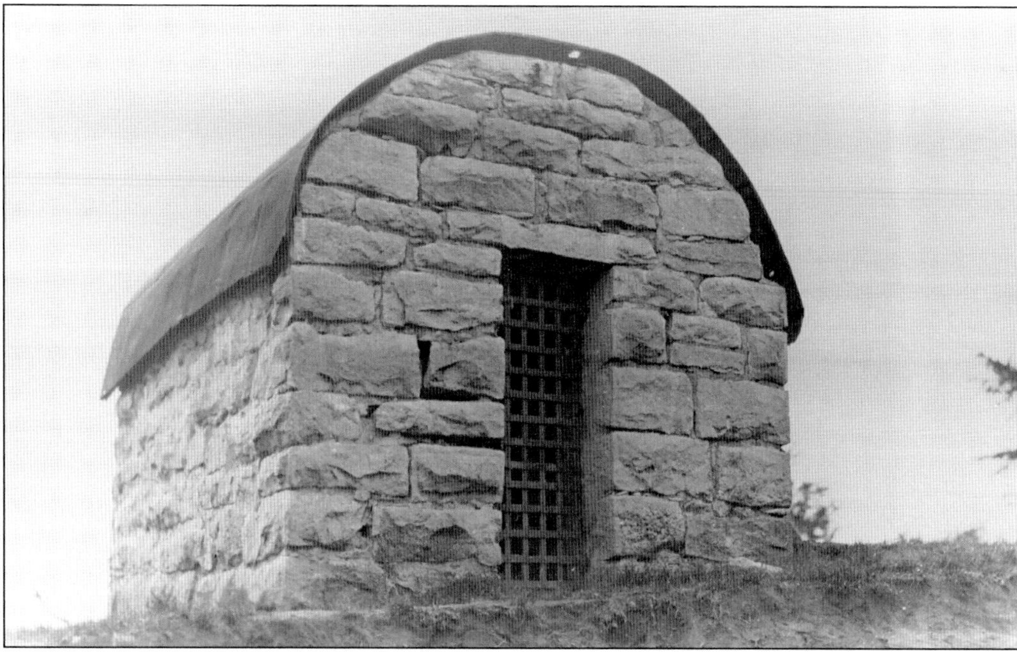

The one-room stone calaboose, built in 1873, is said to have housed just one prisoner in its history. The drunken man was to spend the night in jail, but legend has it that his incessant hollering woke residents of nearby homes. He was released before morning so peace could be restored to the sleepy village. The Arrow Rock State Historic Site maintains the calaboose. (Courtesy of Friends of Arrow Rock.)

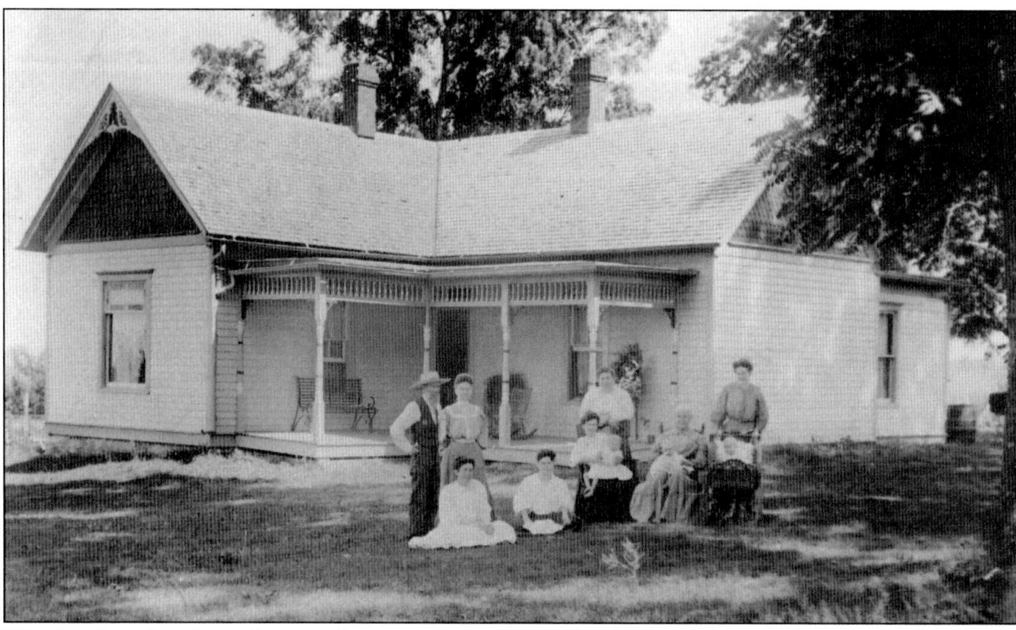

The Lawless family gathers in front of the Victorian-style farmhouse built by patriarch David "Dee" Lawless. The home looks much the same today, thanks to a restoration financed by Lawless descendant Gladys Moehle Thompson and carried out by the Friends of Arrow Rock. (Courtesy of Friends of Arrow Rock.)

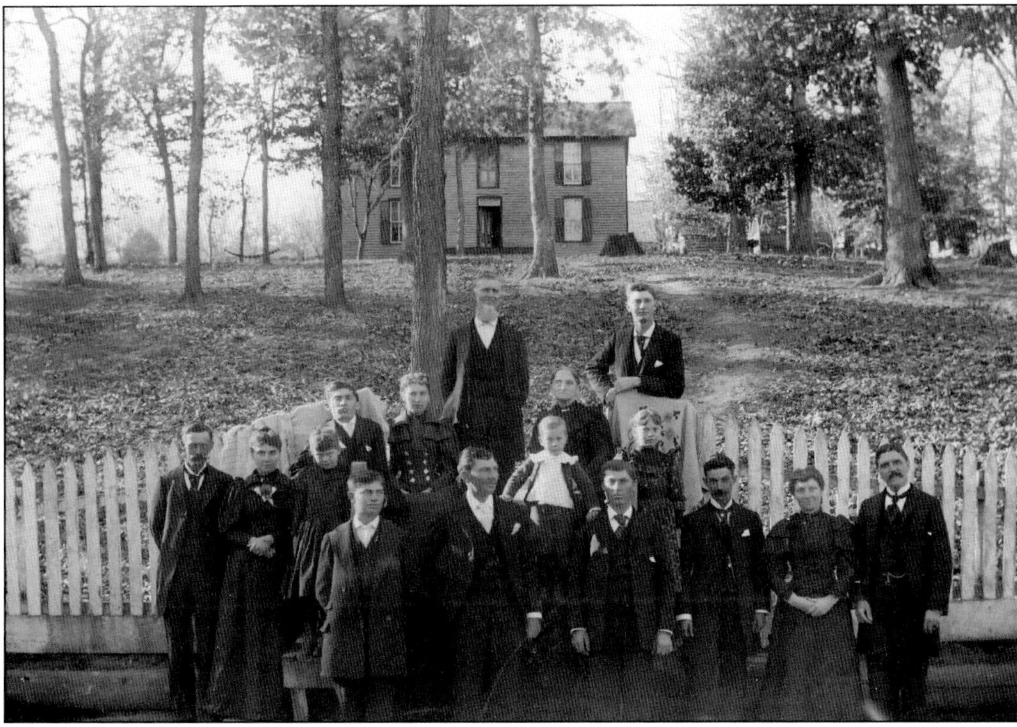

William Bailey Diggs was the patriarch of a prolific and prominent Arrow Rock family. He and his wife, Cynthia, owned a large farm north of Arrow Rock that was the scene for many family gatherings. In the autumn of 1894, sixteen members of the Diggs family gathered for a portrait, including sons Watson (front row, third from left), who owned the Arrow Rock Tavern in the early 1900s, and Bascom (third row, far left), editor and publisher of the *Arrow Rock Statesman* newspaper. The farm was transformed into a winter playground after a heavy snowfall later that same year. (Courtesy of Missouri Department of Natural Resources.)

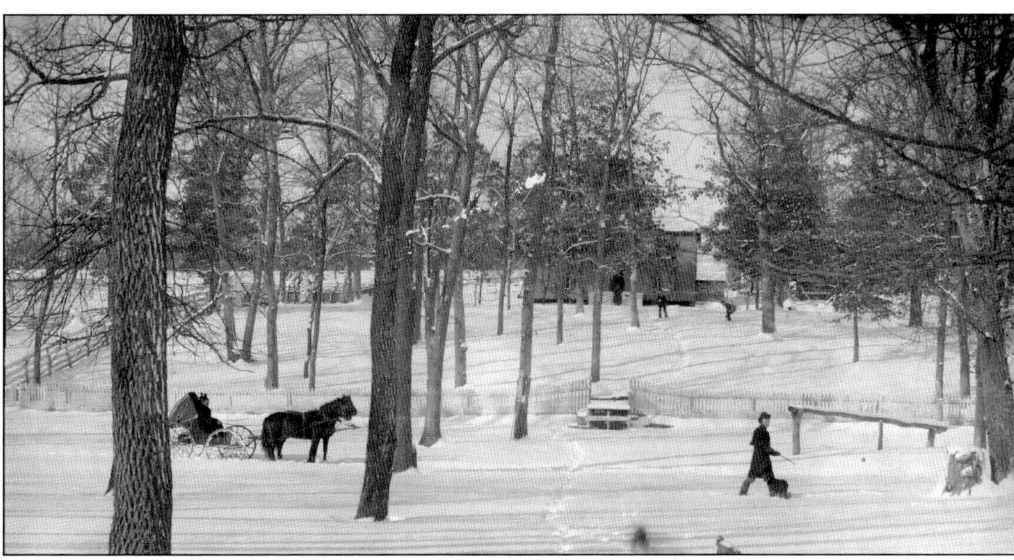

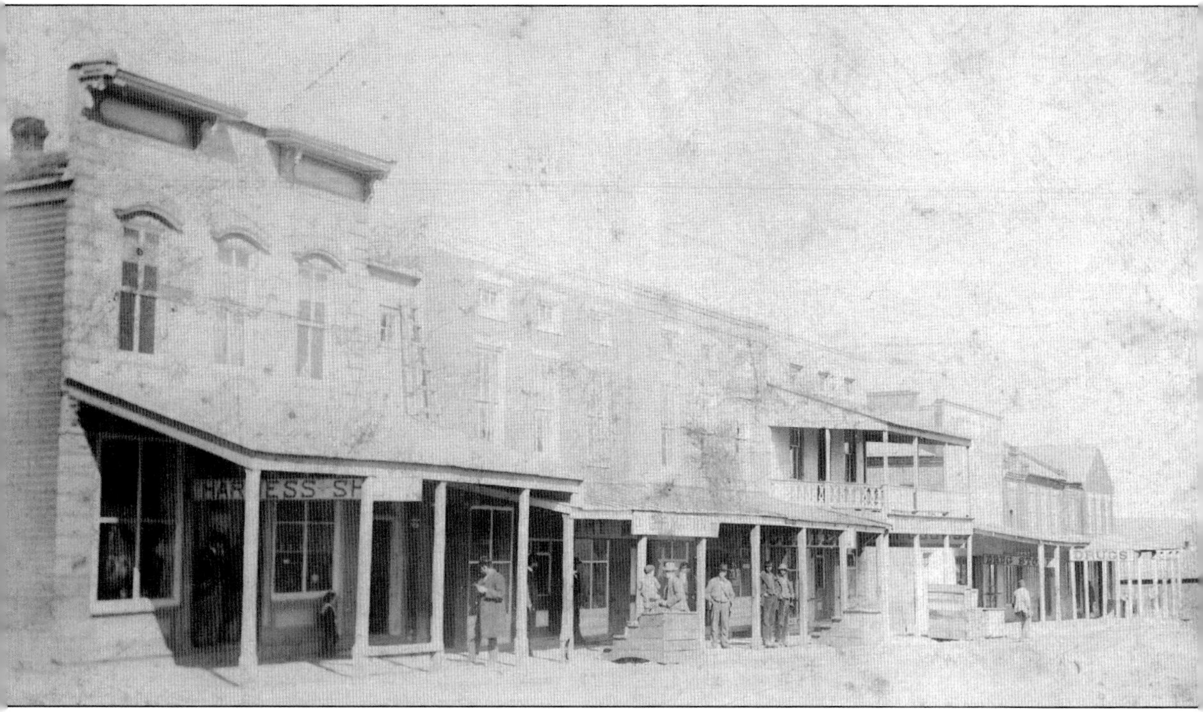

The fire of July 1901 razed most of the buildings along this two-block stretch of Arrow Rock's Main Street. In her diary, Arrow Rock postmaster Leona Gilpin blamed the fire on "three half-witted boys in a half-witted man's drug store." Other accounts are less accusatory, blaming the fire on a fallen lantern in J.W. Wheeler's drugstore. This was the second major fire to strike Arrow Rock after the Civil War. The first, in December 1872, destroyed several residences and nearly two blocks of businesses. The 1901 fire was the final, painful blow for many business owners who had suffered through a long decline following the Civil War when Arrow Rock's Confederate leanings cost the town in both economic strength and political influence. Many of those who clung to the hope of a recovery abandoned that faith in the face of this new devastation. (Courtesy of Friends of Arrow Rock.)

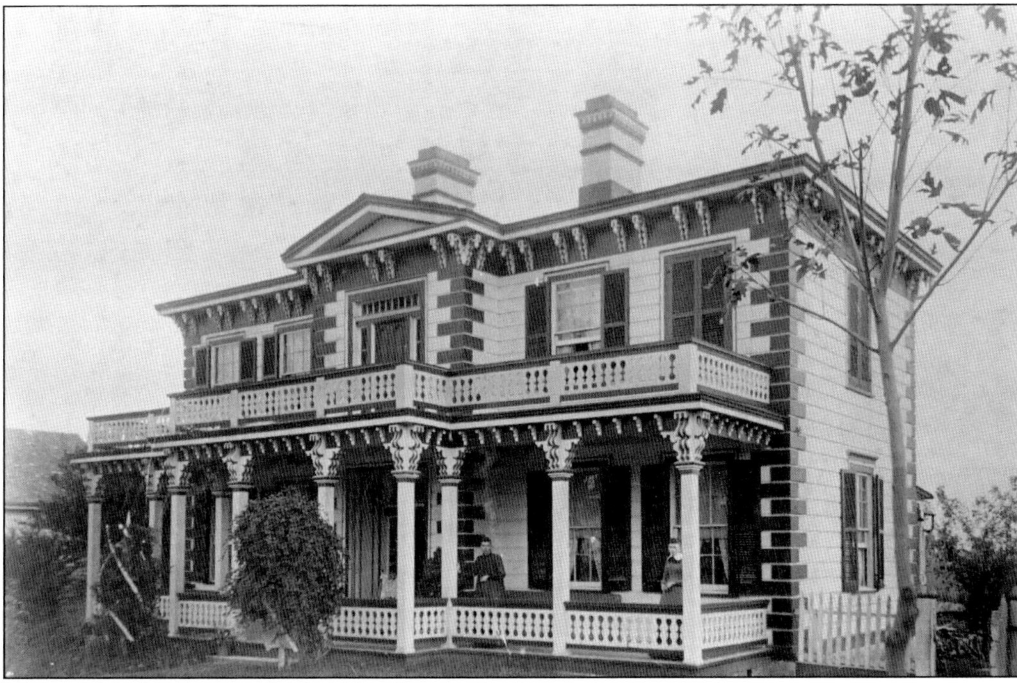

Samuel McMahan was a successful Arrow Rock merchant. His dry goods store was located across from the Arrow Rock Tavern on the boardwalk, and his home, a grand Italianate mansion (above), was just two blocks west on Main Street. McMahan's Missouri roots reached back to the early 1800s; his grandfather was killed in an Indian raid near the mouth of the Lamine River on Christmas Day in 1814. In 1882, McMahan moved his family from the country to town so he could open his store (below), which sold clothing and fancy goods. The dry goods store was completely destroyed by the fire of 1901. (Courtesy of Missouri Department of Natural Resources.)

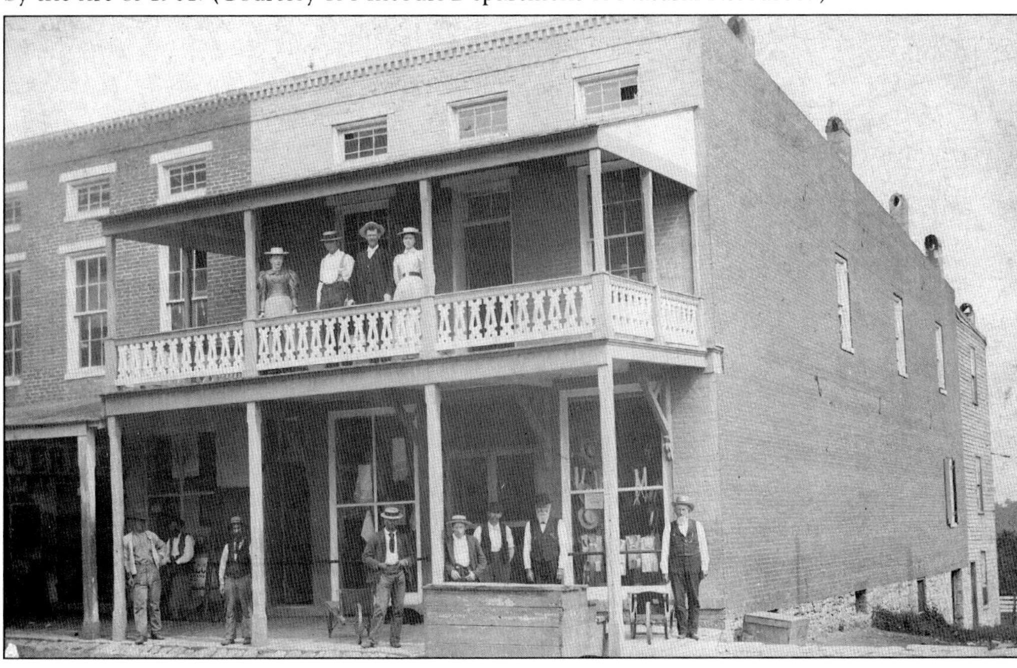

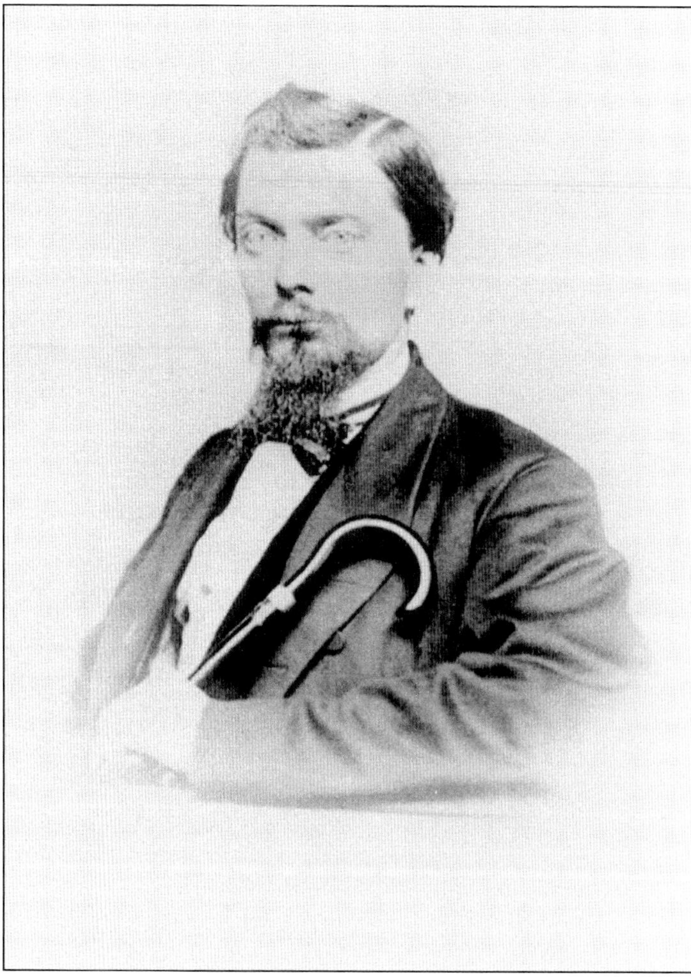

Jay Marcellus Potter was an early Arrow Rock merchant who believed in diversifying his inventory. His combination stage office/post office/store, located at lot 2 on the public square in 1870, sold books, tobacco, toys, notions, and even insurance. Sadly, the entrepreneurial Potter died at age 32. (Courtesy of Missouri Department of Natural Resources.)

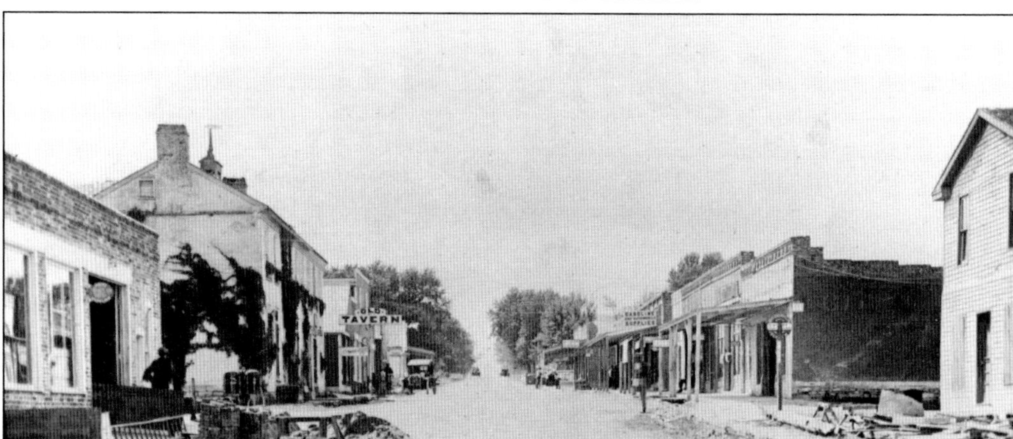

By 1915, Arrow Rock's once-booming business district had shrunk to just a few blocks. Some of the two- and three-story commercial buildings damaged or destroyed in the fires of 1872 and 1901 were rebuilt as single-story structures; some were not rebuilt at all when their owners chose to relocate to other towns. (Courtesy of Friends of Arrow Rock.)

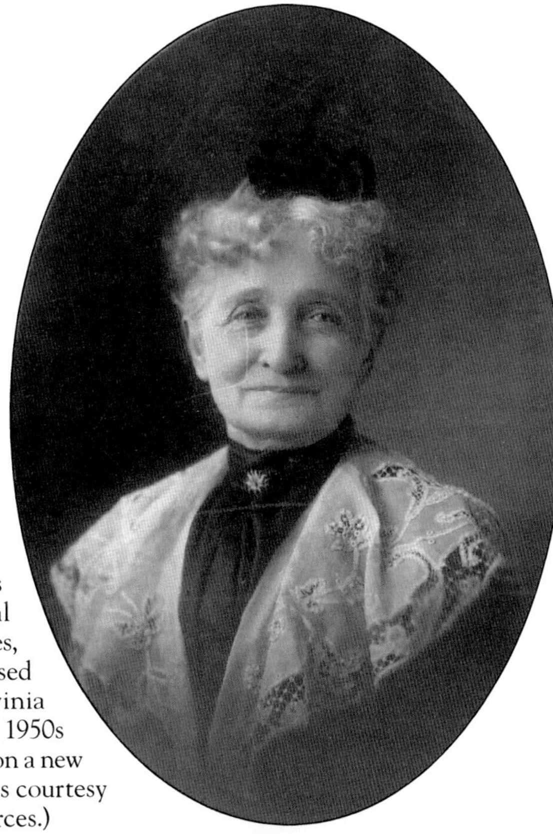

Lavinia Pearson Bradford, the granddaughter of Dr. John Sappington and stepdaughter of Gov. Claiborne Fox Jackson, was married to Dr. Charles Bradford. The Bradfords bought a small house on Main Street in the early 1840s and expanded it to become a Greek Revival showplace to house their large family. Charles, who was in frail health for many years, passed away in 1862 at age 42. The widowed Lavinia lived into her 80s and did not remarry. The 1950s restoration of the Bradford home set in motion a new era of preservation in Arrow Rock. (Images courtesy of Missouri Department of Natural Resources.)

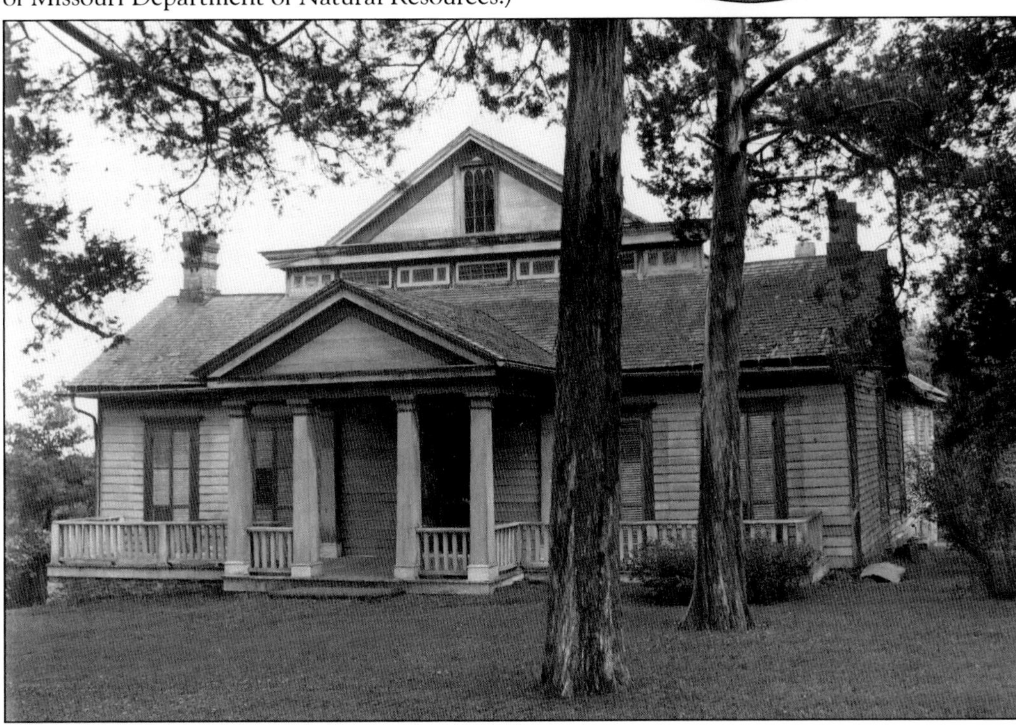

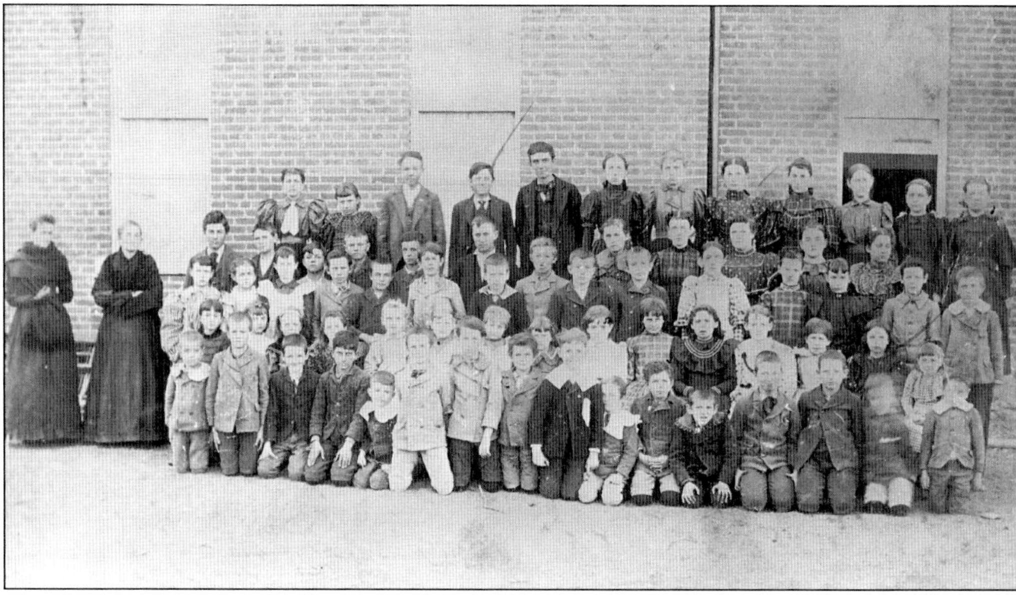

Two teachers, Jessie Kiebler and Anna McMahan, shared the responsibility and the rewards of educating the youth of Arrow Rock in 1898. The school building, located on the west end of Main Street, was constructed in 1892, and it was destroyed by a fire in 1909. (Courtesy of Missouri Department of Natural Resources.)

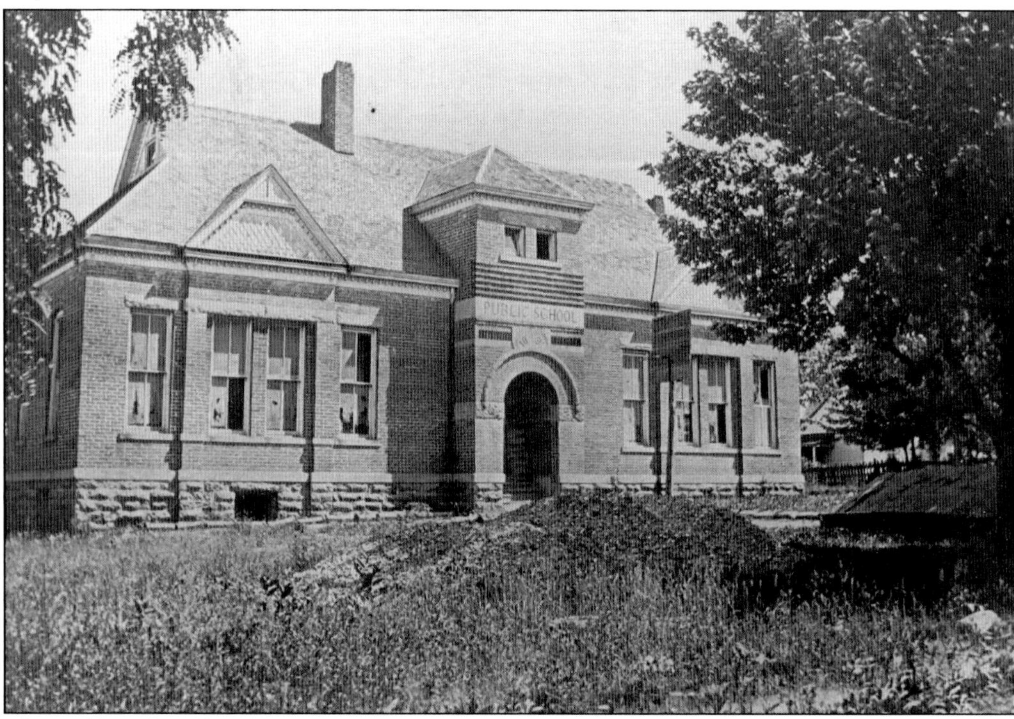

This public school building was constructed in 1910 with the proceeds from a $10,000 insurance policy. The building replaced Arrow Rock's original school building that fire destroyed the previous year. This building, too, would be short lived; it burned to the ground in 1928. (Courtesy of Missouri Department of Natural Resources.)

In her diary, postmaster Leona Gilpin surmised that the 1928 Arrow Rock School fire, which started around noon on a cold February day, was set by two or three small boys. It is more likely the fire started in the flue of the wood stove. The school served all grades in a single building and, at the time of the fire, employed three teachers. (Courtesy of Missouri Department of Natural Resources.)

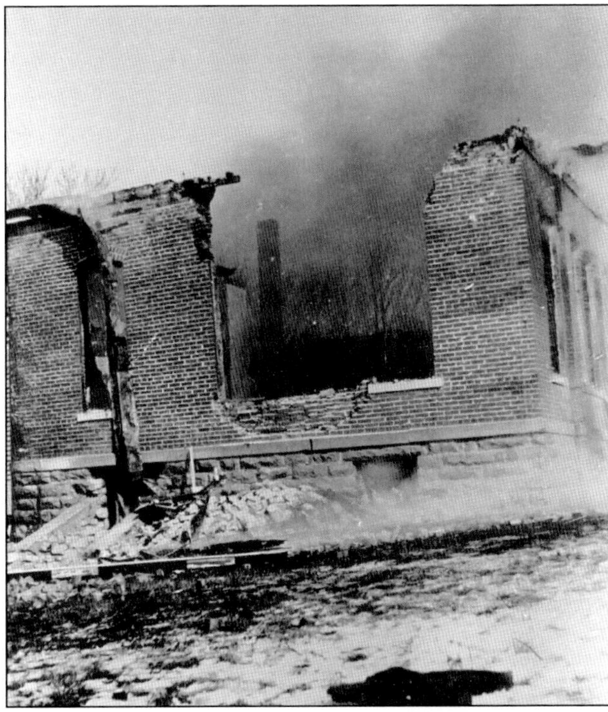

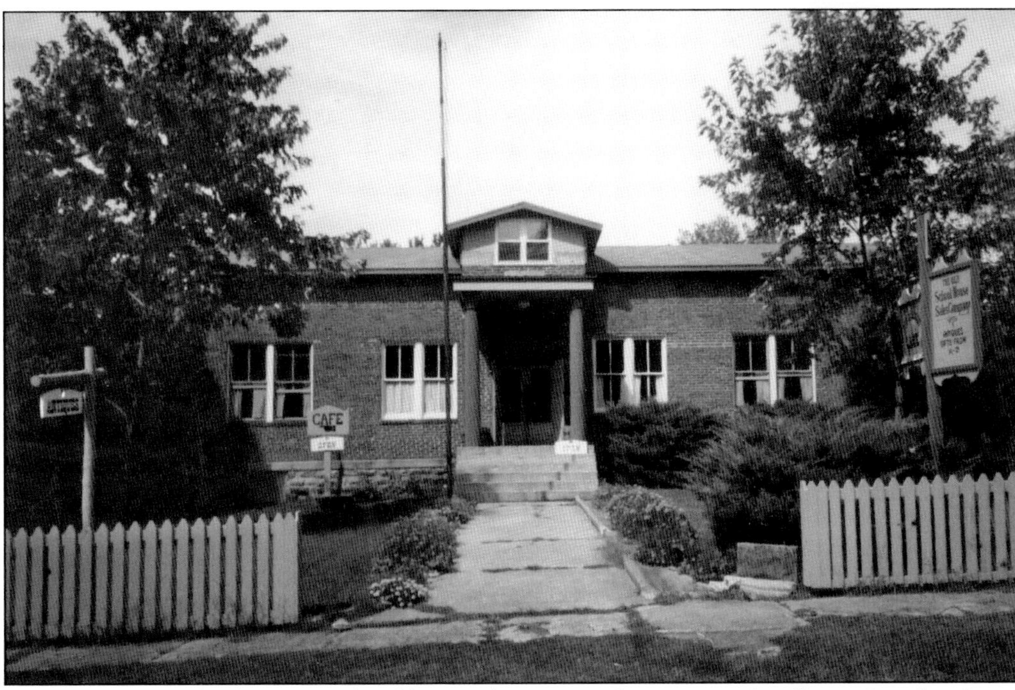

The schoolhouse built in 1928 fared better than its predecessors and still stands today. It was constructed on the footprint of the burned building it replaced and housed the high school and two elementary classrooms on the main level with a lunchroom in the basement. The Arrow Rock School closed in 1968. The building now functions as community and meeting space. (Courtesy of Missouri Department of Natural Resources.)

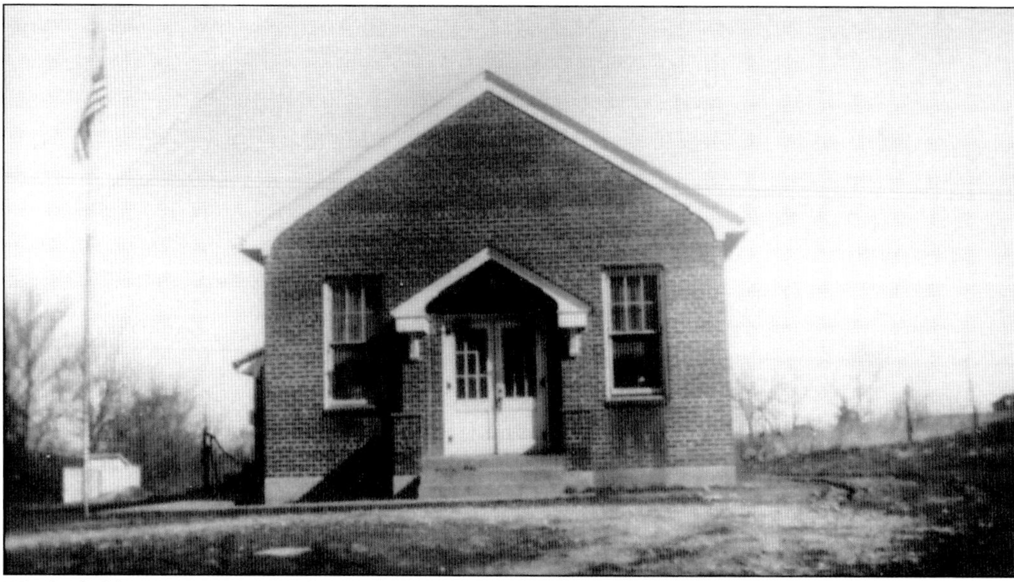

Black children in Arrow Rock were not privy to a formal education until after the Civil War. The first black school in Arrow Rock, founded in 1869, held classes in Brown's Chapel. In 1890, the school moved to a dedicated building on the northeast side of town. This 1939 brick structure replaced an earlier school building that burned down. (Courtesy of Missouri Department of Natural Resources.)

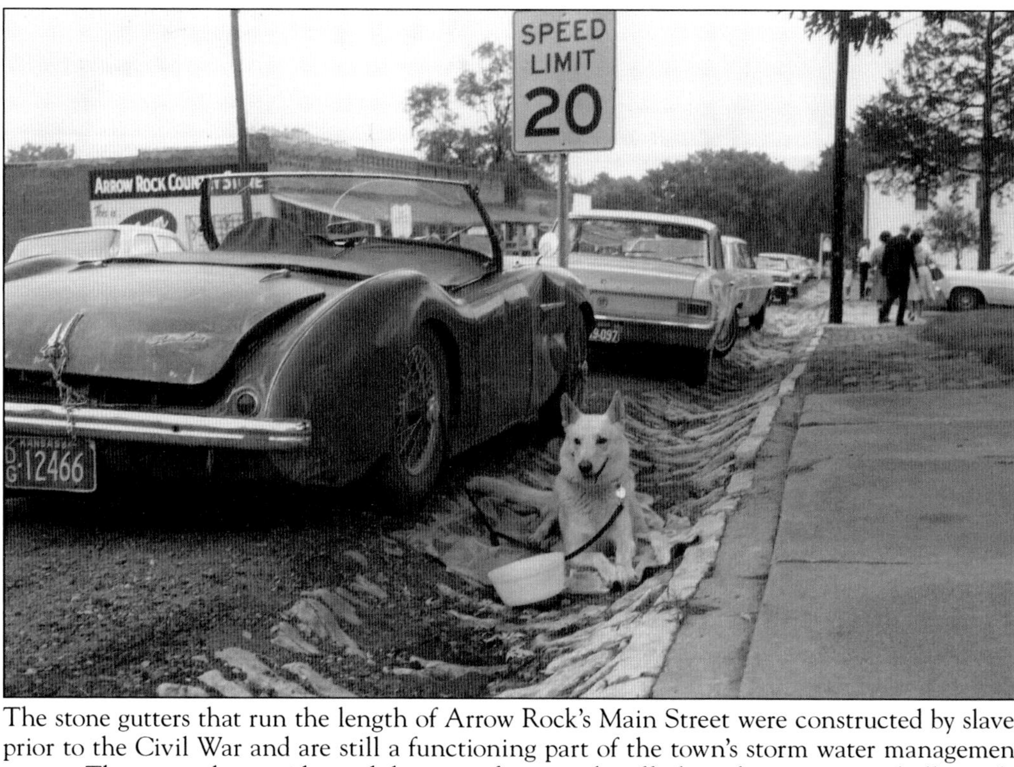

The stone gutters that run the length of Arrow Rock's Main Street were constructed by slaves prior to the Civil War and are still a functioning part of the town's storm water management system. The gutters have withstood the tests of time and traffic but often present a challenge for low-riding modern vehicles. (Courtesy of Friends of Arrow Rock.)

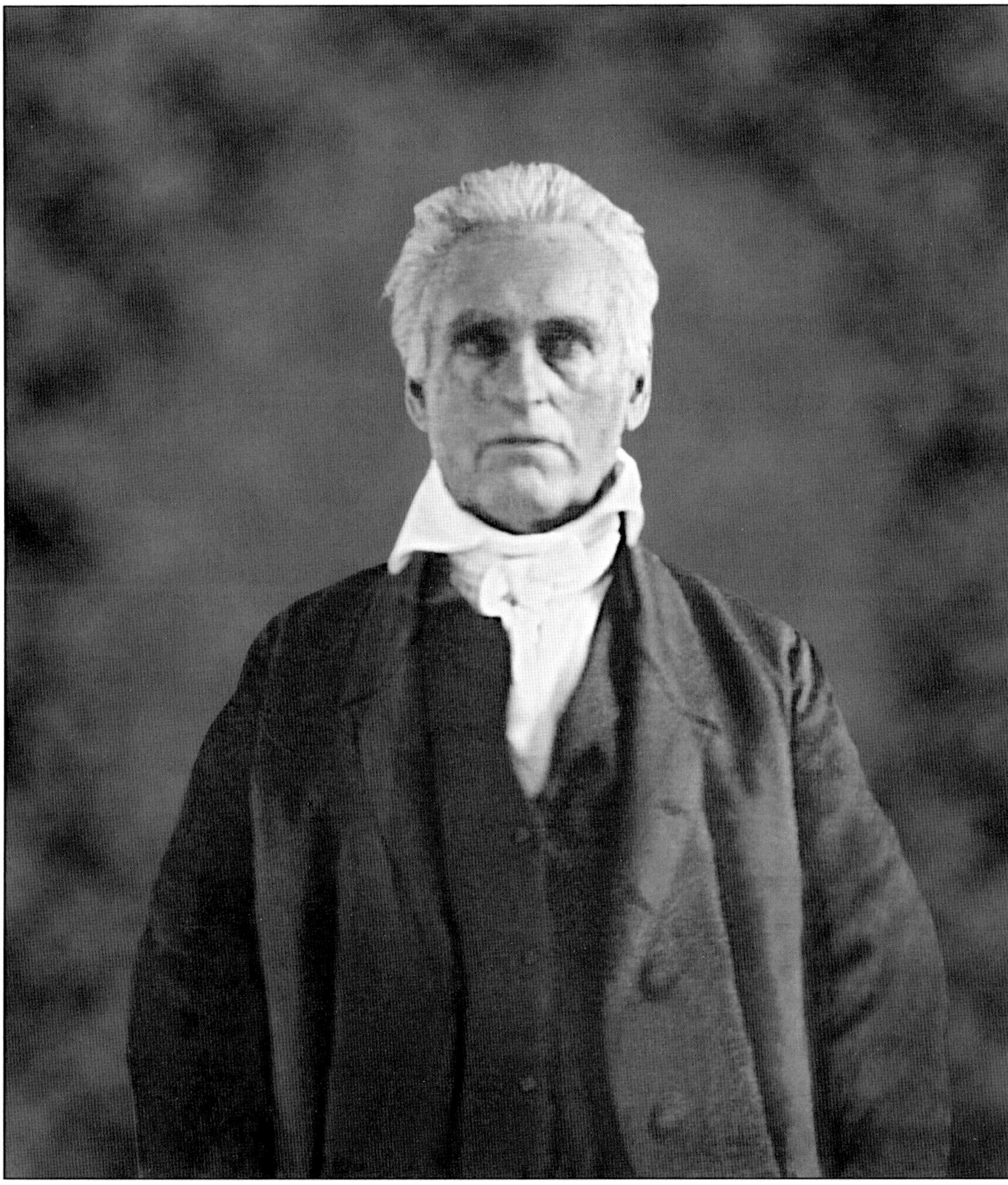

Dr. John Sappington arrived in the area in 1819 and became Saline County's first physician. His innovative treatment of malaria using quinine—as opposed to the common practices of bleeding, purging, and puking used by other physicians of his era—put him at odds with the medical establishment but saved countless lives. He began the manufacture of Dr. John Sappington's Anti-Fever Pills in 1832 and showed a flair for entrepreneurship by marketing his pills across the country through his company, Sappington and Sons. The pills earned Sappington a fortune, and quinine became the accepted standard of treatment for malaria for the next 100 years. In 1844, Sappington wrote *The Theory and Treatment of Fevers*, the first medical book published west of the Mississippi. In the book, Sappington revealed the formula for his anti-fever pills, which made his business vulnerable to competition. In his later years, Sappington left medicine behind and focused on agricultural pursuits. (Courtesy of the Friends of Arrow Rock.)

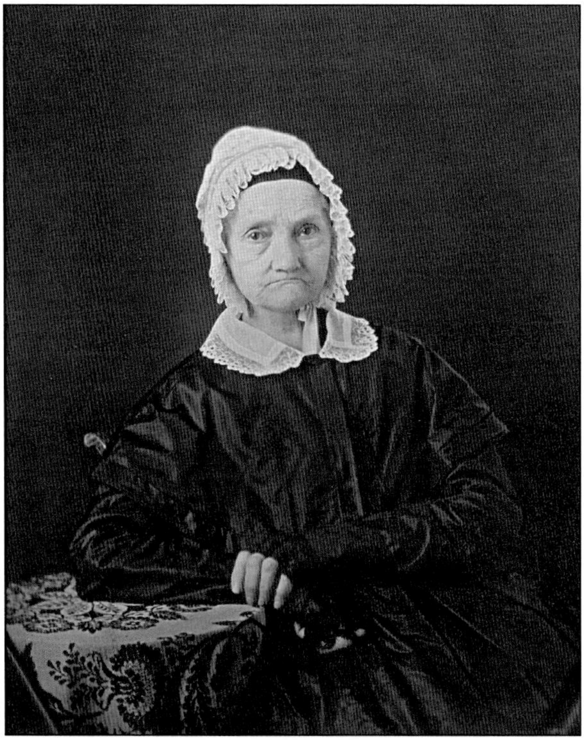

Dr. John Sappington's wife, Jane Breathitt, was born into an influential Kentucky family. Her brother John became Kentucky's 11th governor, and brother Roger was the secretary to Pres. Andrew Jackson. She married Sappington in 1804, and the couple had nine children. Their family legacy included two sons-in-law and one grandson who served as governors of Missouri. (Courtesy of the Friends of Arrow Rock.)

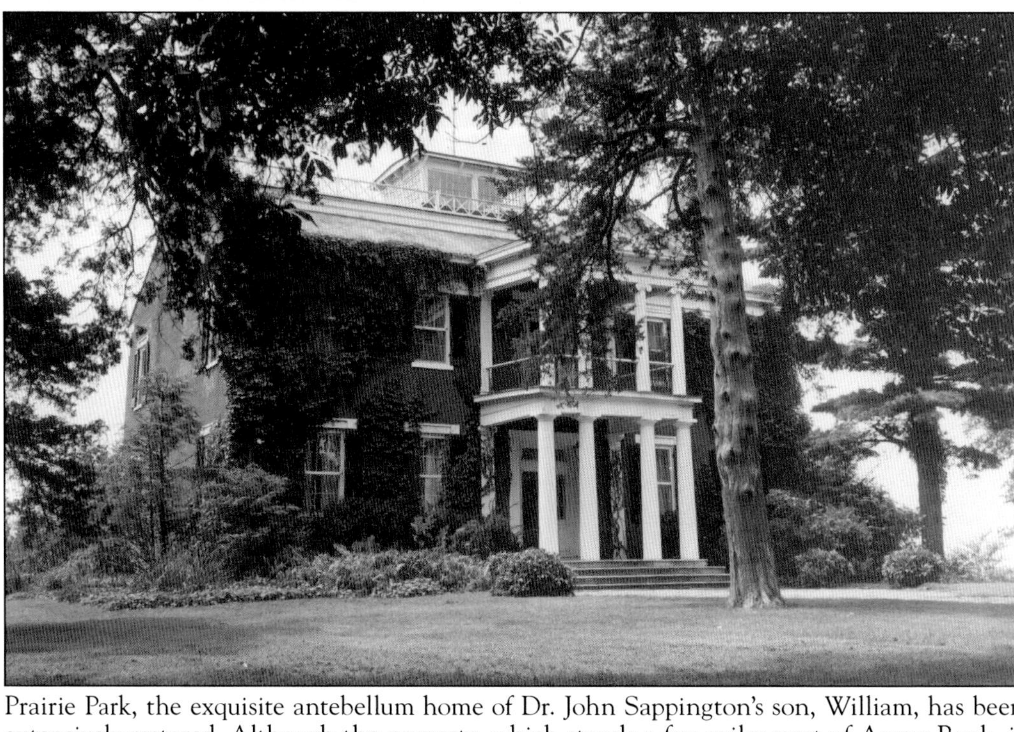

Prairie Park, the exquisite antebellum home of Dr. John Sappington's son, William, has been extensively restored. Although the property, which stands a few miles west of Arrow Rock, is privately owned, it is available for tours and is often the venue for Arrow Rock's most elegant occasions. (Courtesy of Friends of Arrow Rock.)

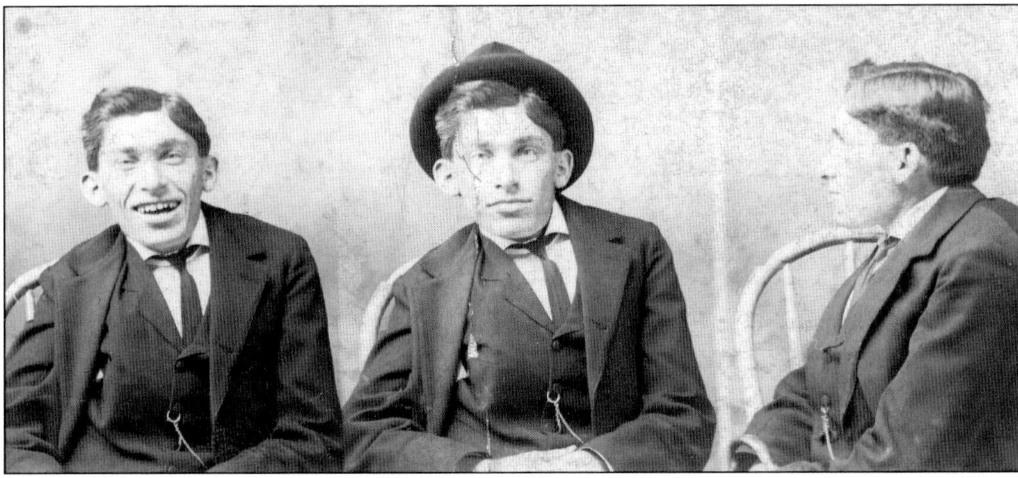

Bascom Diggs was editor and publisher of the *Arrow Rock Statesman* from 1897 to 1918. He purchased the newspaper in partnership with his brother I.O. but became sole owner in 1898 when his brother left to run a newspaper in Hartville, Missouri. Bascom's growth was stunted by a childhood accident, but that didn't prevent him from becoming one of Arrow Rock's most influential citizens. (Courtesy of Missouri Department of Natural Resources.)

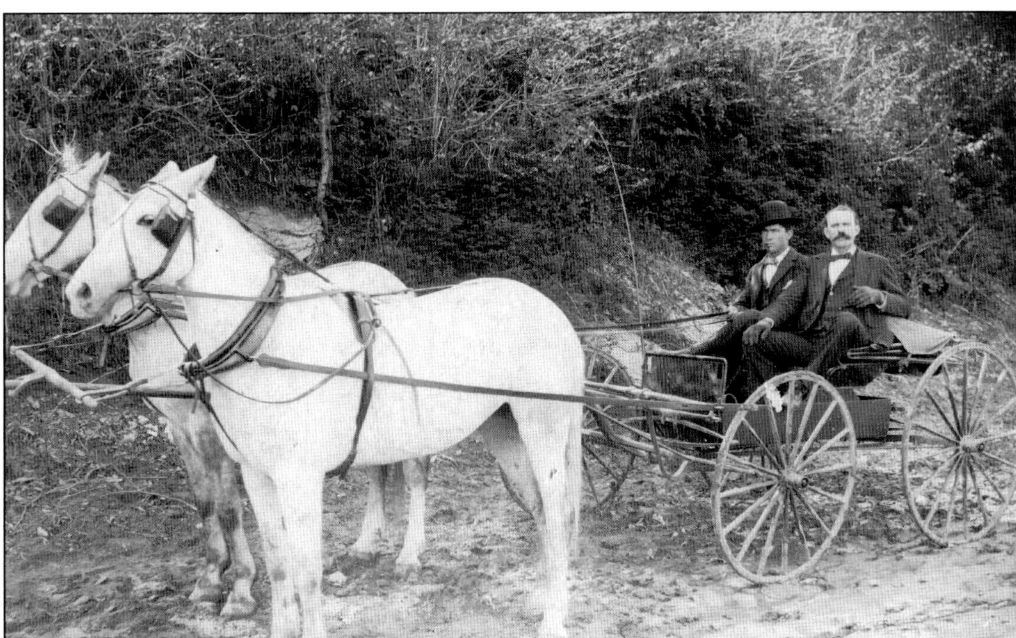

Saunders Townsend (on right), seen here at Big Spring with his son Walter, was a successful farmer who lived near Arrow Rock. In his book *Along the Old Trail,* Arrow Rock historian T.C. Rainey described Townsend as "a very strong man physically, with a temper not safe to trifle with; very positive in his convictions and very free to express them." (Courtesy of Missouri Department of Natural Resources.)

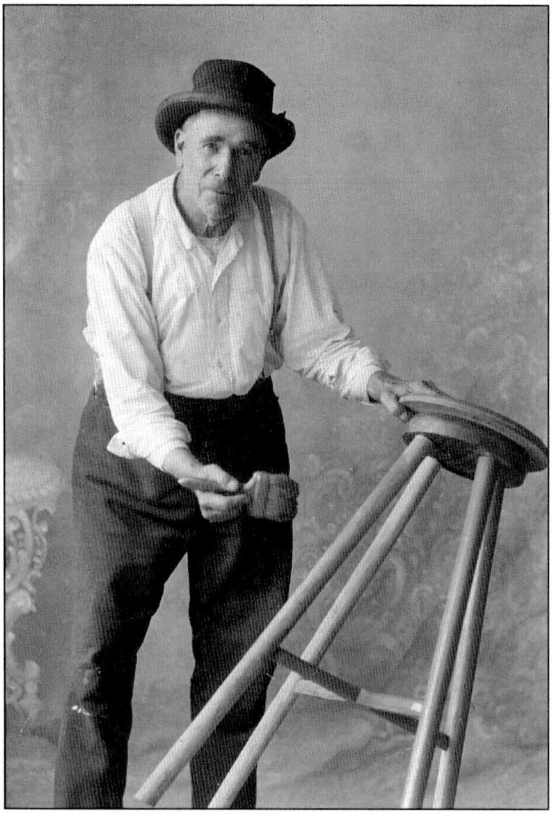

Ed Miller, a painter in Arrow Rock during the latter years of the 1800s, has not been remembered in local history like his sister-in-law, Nannie Sites, the famously pampered wife of the local gunsmith. Ed and his wife, Amanda, lived at the corner of Fourth and High Streets. He operated a paint shop out of the rear of his home. (Courtesy of Missouri Department of Natural Resources.)

The Latch House, a small frame home on the corner of Fourth and High Streets, is one of several homes with competing claims of being the oldest home in Arrow Rock. The modest home was purchased in 2009 by the Arrow Rock town government for use as the city hall. (Courtesy of Missouri Department of Natural Resources.)

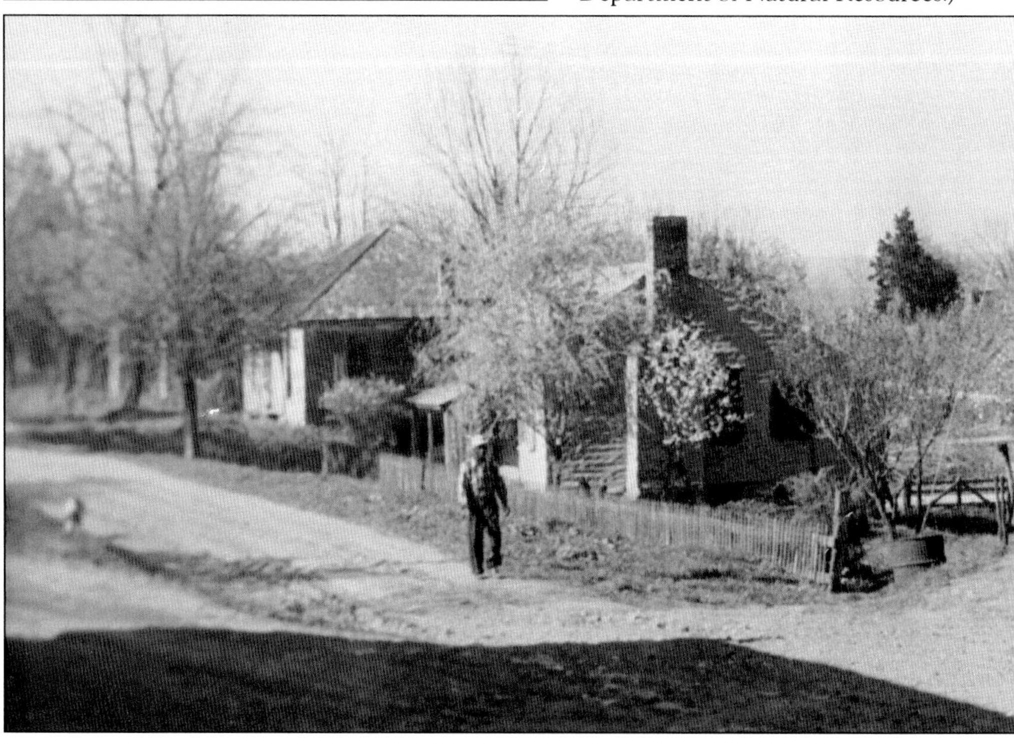

In 1917, it was considered a patriotic obligation to purchase Liberty Bonds in support of the American troops and the allied effort in World War I. A wave of national pride swept through Arrow Rock when hundreds of citizens flocked to Main Street to participate in a Liberty Bond drive. (Courtesy of Missouri Department of Natural Resources.)

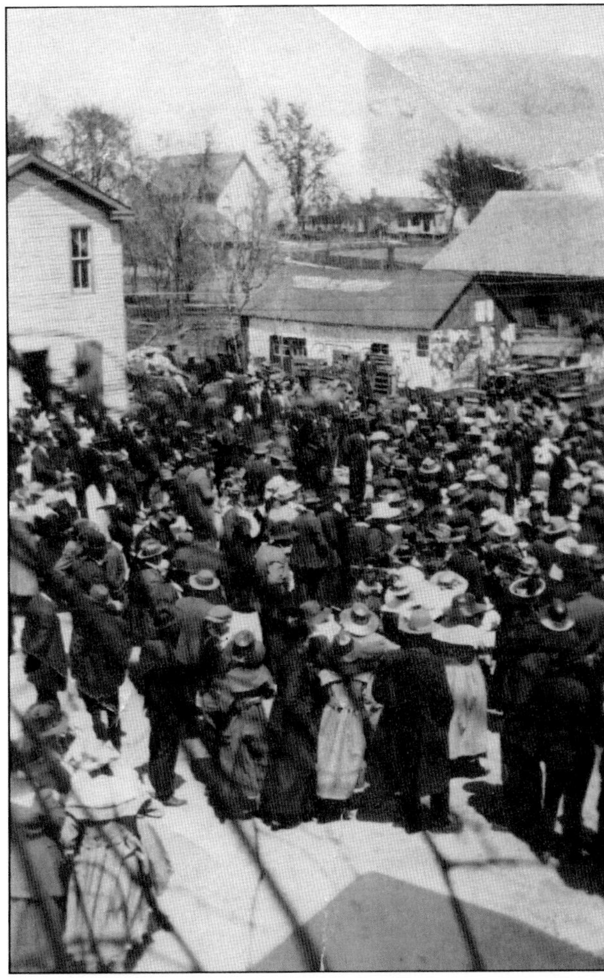

At different times in their history, two Arrow Rock businesses were dubbed the Arrow Rock Hotel: the building more commonly recognized as the Arrow Rock Tavern and this large home three blocks west on Main Street. The property, which is now operated as a bed and breakfast, continues to be a restful place for travelers. (Courtesy of Missouri Department of Natural Resources.)

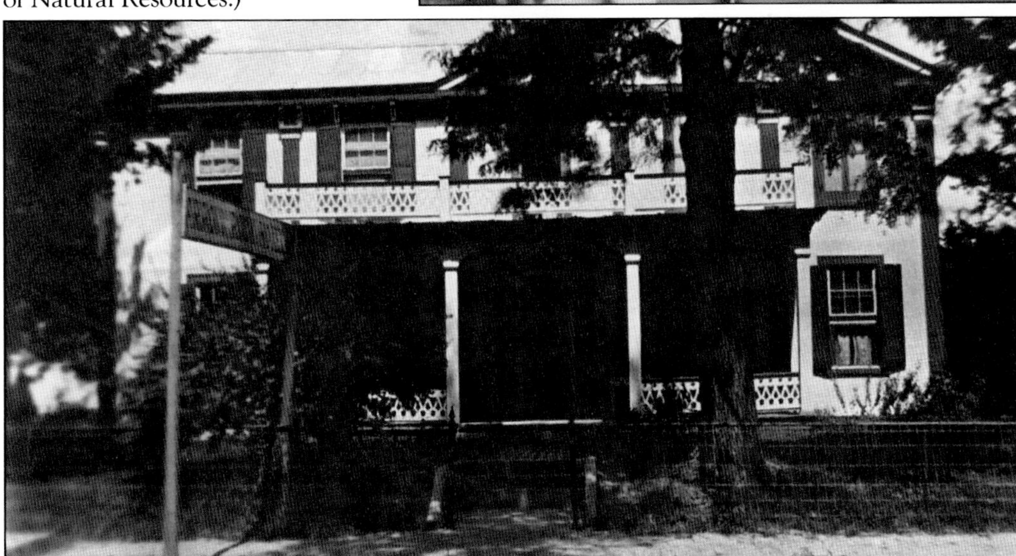

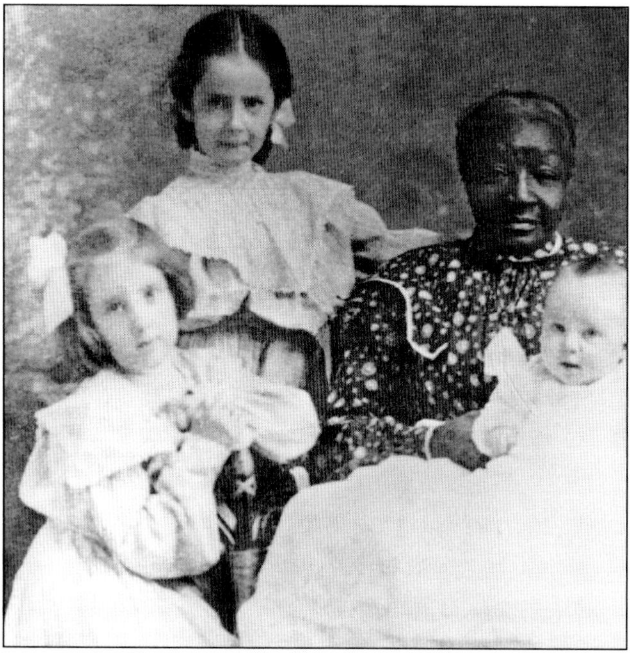

Although the Withers family appreciated the role of their African American servant enough to include her in a photograph with their children—Ida, Flora, and I.C.—the fact that she was identified as "Black Mammy Thompson" indicates that, in 1890, racial equality was a concept whose time had not yet come. (Courtesy of Missouri Department of Natural Resources.)

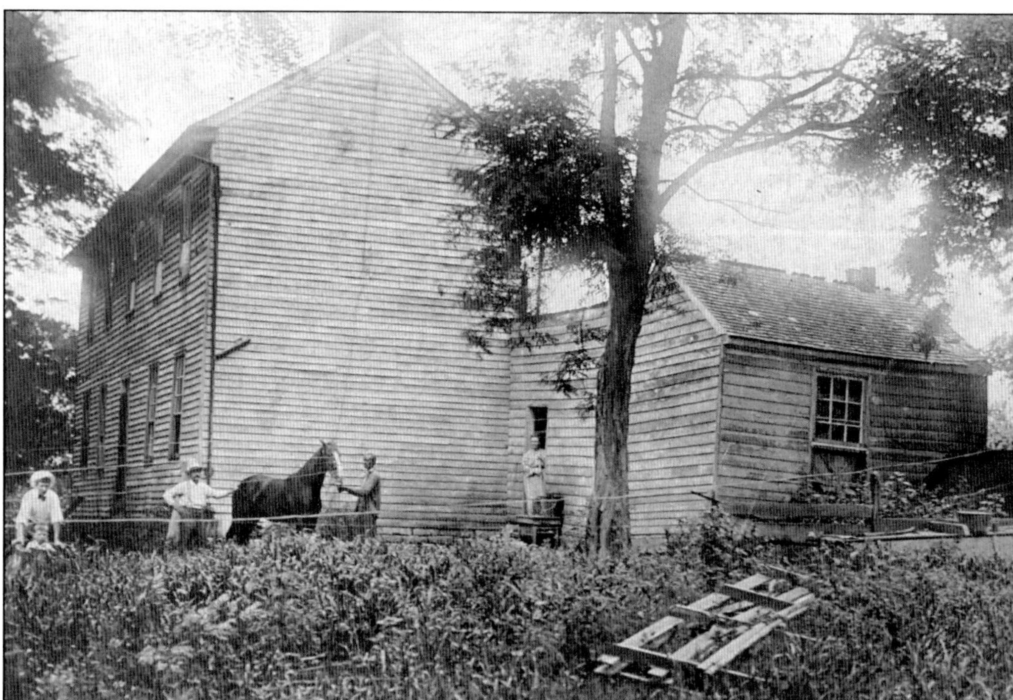

South Carolina–born O.B. Pearson ran a plantation near Arrow Rock. There is little question about his loyalties in the Civil War. In the 1850s, he partnered with future Confederate governor Claiborne Fox Jackson to ship locally produced agricultural products, horses, and mules to the cotton-growing and slave-dependent Natchez district of Mississippi. Pearson himself owned 28 slaves, according to the 1860 census slave schedule. (Courtesy of Missouri Department of Natural Resources.)

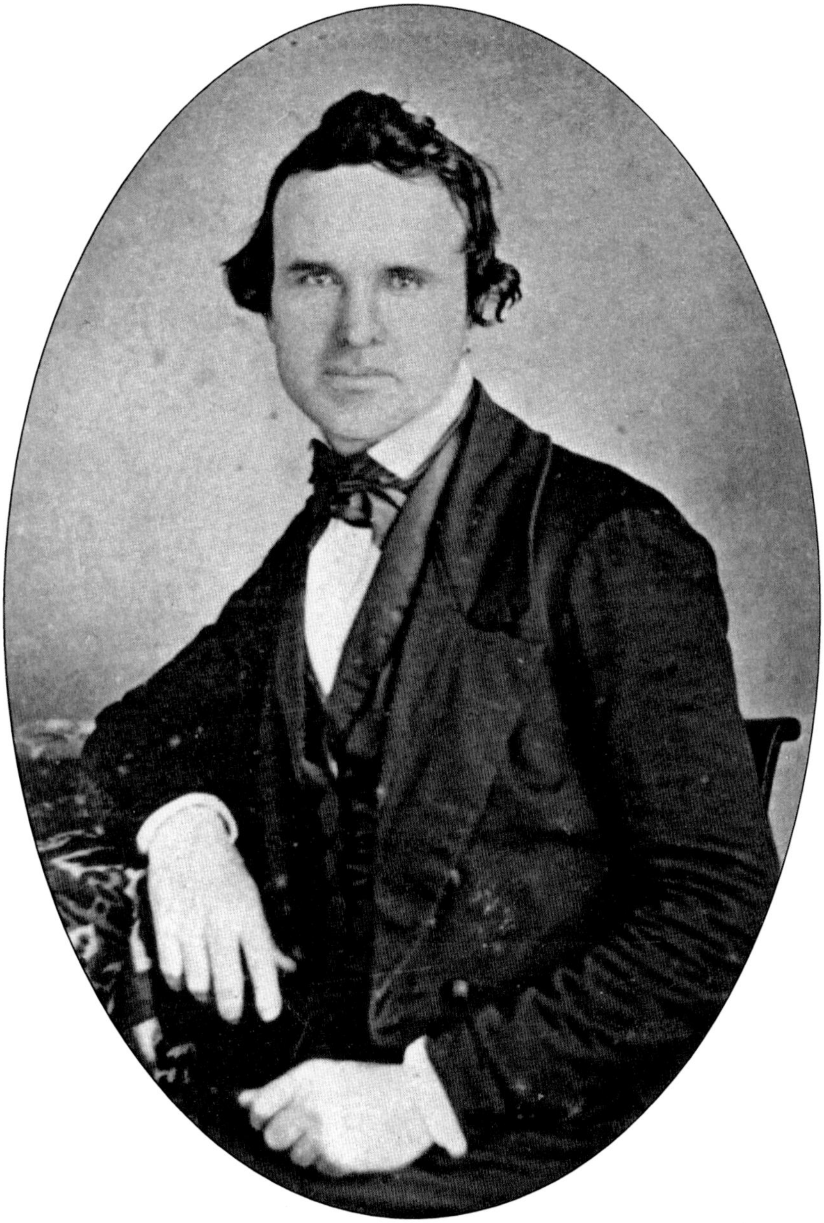

Artist George Caleb Bingham is Arrow Rock's most famous citizen. He served as a judge in the town's first election in 1840 and as chairman of the town board of trustees in 1847. He was seldom at home because it was difficult to make a living as a painter in Arrow Rock, but his affection for the town was clear in both his writings and in his art, which often featured local people and places. Bingham made most of his money from portrait painting, but it is in his genre paintings of everyday life where his talent for storytelling is most evident. Bingham was active in Unionist politics and often used his canvases as vehicles for political opinion. He was also a prolific letter writer and freely shared his views to friends, political foes, and the media. He ran for statewide office on several occasions and was elected to the Missouri Legislature in 1848, then appointed state treasurer in 1862. He died in 1872 and is buried in Kansas City. (Courtesy of Friends of Arrow Rock.)

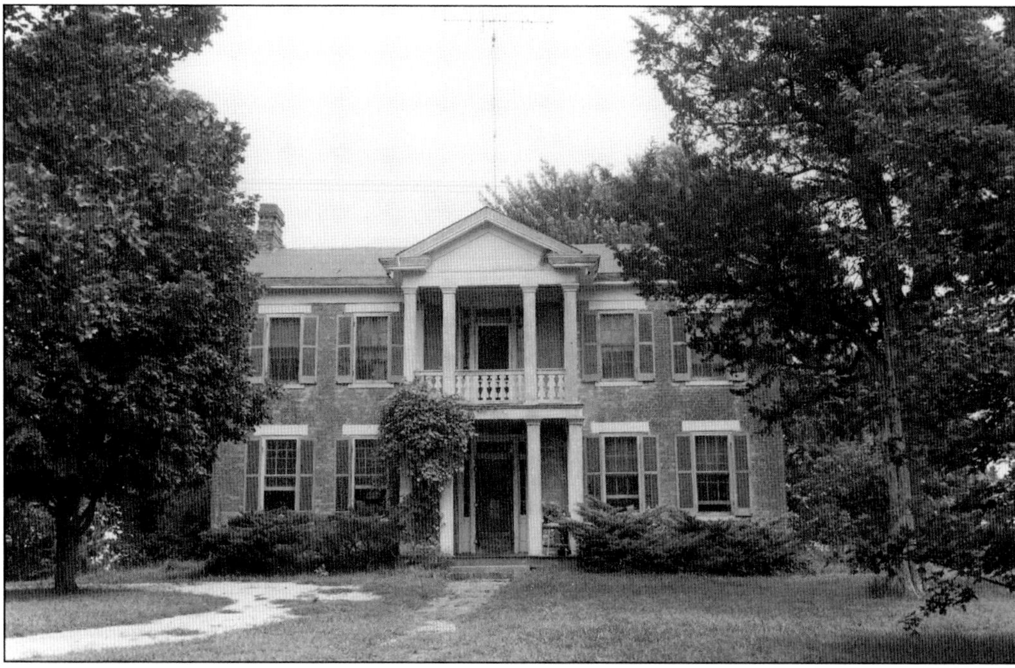

The Henry Hogge home, built in 1867, still stands today. The house was constructed on the site of an earlier home from where it is said owner Daniel Watts watched shots being fired at Arrow Rock from a Yankee steamboat during the Civil War. (Courtesy of Friends of Arrow Rock.)

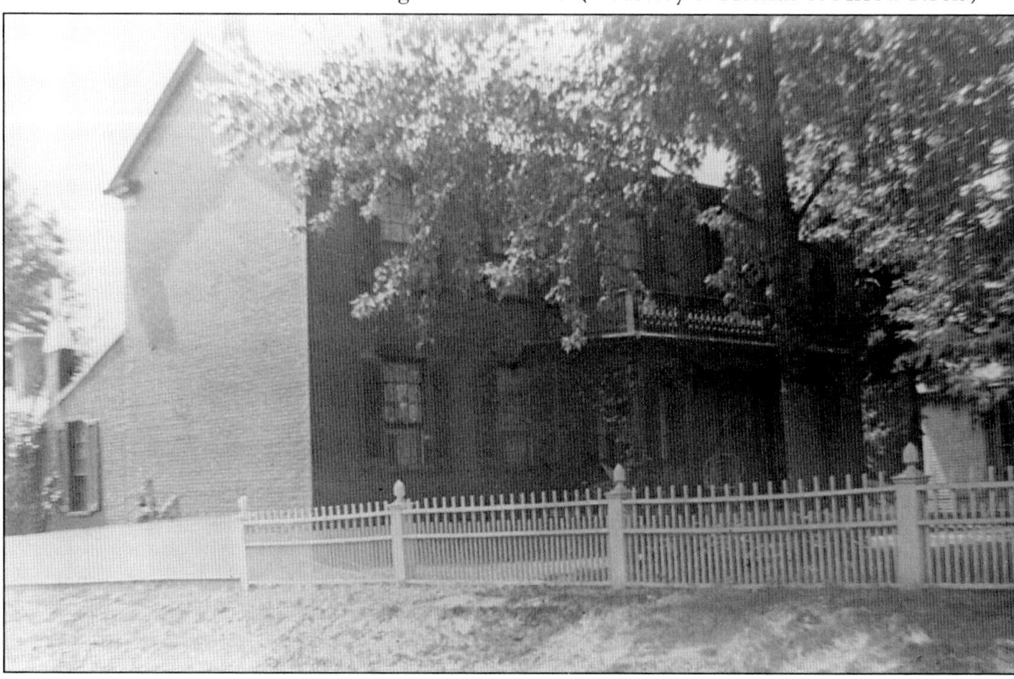

This stately brick home on Main Street, constructed in 1840 by Dr. William Price, still impresses visitors. In 1912, it was the home of the John McGuffin family. McGuffin owned the local hardware store. A niece, Georgia Stean, was orphaned at age 6 and lived with the McGuffins until her 1913 marriage. (Courtesy of Missouri Department of Natural Resources.)

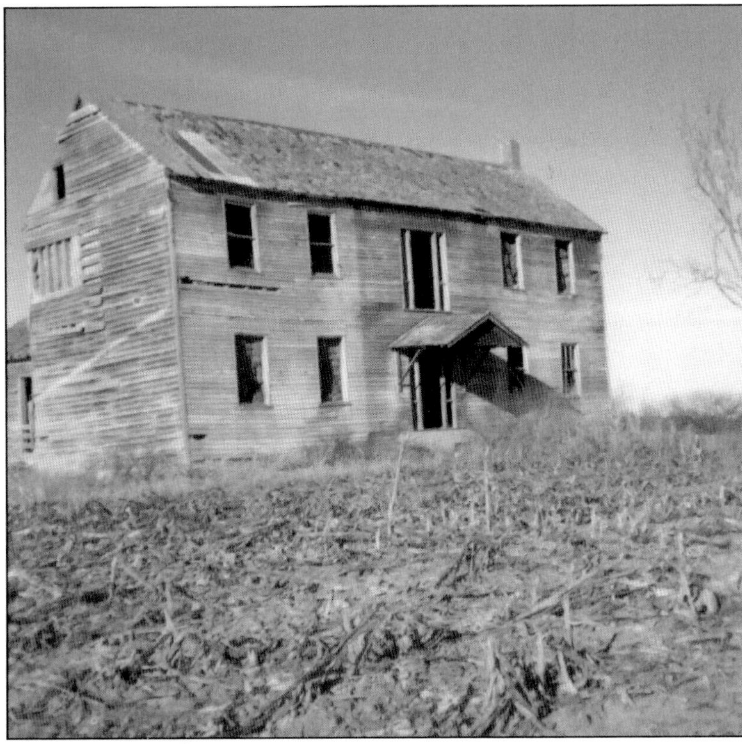

Meredith Miles Marmaduke, a successful farmer and son-in-law of Dr. John Sappington, lived in this home southwest of Arrow Rock. He was elected Missouri's lieutenant governor in 1840 and became the state's eighth governor when his predecessor, Thomas Reynolds, committed suicide nine months before the end of his term. By 1973, Marmaduke's home had been relegated to use as a hay barn. (Courtesy of Thomas B. Hall III.)

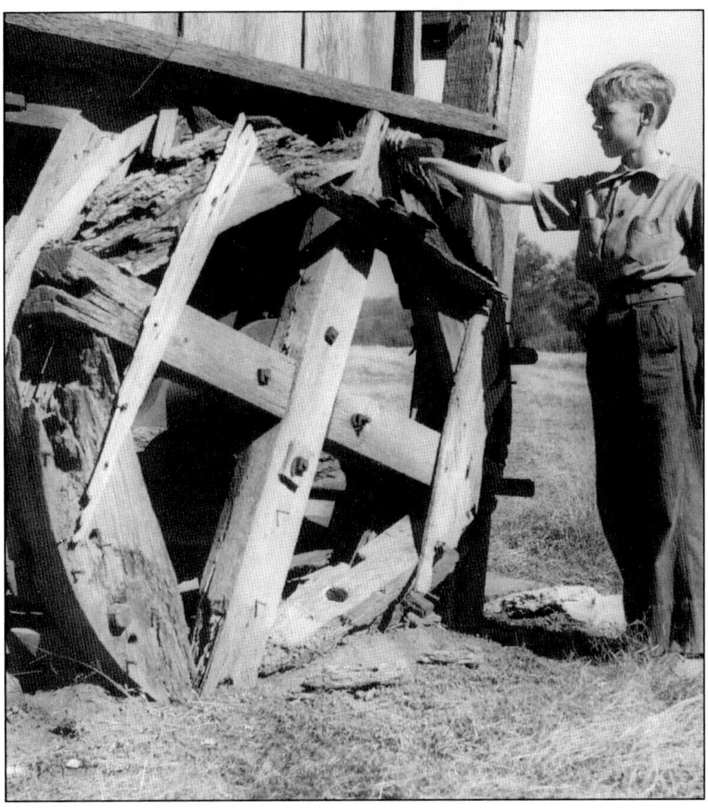

In the mid-1800s, hemp was used in the manufacture of rope and cording for cotton bales. That connection to the South's cotton industry was an important component of Arrow Rock's economy before the Civil War. A hemp press, like this one, was used to press the hemp stalks into bales for ease of shipping. (Courtesy of Missouri Department of Natural Resources.)

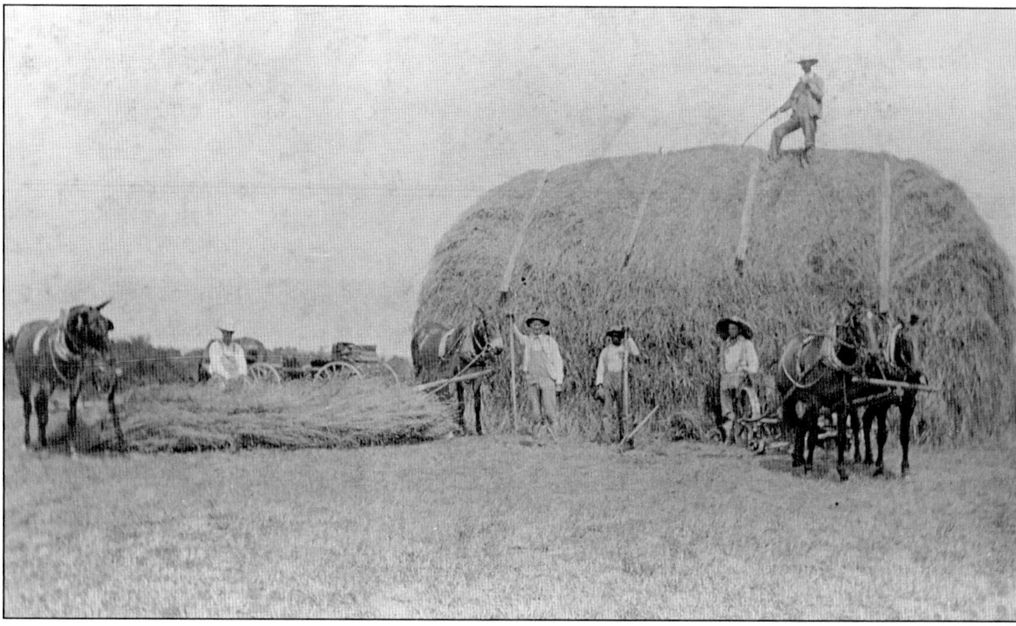

In 1895, it took many men and a few strong mules to gather hay for the winter. Monroe Thomas was among those helping in the field on this day. Like many young men of his era, Thomas helped support his family by working odd jobs. One of his favorite jobs was hauling ice from the frozen river to supply the Arrow Rock Tavern. (Courtesy of Missouri Department of Natural Resources.)

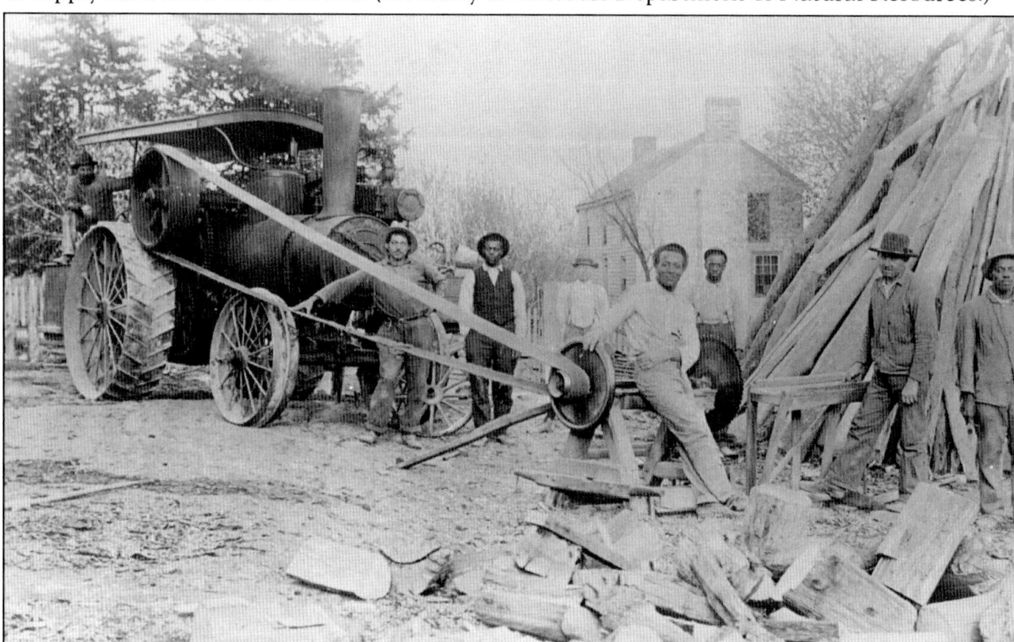

Arrow Rock ran on steam power in 1907 when entrepreneur Daniel Kuhn used local labor to operate his lumber mill. Steam engines were one of the great technological advances of the 19th century and allowed sawmill owners like Kuhn to locate their mills anywhere, not just adjacent to water. This mill was situated on land behind the Arrow Rock Tavern. (Courtesy of Missouri Department of Natural Resources.)

The Arrow Rock Cemetery, one mile west of town, was established in 1849 when the town board paid property owner George Fall $20 for one acre of land. The cemetery was expanded in 1856 and is still open for interments. In this 1914 photograph, members of the Spurlock and McGuffin families examine the damaged grave marker of J.W. Thompson. (Courtesy of Missouri Department of Natural Resources.)

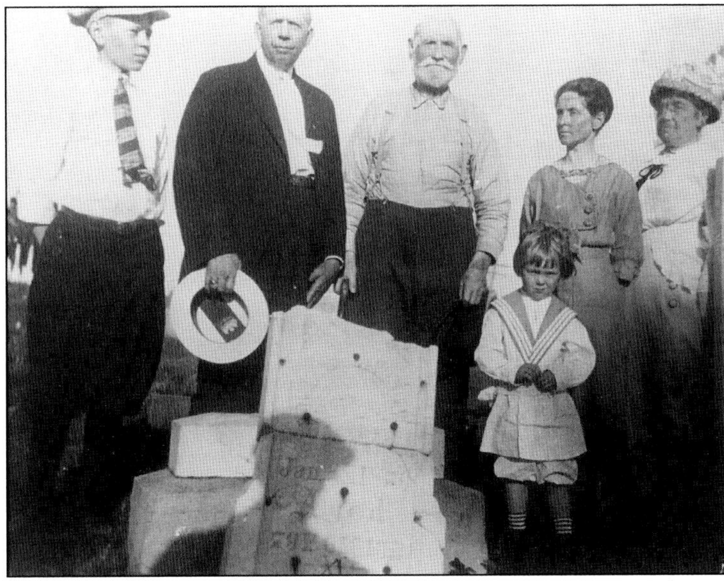

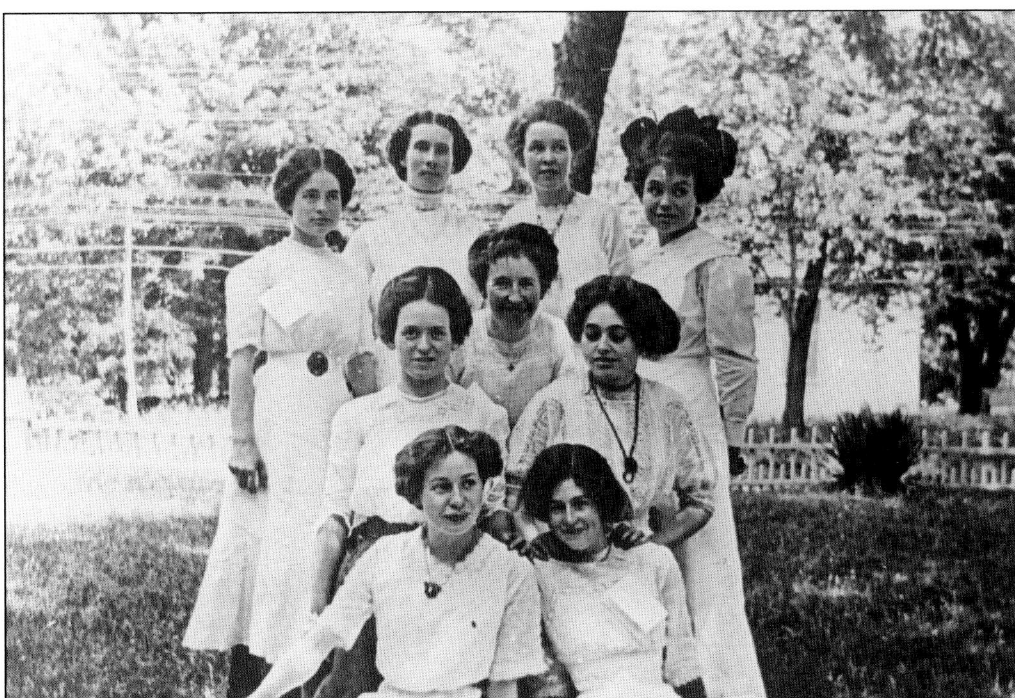

In 1912, these elaborately coiffed young women were at the center of Arrow Rock's social scene. Among those gathered in front of the McGuffin home was Sadie Hogge (rear, second from left) who eschewed marriage for a career as a secretary at the US Capitol. She returned to Arrow Rock after retirement and lived here until her death in 1967 at age 85. (Courtesy of Missouri Department of Natural Resources.)

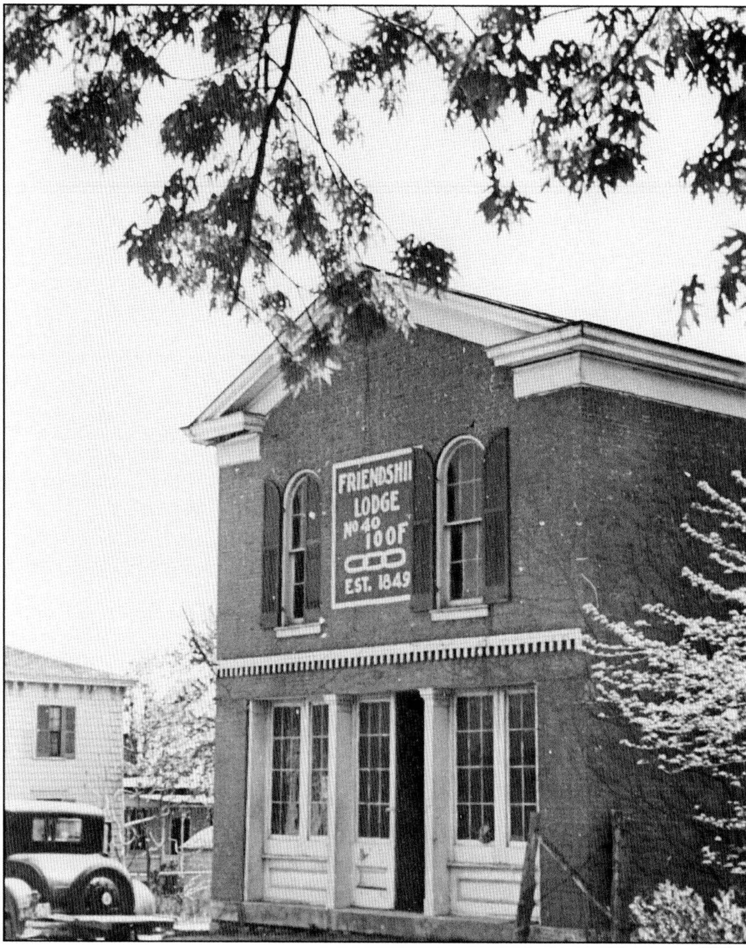

The Independent Order of Odd Fellows (IOOF) was established in England in 1849 as a social organization for the working class. The Arrow Rock chapter spent $3,000 to build its two-story lodge in 1868. George Caleb Bingham was an early member of the chapter. The upstairs was used for meetings until 1927 and is still furnished as it would have looked while active. (Courtesy of Friends of Arrow Rock.)

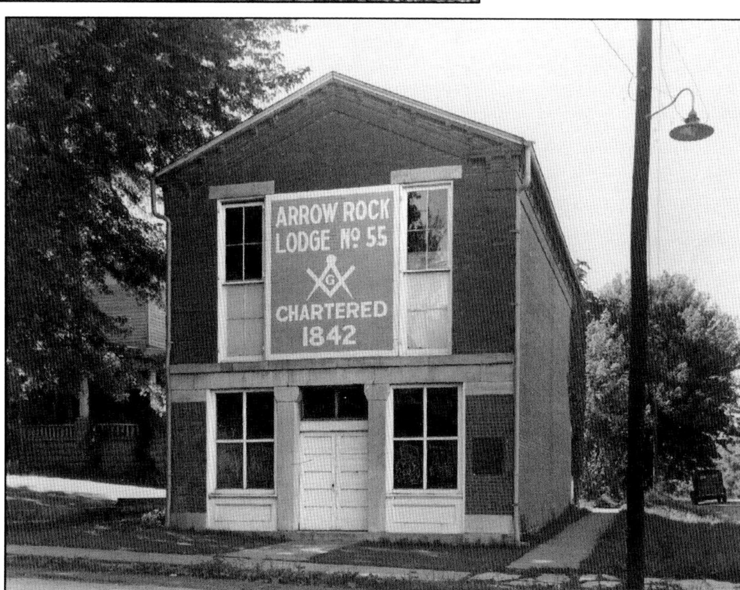

Arrow Rock Lodge No. 55 of the Ancient Free and Accepted Masons was founded in 1842 and built its hall in 1868. The building is across the street and almost an exact mirror of the Odd Fellows Lodge constructed the same year. The Masons, while still active in town, moved their lodge in 2007 and sold this building to the Friends of Arrow Rock. (Courtesy of Friends of Arrow Rock.)

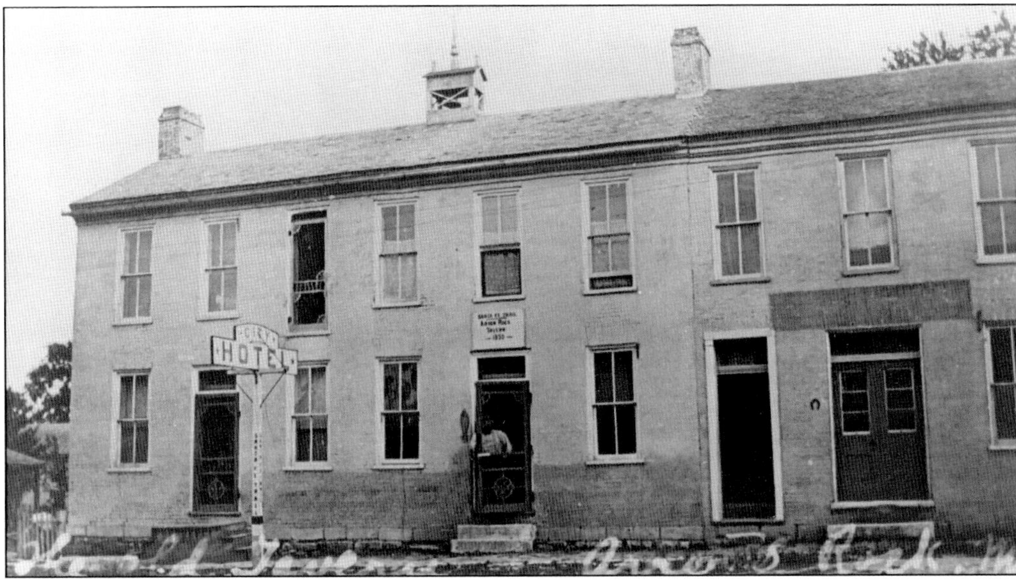

Since Joseph Huston constructed the two-story, Federal-style building in 1834, the Arrow Rock Tavern has been the town's most important and recognizable structure. Although the structure was originally built as a residence for his family, the business-minded Huston recognized the potential in expanding the building to create a hotel and restaurant for travelers and a gathering place for locals. The tavern soon became the place to go to catch up on the political and social discourse of the day. Artist and Arrow Rock resident George Caleb Bingham immortalized the Arrow Rock Tavern's front facade in his 1852 painting *Canvassing for a Vote*. By 1912, the iconic building had fallen into a state of disrepair. (Images courtesy of Friends of Arrow Rock.)

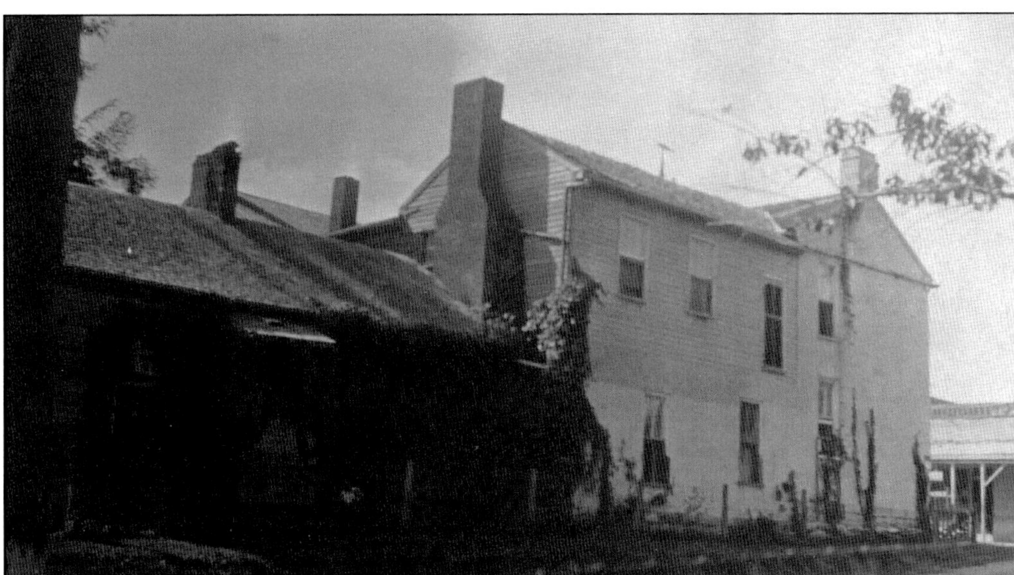

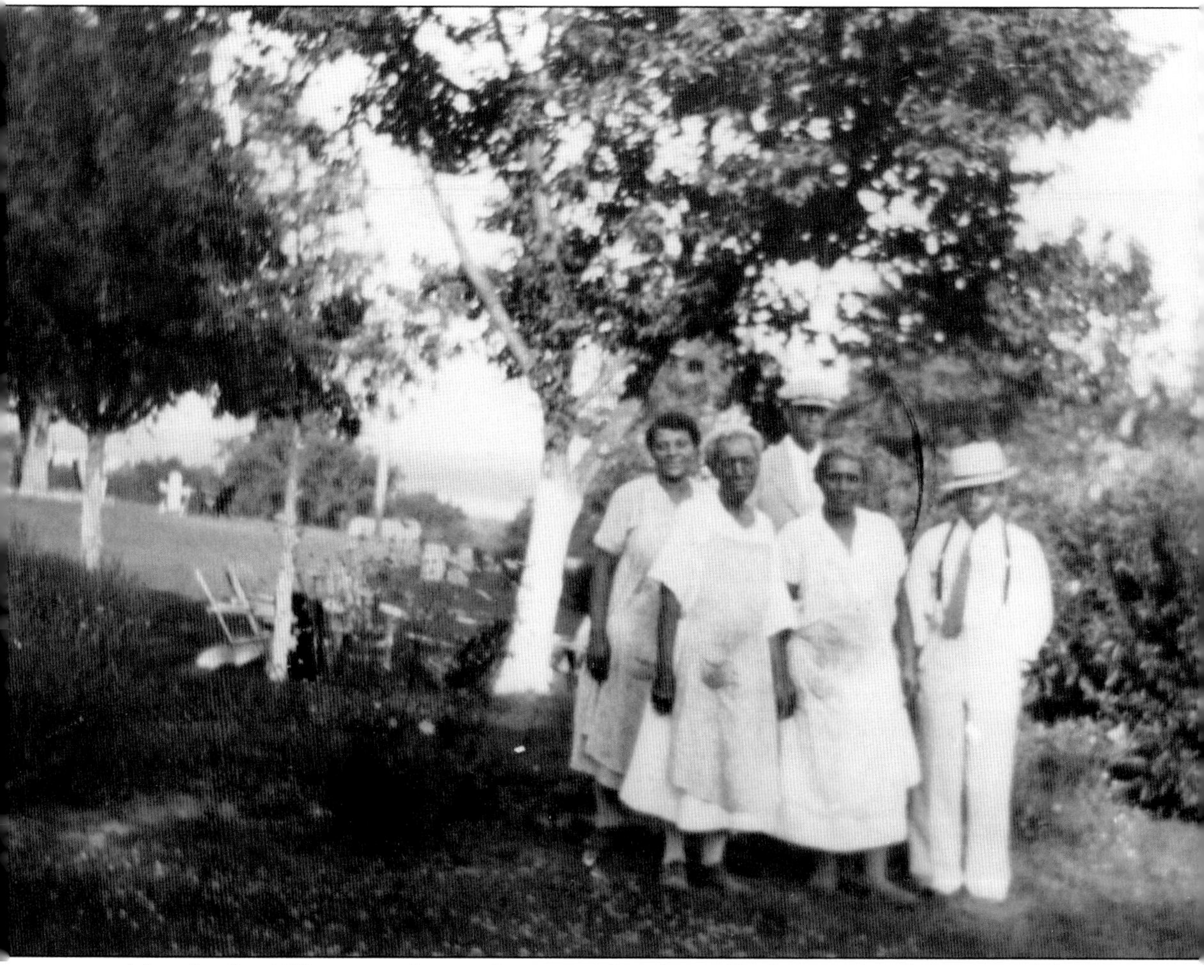

After the Civil War, many former slaves stayed in Arrow Rock to work as laborers and domestic help. Others moved in from defunct hemp and tobacco plantations. In 1912, when Arrow Rock Tavern workers posed for this photograph, African Americans accounted for nearly 50 percent of the town's population. Currently, there are no black residents among the 56 people who live in the village. (Courtesy of Friends of Arrow Rock.)

Two

The New Pioneers

What is so special about Arrow Rock? There is a long list of answers to that question today, thanks to the efforts of people who cared about preservation long before preservation was in vogue.

It began in 1912 with local citizens who formed the Arrow Rock chapter of the National Old Trails Road Association. The association aimed to connect old pioneer and Indian trails to create a highway stretching across the United States. In those days, many of the roads were still made of dirt; traveling was slow and difficult. To make it worth the trip, local associations, like the one in Arrow Rock, created interesting attractions along the way. In Arrow Rock, that attraction was a museum room in the Arrow Rock Tavern.

A few years later, the Daughters of the American Revolution took the next step. They put pressure on the Missouri Legislature and came away with enough money to repair and restore the Arrow Rock Tavern. Missouri's lawmakers had just one condition: the DAR had to manage the property, a responsibility the organization accepted with enthusiasm.

The state was so impressed with the tavern's revival that it established a state park on land surrounding the building. The park quickly expanded and became a tourist attraction in its own right.

By mid-century, the beautified tavern and the Arrow Rock State Park were thriving, but homes and buildings throughout the village were suffering from neglect. One home, a crumbling Greek Revival, whose days of grandeur were long gone, caught the eye of Bill and Cora Lee Miller. There were plenty of naysayers who warned them away from the restoration project, but the Millers were determined. Their transformation of the Miller-Bradford House inspired others, and a preservation revolution was underway.

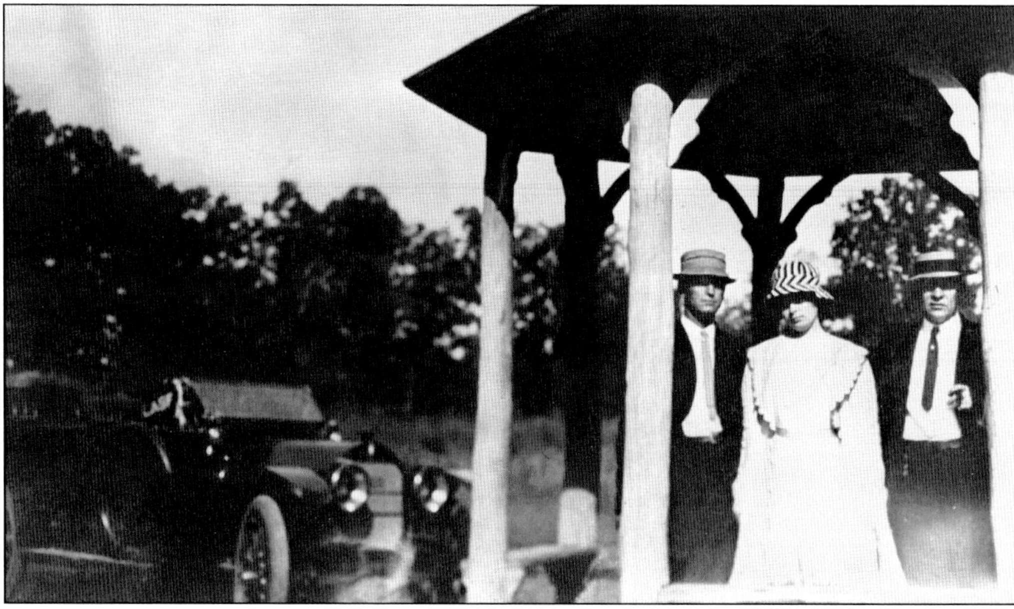

The National Old Trails Road Association was established in 1912 to promote a New York-to-California autoroute that connected old pioneer and Indian trails. Local chapters along the route, like the one in Arrow Rock, sought to capture the interest of travelers with attention-grabbing attractions. These association members were on their way to a meeting in Arrow Rock in 1915. (Courtesy of Missouri Department of Natural Resources.)

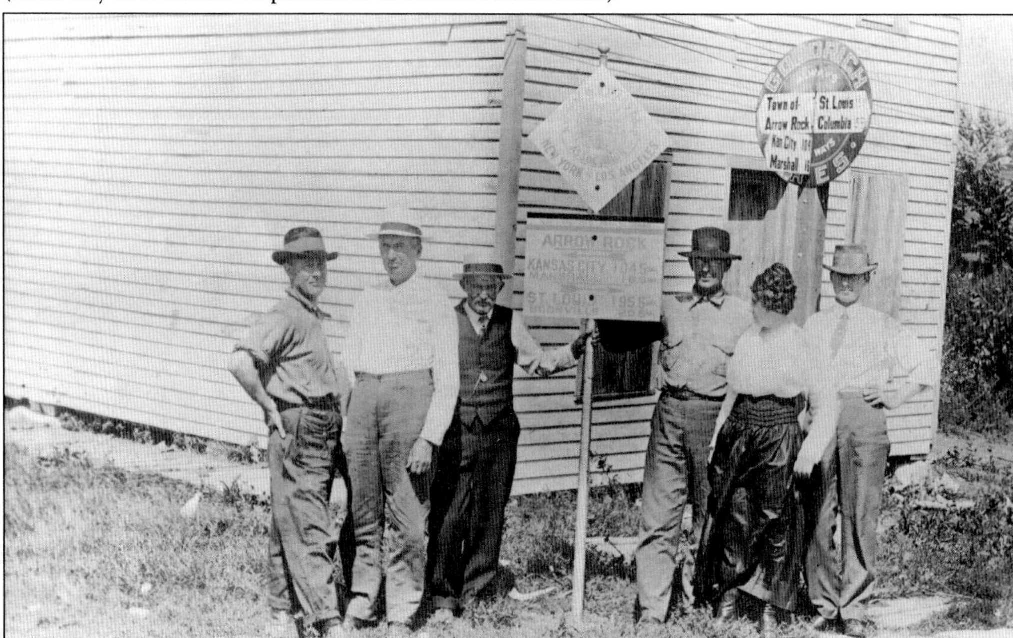

Arrow Rock was a convenient stop for cross-state travelers in the early 1900s, but by 1926, parts of the National Old Trails Road had been absorbed into US Route 66. The road through Arrow Rock was not included on that celebrated cross-country route. (Courtesy of Missouri Department of Natural Resources.)

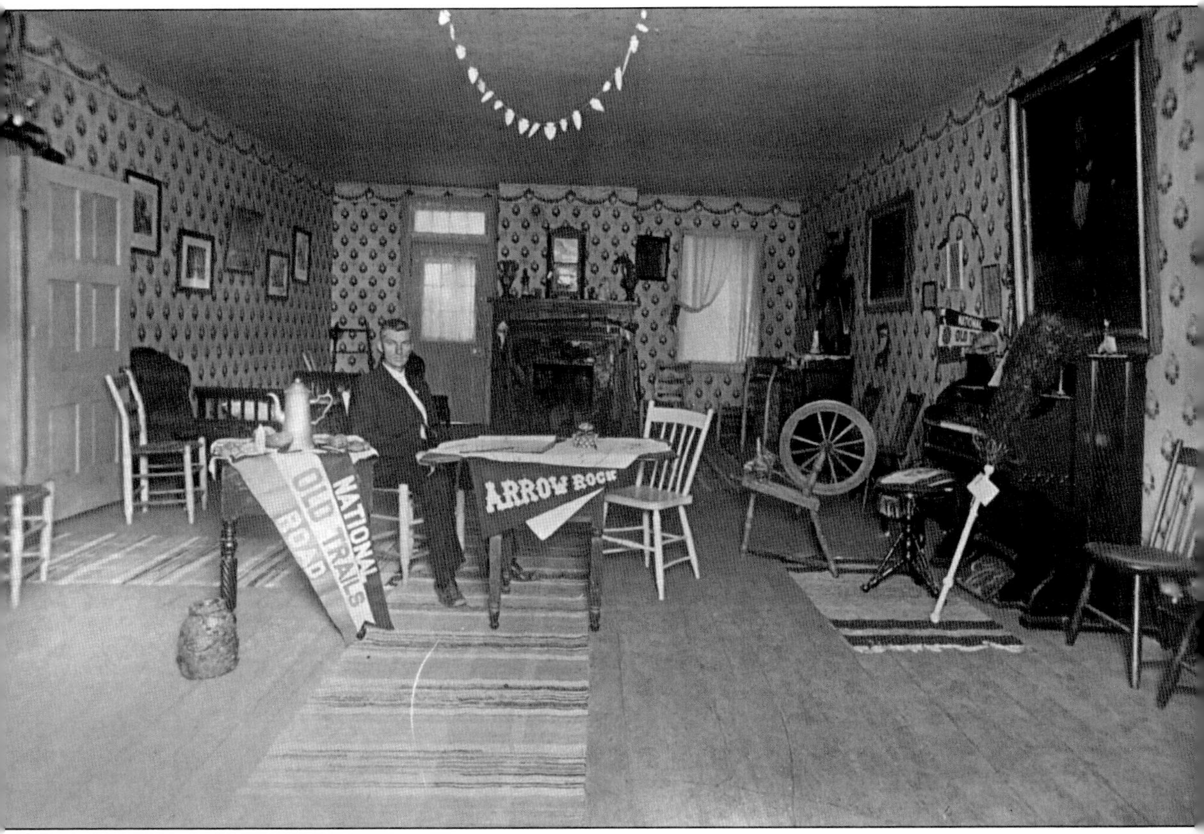

In 1912, the National Old Trails Road Association established a museum room in the Arrow Rock Tavern, owned at the time by Watson Diggs (pictured). A 1919 article in *American Motorist* magazine offered a rather romanticized description of the tavern: "The Arrow Rock tavern, on a high bluff on the Missouri river, was built in 1830 of bricks burned by slaves. The interior construction is in conformity with the idea of the old-time roadway inn, large fireplaces and windows, a commodious reception room with a high mantel, big antlers above, the woodwork throughout being of solid walnut." In the early days of historic preservation, artifacts did not always relate to the place they were displayed, as was the case with an item described in the article: "One interesting feature shown guests in this old stopping place is Daniel Boone's fiddle, which was given him by the black man who was with him during the final hunting trips of the noted pioneer." (Courtesy of Missouri Department of Natural Resources.)

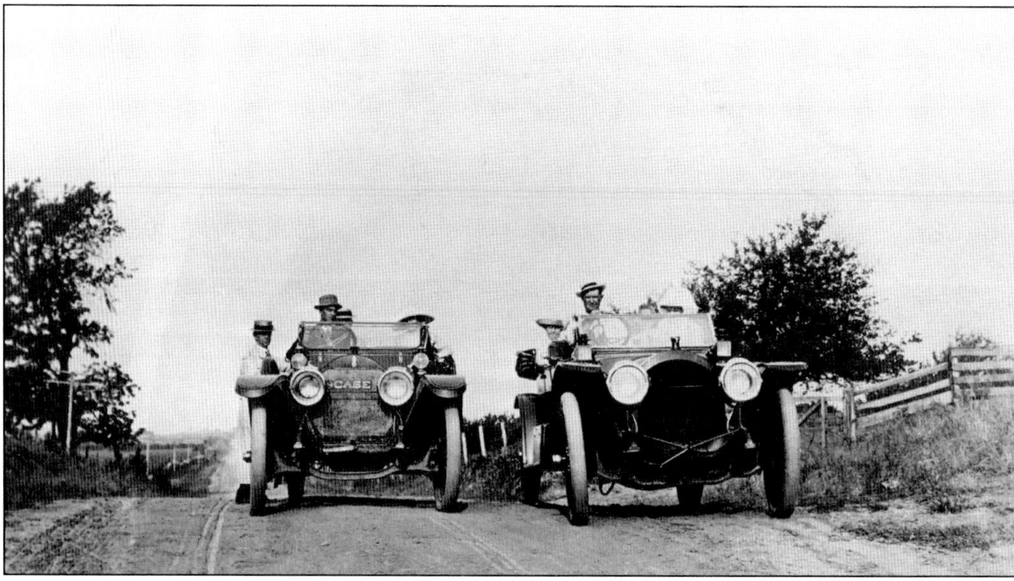

In 1914, the highway to Arrow Rock was made of dirt, but that did not deter this fun-loving group. The car on the left is full of Hogge family members, including driver Henry, plus Sadie, Albert (on running board), and Simon. Frank Brockway drives the other car. The National Old Trails Road Association soon kicked off a campaign to "Get Missouri out of the Mud" by paving its highways. (Courtesy of Friends of Arrow Rock.)

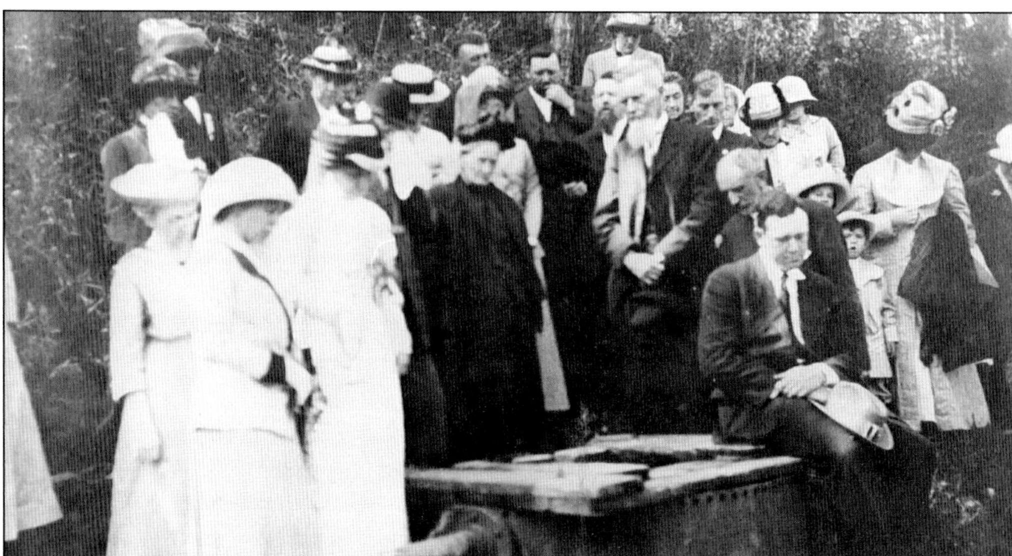

Early Arrow Rock preservationists recognized that Big Spring, a water source for pioneers heading west, was a historical highlight of the village. The National Old Trails Road Association held a meeting there in 1913. T.C. Rainey, the white-bearded man in the center, was among the first to document Arrow Rock's history in his book *Along the Old Trail*. (Courtesy of Missouri Department of Natural Resources.)

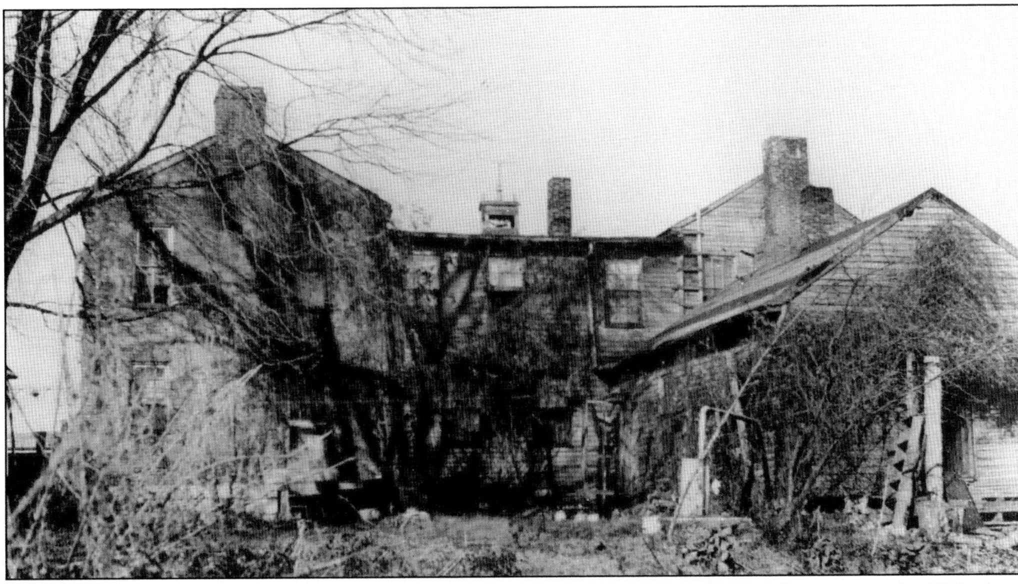

The Arrow Rock chapter of the Daughters of the American Revolution, known as the "Mothers and Daughters" chapter, was established in 1921 and led by the formidable Nettie Morris Dickson. The group wasted no time finding a project; they set out to restore the Arrow Rock Tavern, and by 1923, the group had secured funding for the project. (Courtesy of Friends of Arrow Rock.)

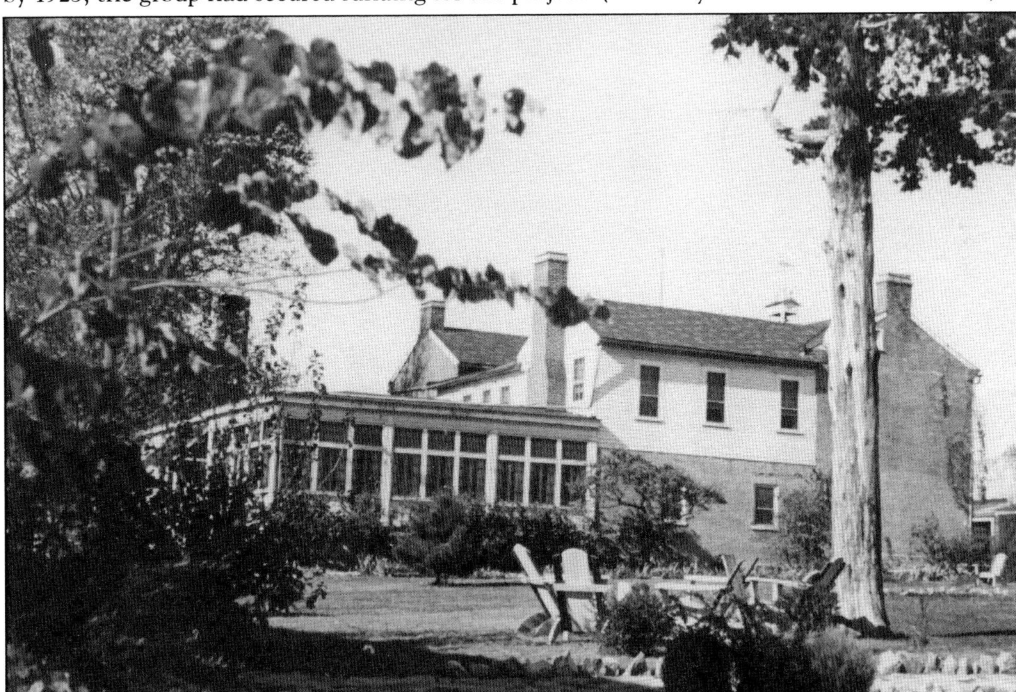

The Daughters of the American Revolution persuaded the Missouri Legislature to purchase the Arrow Rock Tavern for $5,000, and the ladies oversaw the building's restoration. The state appointed the DAR as permanent custodian of the property, including its restaurant and lodging businesses. The restoration was completed in 1926. (Courtesy of Friends of Arrow Rock.)

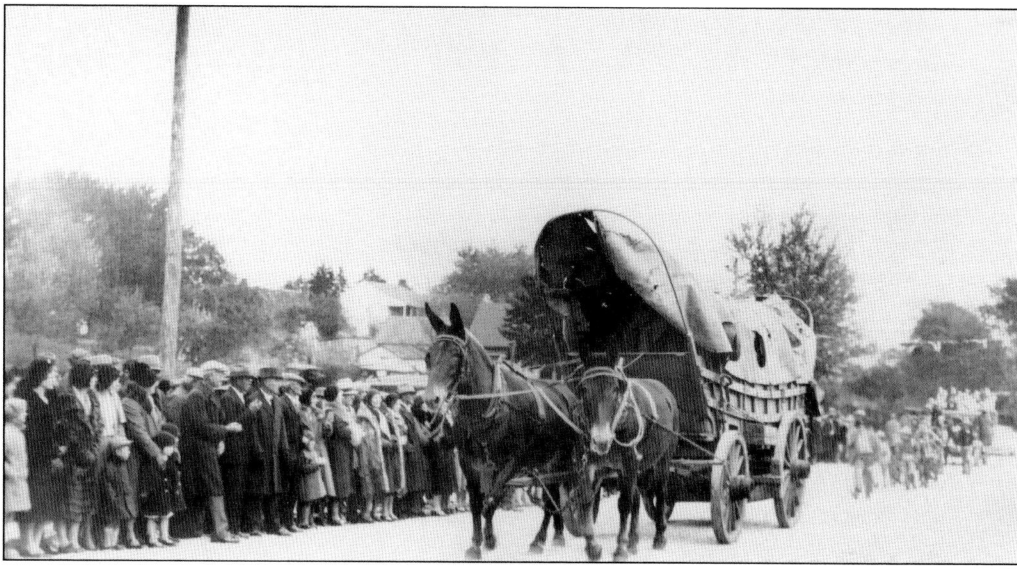

Historical dates tended to get a bit muddied when the notion of preservation was first gaining traction in Arrow Rock. Although later research confirms the construction date of the Arrow Rock Tavern as 1834, the Daughters of the American Revolution celebrated the building's centennial with a weekend-long celebration in 1930. The centennial events included a parade that featured floats from regional DAR chapters. Each float represented a different period in Arrow Rock's history, from the first episode, featuring "Indian chief and braves on ponies," to the twelfth, recognizing the age of the airplane. (Above, courtesy of Arrow Rock Chapter, DAR; below, courtesy of Friends of Arrow Rock.)

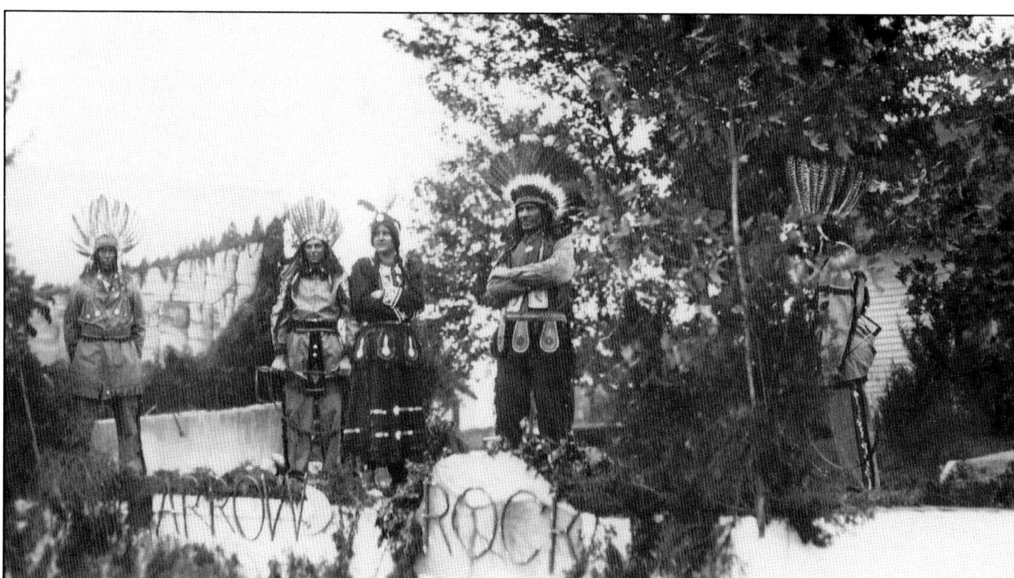

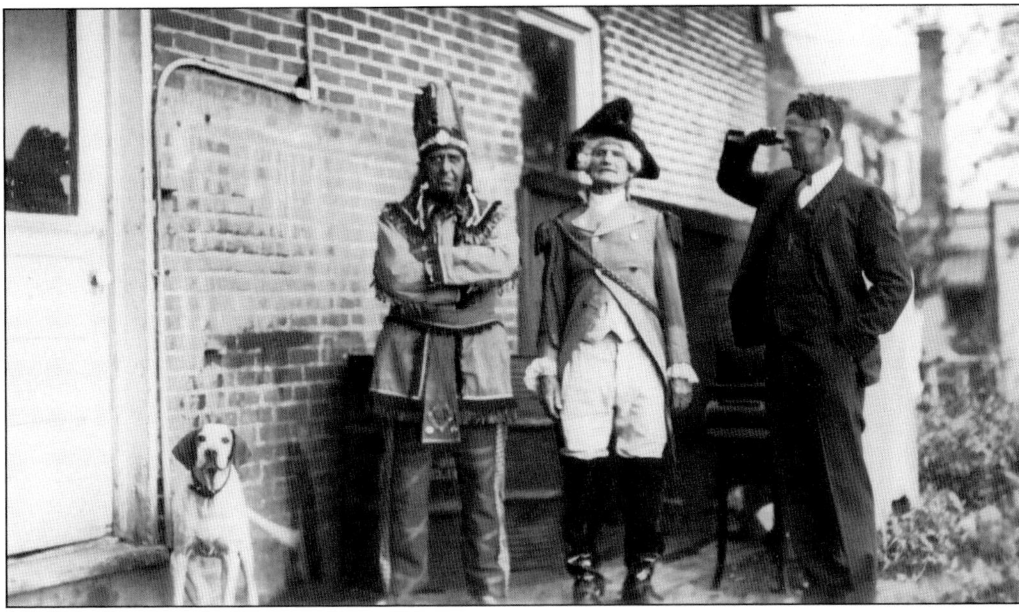

The Daughters of the American Revolution parade in honor of the Arrow Rock Tavern's centennial, titled *From Oxcart to Airplane,* made for some intriguing meetings between famous Americans, including this one between Apache leader Geronimo, portrayed by Russell Davis, and Pres. George Washington, portrayed by Bill Gibson. Local resident George Pearson gives these national icons a salute. (Courtesy of Arrow Rock Chapter, DAR.)

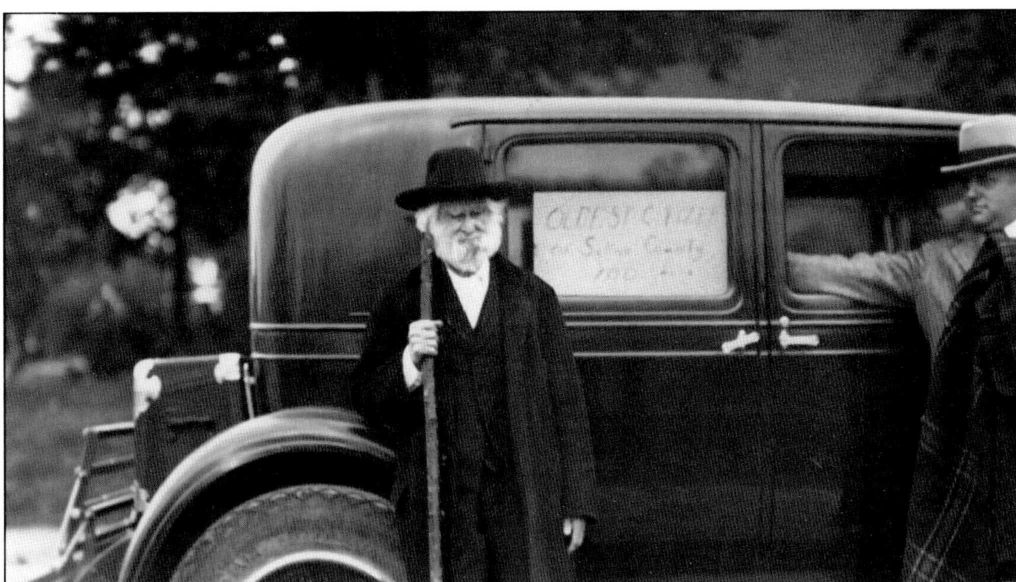

One-hundred-year-old Jacob Keithly, Saline County's oldest citizen, was an honored guest at the Arrow Rock Tavern centennial parade. Keithly, a father of eight, fed his family using innovative farming techniques that included cultivation of a variety of hearty fish species in multiple ponds and construction of a chilled stone barn cooled by a natural spring. Keithly died at age 103. (Courtesy of Friends of Arrow Rock.)

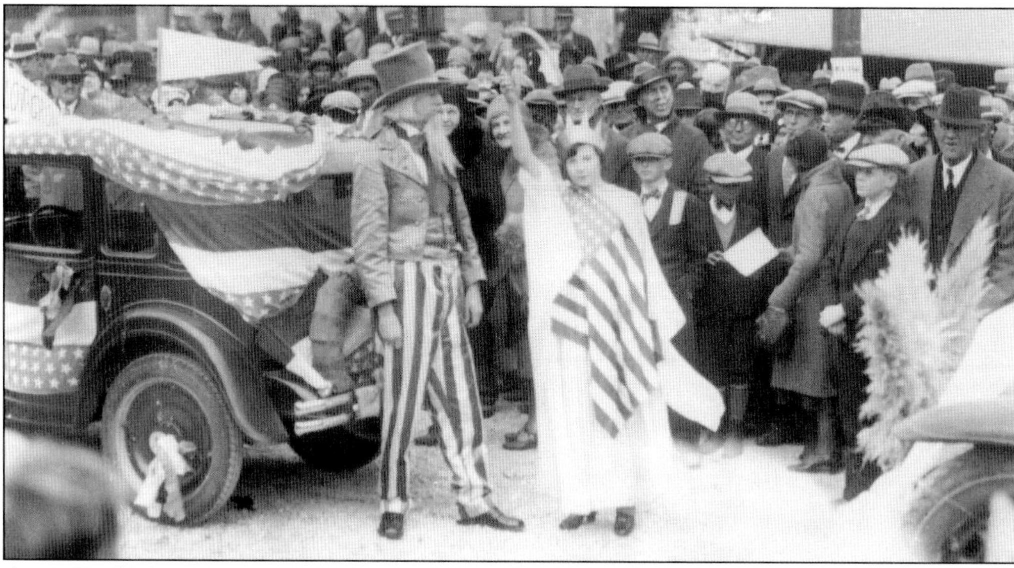

Arrow Rock's Mary Lou Pearson was elected Centennial Queen of the Daughters of the American Revolution's Arrow Rock Tavern Centennial Parade. As queen for the day, Pearson won an escort from Uncle Sam, and the patriotic pair rode in style down the Main Street parade route. (Courtesy of Arrow Rock Chapter, DAR.)

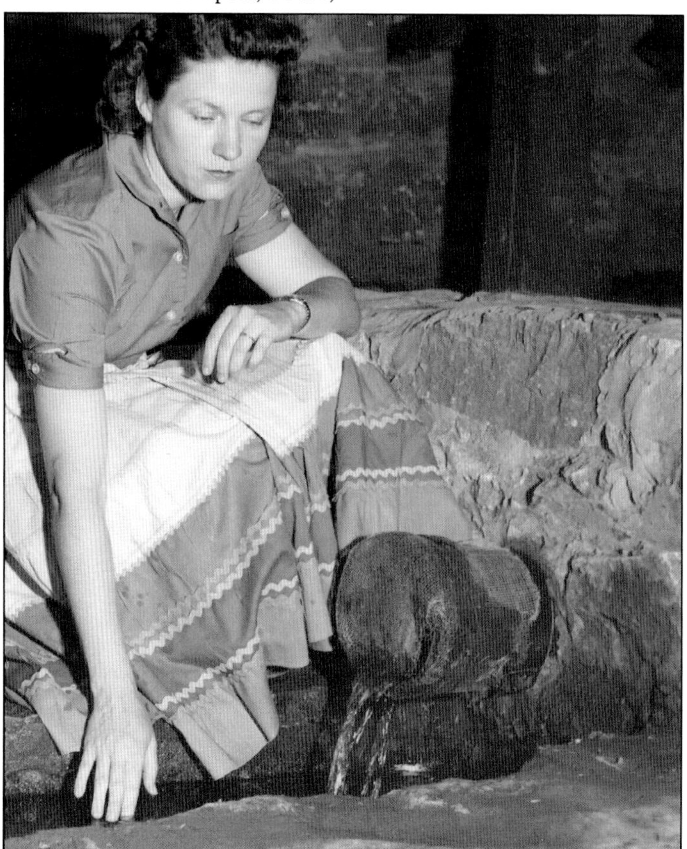

Twenty-five years after Mary Lou Pearson held court in the centennial parade, another woman by the same name was employed as hostess of the Arrow Rock Tavern. Pearson, seen here at the Big Spring, enjoyed a longer tenure than many who served in that position. Some would last only a few months before the challenges of tavern management had them seeking employment elsewhere. (Courtesy of Missouri Department of Natural Resources.)

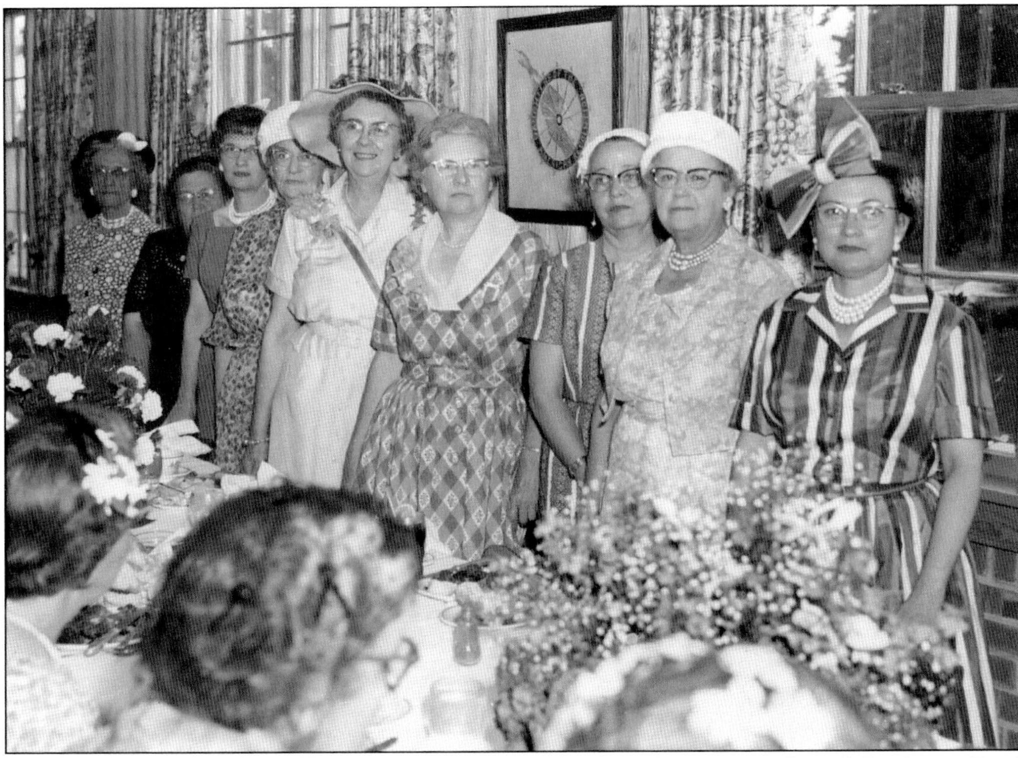

The Daughters of the American Revolution continued to serve as caretaker of the Arrow Rock Tavern until 1985. The members of the organization also took on the responsibility of historical interpretation, which they accomplished through tours and with rooms decorated by area chapters with period furnishings. Here, DAR officers pose for a photograph during a 1961 luncheon. (Courtesy of Friends of Arrow Rock.)

A nursery was among the Arrow Rock Tavern rooms staged by the Daughters of the American Revolution. The room was filled with old-fashioned toys and decorations, and in 1955, it made a favorable impression on young Martha and Al Swisher, who found the furnishings to be just their size. (Courtesy of Missouri Department of Natural Resources.)

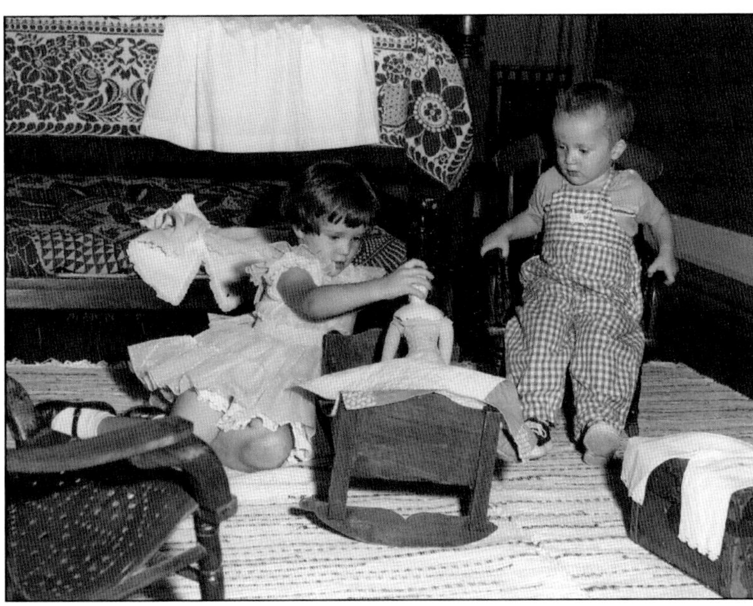

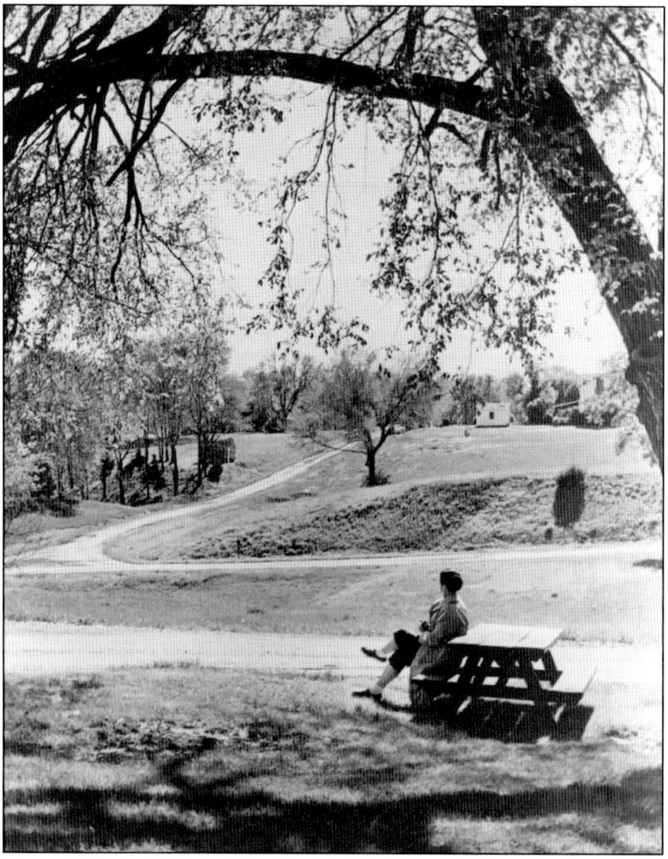

The DAR's successful restoration of the Arrow Rock Tavern prompted the state to establish Arrow Rock State Park in 1926 on land surrounding the building. The park gradually expanded its holdings to include Big Spring, the calaboose, and the Academy Boarding House. In 1976, the state changed Arrow Rock's designation to state historic site, reflecting a new focus on the town's historical importance. (Courtesy of Missouri Department of Natural Resources.)

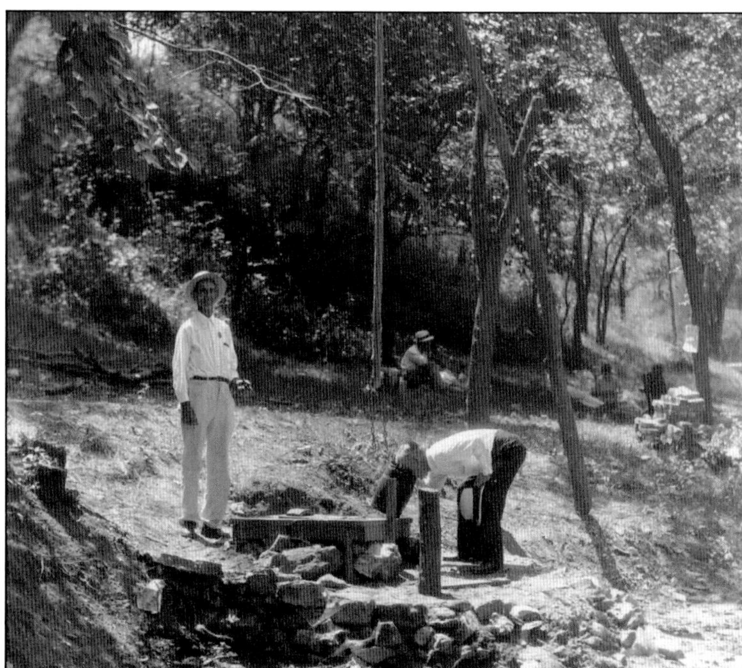

When the Arrow Rock State Park was established in the mid-1920s, Big Spring became a highlight of the new tourist destination. Workers built fences and shelters to protect the integrity of the spring and occasionally took a refreshing drink of the cold water. (Courtesy of Missouri Department of Natural Resources.)

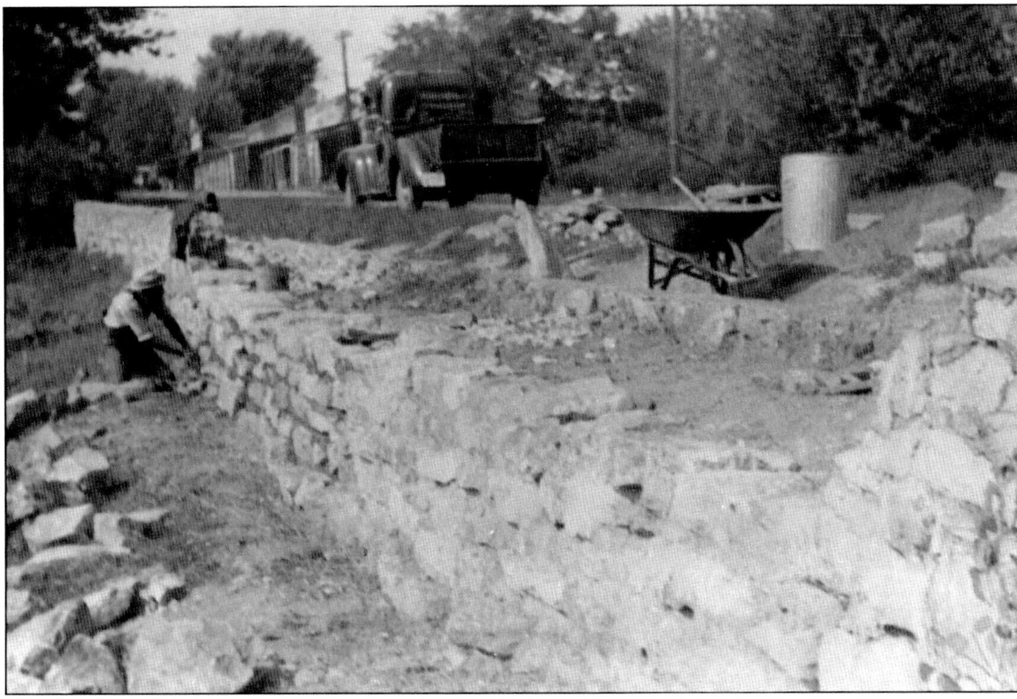

The Works Progress Administration was established in 1935 as part of Pres. Franklin Roosevelt's job-creating New Deal. Works Projects Administration (WPA) workers completed several large projects for the Arrow Rock State Park. One project was the repair and extension of a stone retaining wall that stretches for two blocks alongside Main Street's east end. A portion of the wall dates from the 1840s. (Courtesy of Missouri Department of Natural Resources.)

Little is known of Jacob and Mary Shroyer, who are buried on land now managed by the Arrow Rock State Historic Site. The elaborate gazebo over the two isolated graves was constructed in the 1930s through the WPA. Morris Pearson, superintendent of the Arrow Rock State Park, is seen inspecting the site in 1955. (Courtesy of Missouri Department of Natural Resources.)

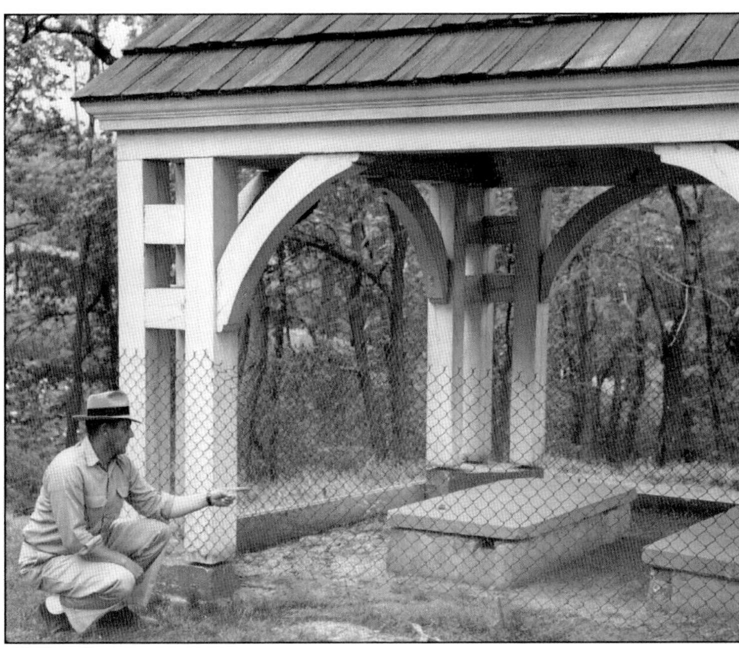

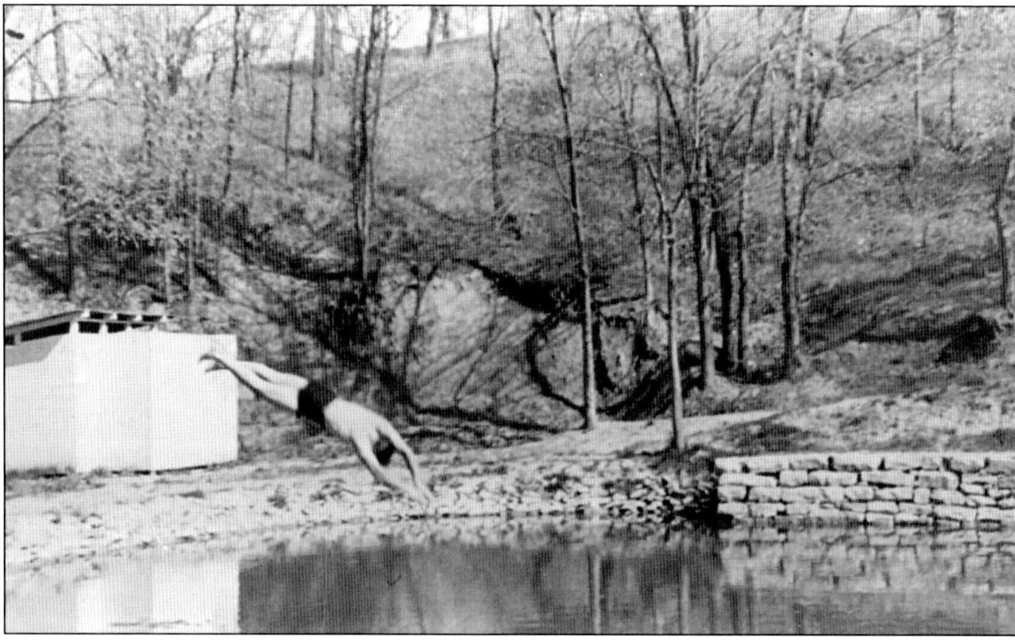

The swimming pool just downstream from Big Spring was a summertime attraction for those bold enough to dive into the chilly water. It was built in 1935 as a WPA project, along with a stone bridge that spans the stream. The pool was destroyed by a flood in 1961, but remnants of the pool's stone walls are still visible. (Courtesy of Missouri Department of Natural Resources.)

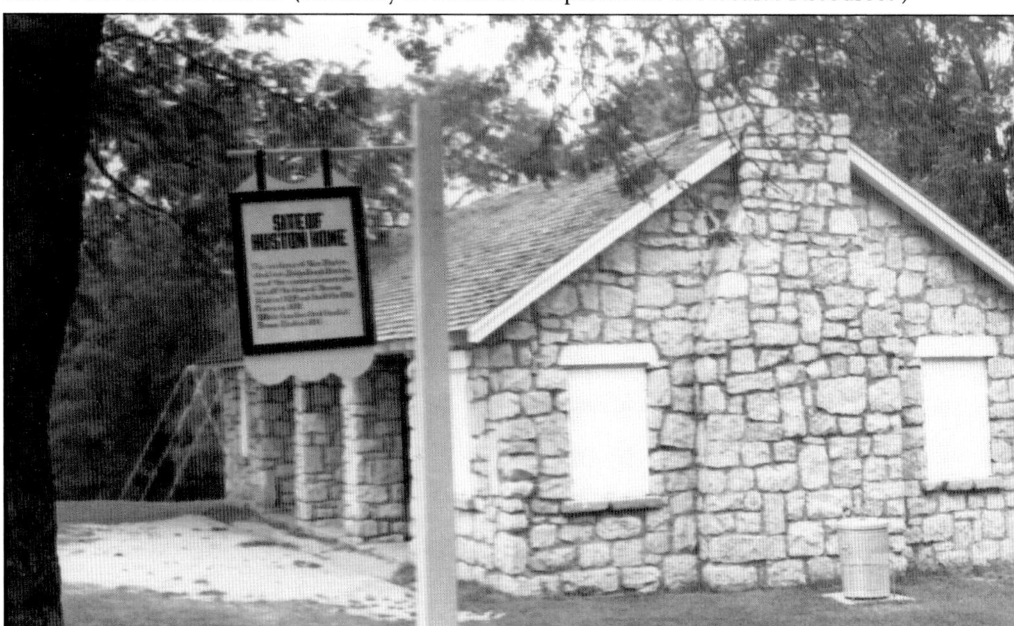

WPA laborers constructed Arrow Rock State Park's stone shelter house on a hill south of town in 1936. The spot had once been the site of Samuel Huston's home. Samuel, son of town founder and Arrow Rock Tavern proprietor Joseph Huston, was known to be somewhat irrepressible in his youth but matured into a respected businessman and mill owner. (Courtesy of Friends of Arrow Rock.)

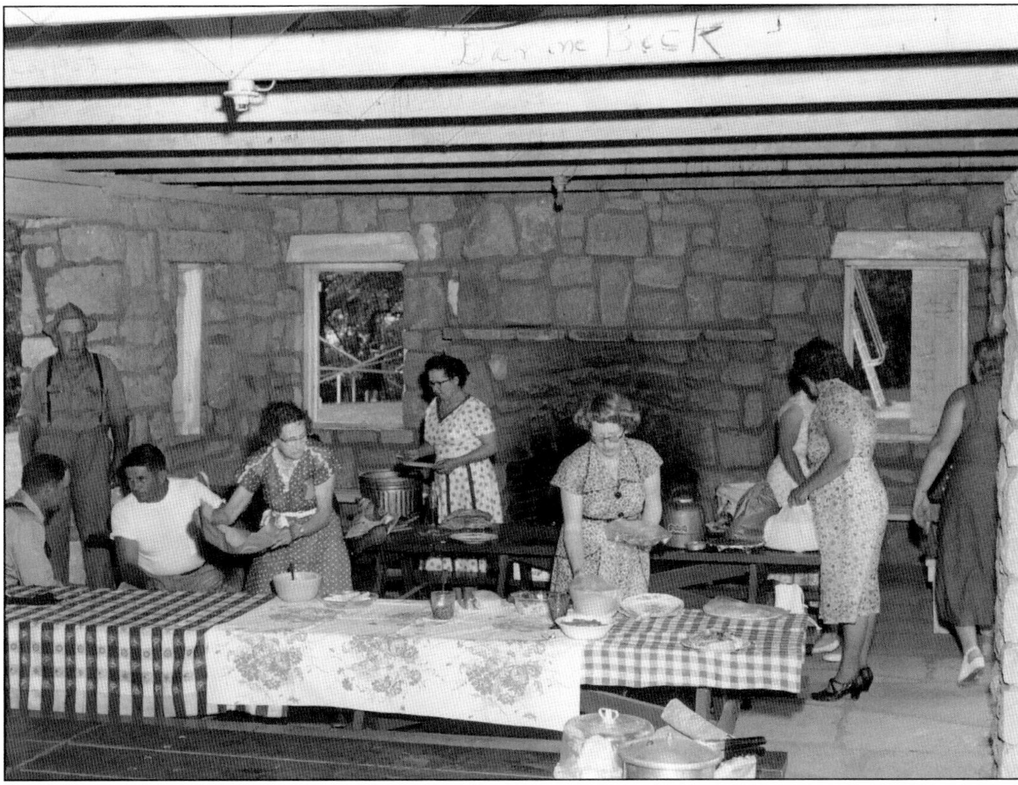

The Arrow Rock State Historic Site shelter house has been used for family reunions, wedding receptions, and community gatherings for decades, and appears virtually unchanged from the way it looked when this group of friends got together for a potluck picnic in 1955. The adjacent playground, on the other hand, has changed dramatically since the 1950s, when the metal slide got sizzling hot in the summer sun and swing chains pinched many a tender finger as youngsters tried to discover how high they could fly. Families who visit the playground today will find safer, modern play structures. (Courtesy of Missouri Department of Natural Resources.)

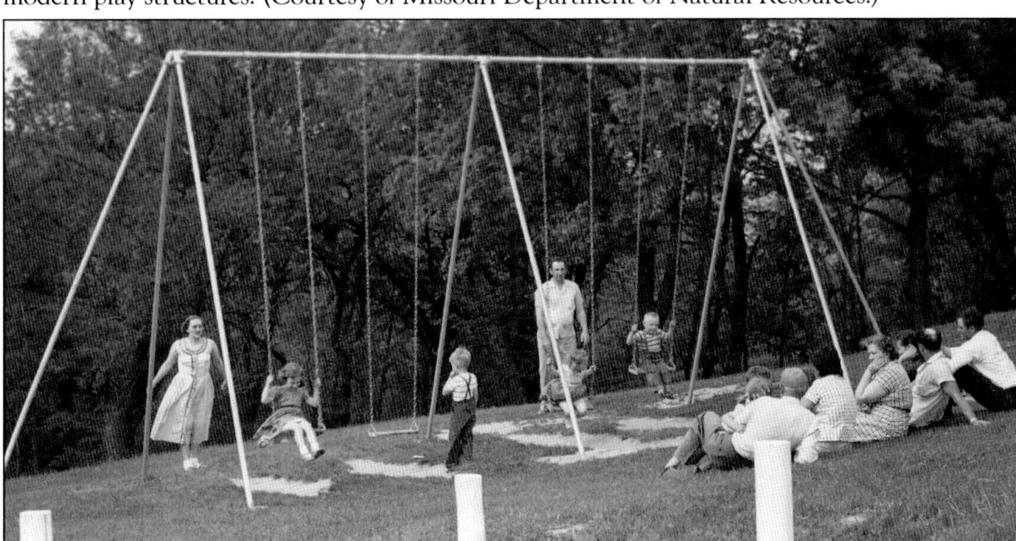

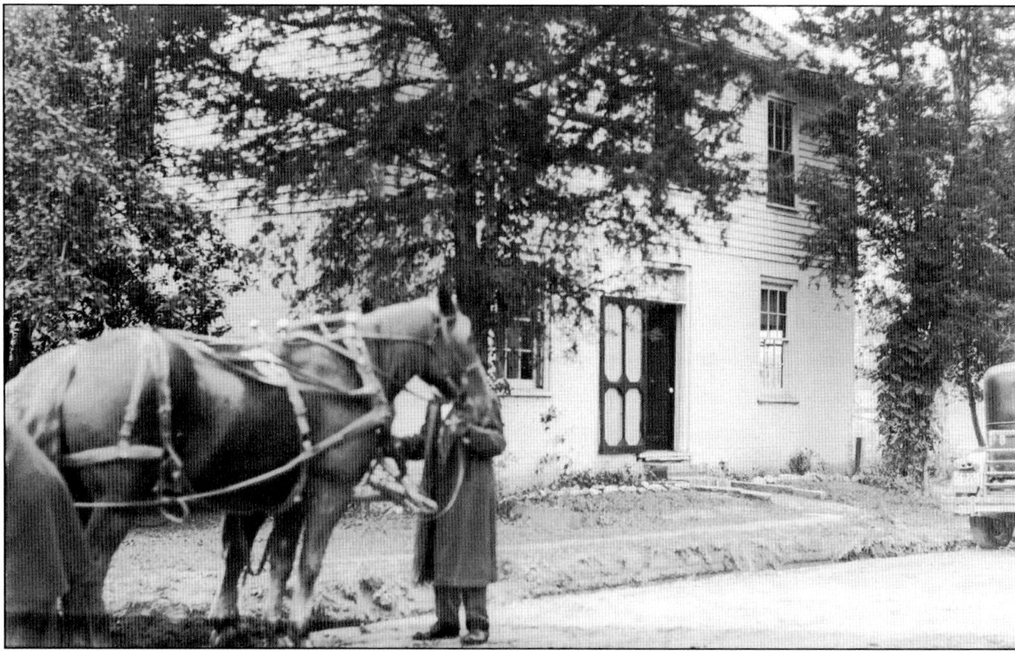

Artist George Caleb Bingham built his Arrow Rock home in 1837. In 1930, the home was a two-story structure. It was believed at the time that the second story was added after the Bingham family left Arrow Rock. To restore the home's authenticity, the State of Missouri had the second story removed using labor available through the WPA. Unfortunately, structural analysis was not as precise in the 1930s as it is today. It has since been determined that the substantial stone foundation was built to support a two-story structure. (Above, courtesy of Arrow Chapter, DAR; below, courtesy of Missouri Department of Natural Resources.)

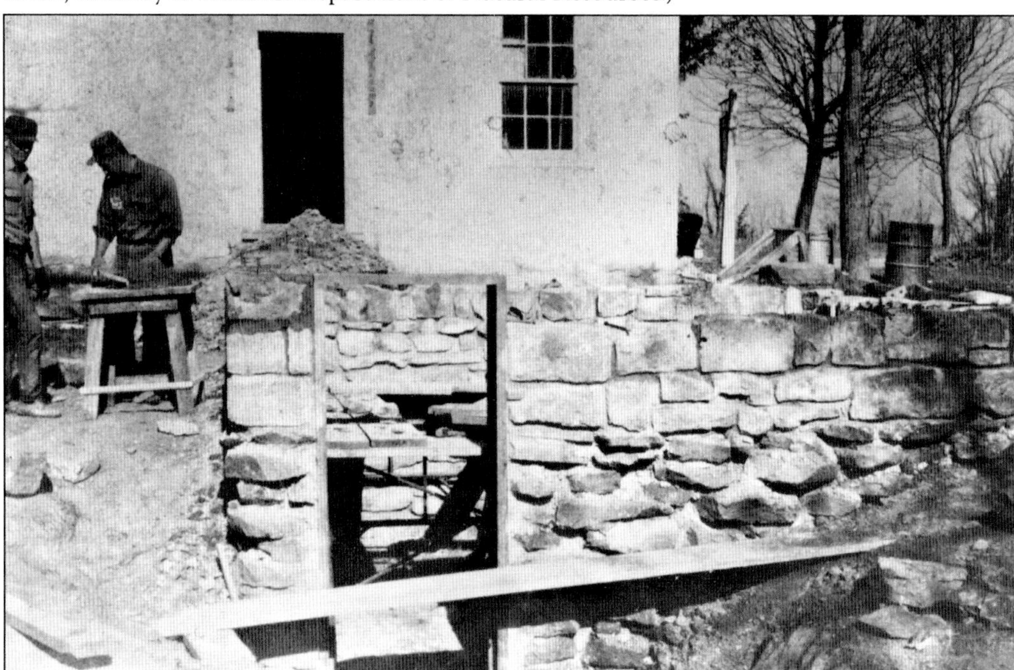

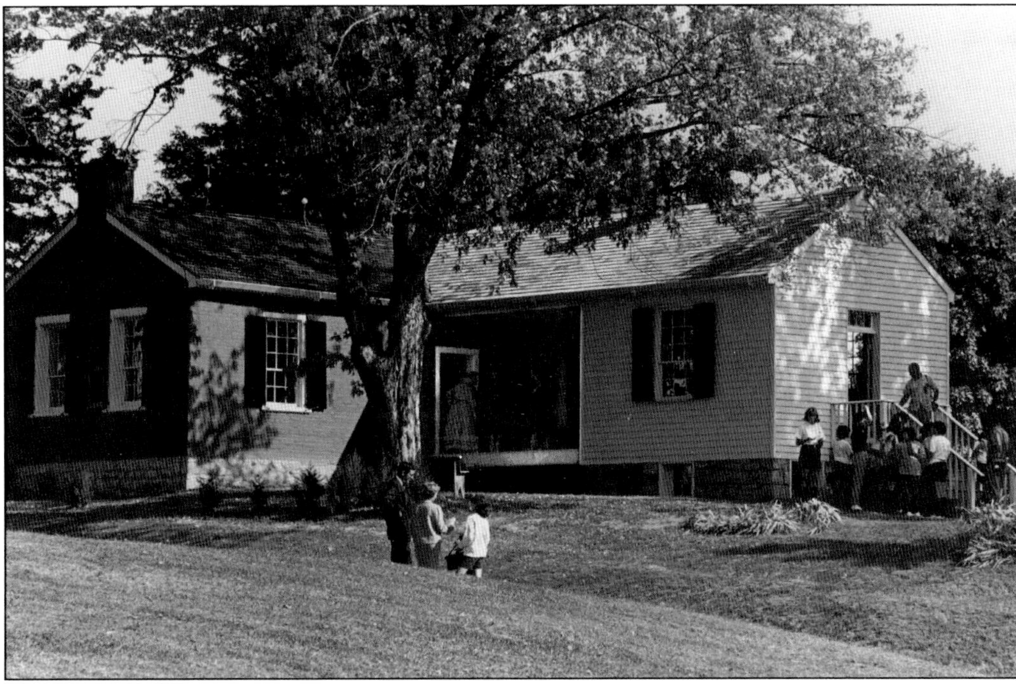

In 1964, State Park officials directed a second restoration of the George Caleb Bingham Home. Architectural studies of the property indicated the home had once included a kitchen building attached to the main house with a dogtrot. Those structures were rebuilt with such care, few visitors realize they are modern recreations. The previously removed second story was not reconstructed because of concerns about stairwell placement. (Courtesy of Friends of Arrow Rock.)

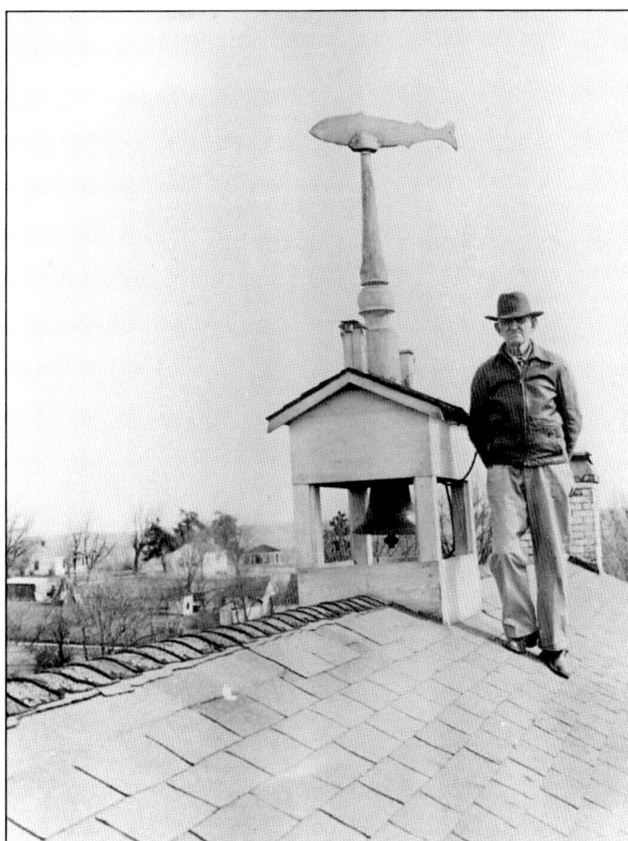

Lester Dickson served as superintendent of the Arrow Rock State Park from 1943 until 1954. One of his duties was to inspect the buildings in his care. Here, he looks at the cupola atop the tavern roof. The fish-shaped weather vane has since been replaced with a replica. The original is held by the Arrow Rock State Historic Site. (Courtesy of Friends of Arrow Rock.)

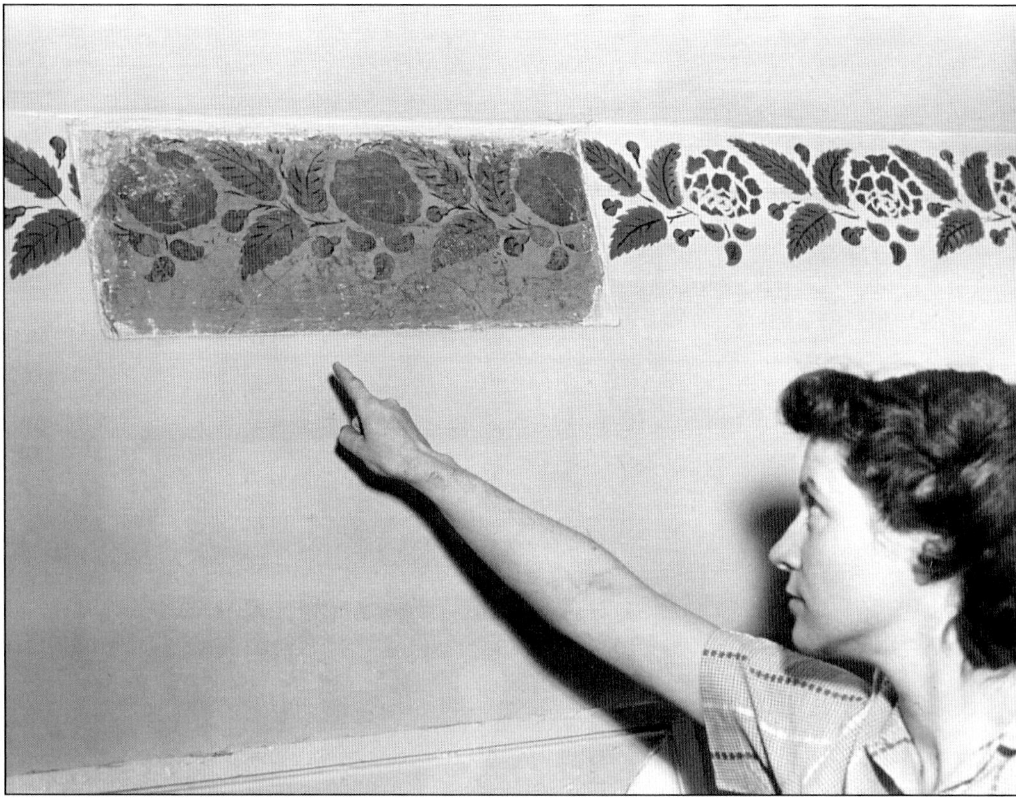

The State of Missouri undertook a major restoration project of the tavern in 1955. The aim was to bring back as much of the original interior as possible. Stenciling discovered on the walls of the upstairs ballroom by tavern hostess Mary Lou Pearson was carefully reproduced. A section of the original stenciling was preserved and remains visible for comparison. (Courtesy of Missouri Department of Natural Resources.)

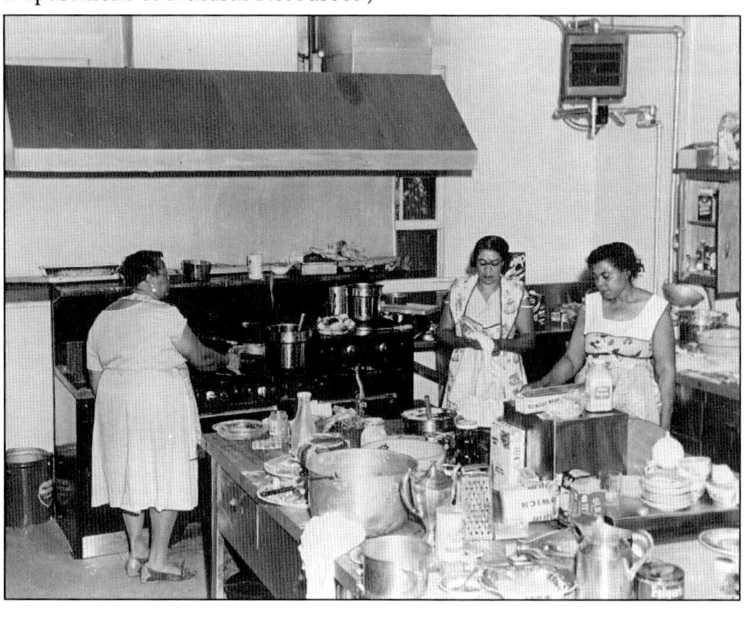

The kitchen in the Arrow Rock Tavern was not a model of organization in 1958, but it did turn out excellent food that kept diners coming back for more, thanks to the efforts of cooks Georgia Woods, Francis Edwards, and Ruth Banks. The tavern was renowned throughout the state for its pan-fried chicken dinners. (Courtesy of Missouri Department of Natural Resources.)

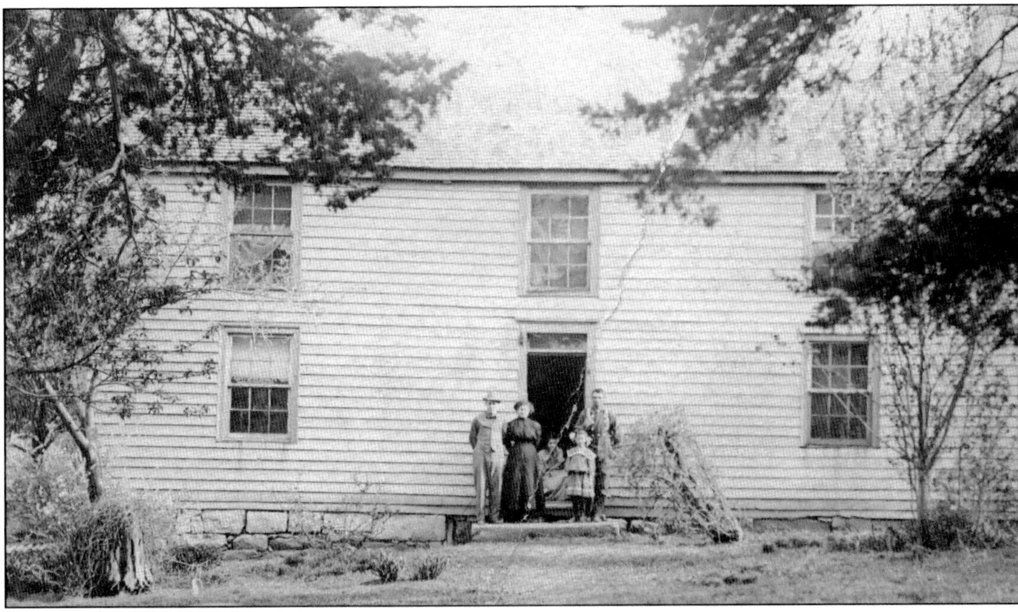

The Academy Boarding House, built in 1829, served as housing for students of the adjacent Arrow Rock Female Seminary (no longer standing) beginning in 1843. Multiple entities tried operating a school at this site, with the last one closing for good in 1861 at the outset of the Civil War. After that time, the building served as a family residence. The Arrow Rock State Park restored the Academy Boarding House in 1956, temporarily stripping off the exterior siding during the process to reveal the logs underneath. In 1962, the interior underwent modernization with the additions of plumbing, electricity, a kitchen, and bathroom to become a residence for the park superintendent. The interior has since been restored to its original 19th-century appearance. (Images courtesy of Friends of Arrow Rock.)

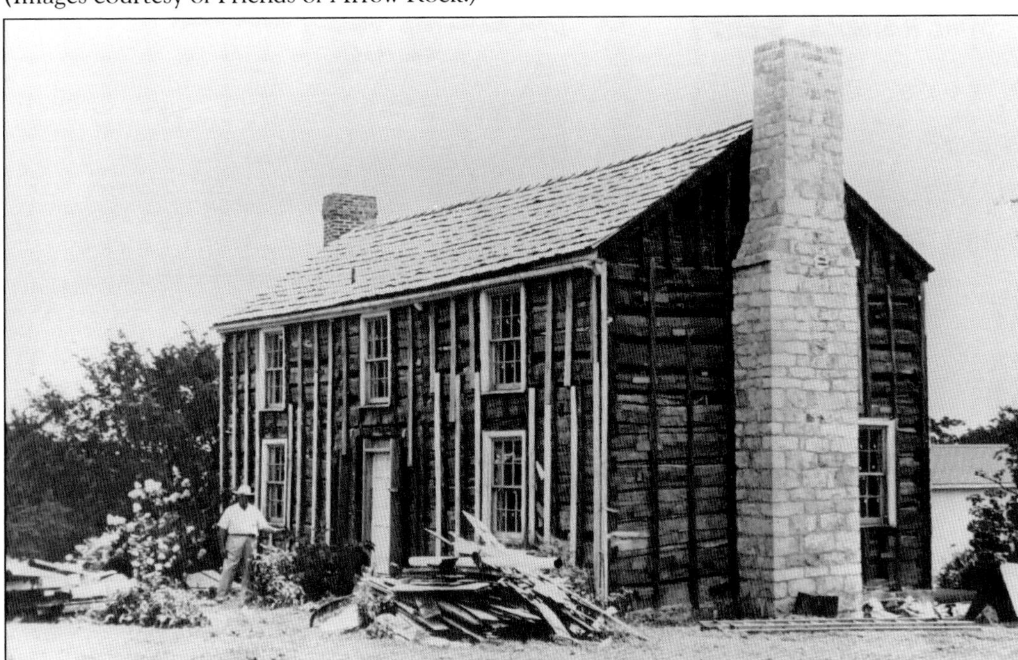

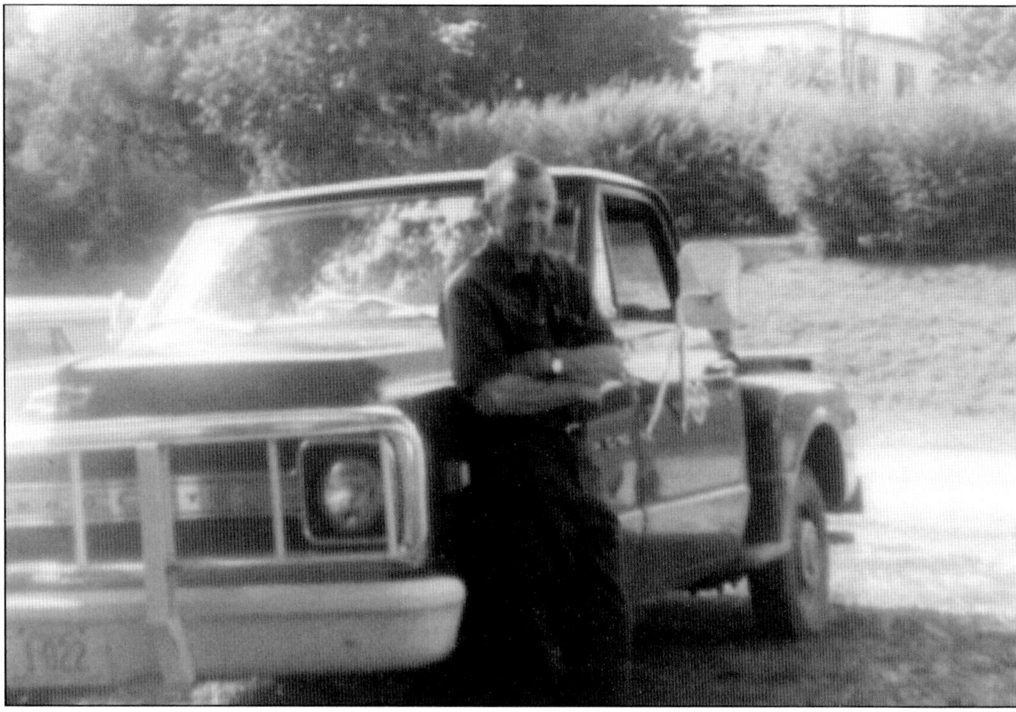

Local native Robert Stith became Arrow Rock State Park superintendent in 1959. As the park's only full-time employee, he kept busy with maintenance and public relations responsibilities. For a time, he was also responsible for Boone's Lick State Park across the river. Boone's Lick is a short distance from Arrow Rock "as the crow flies" but a 30-mile trip by car (or Chevy pickup). (Courtesy of Elaine Breshears.)

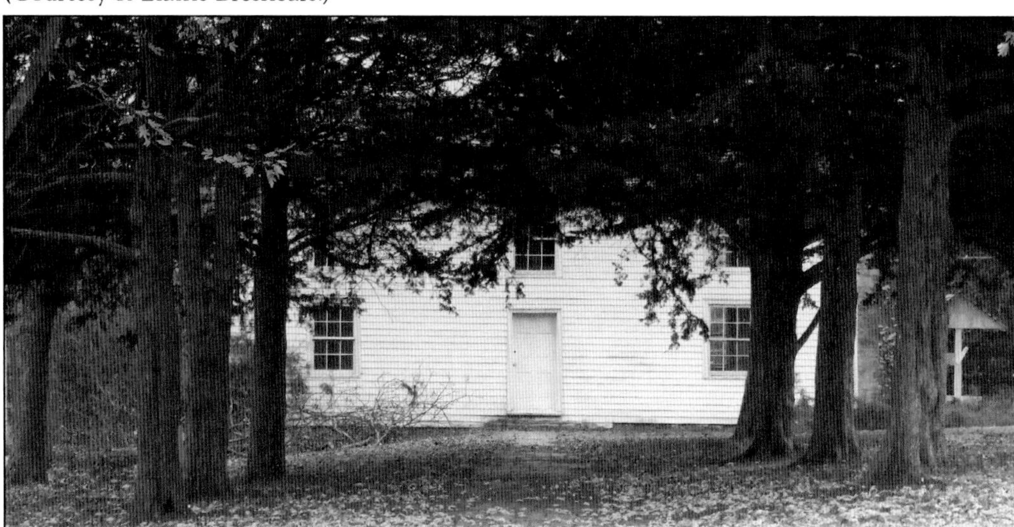

Arrow Rock State Park superintendent Robert Stith planted cedar saplings in front of the Academy Boarding House shortly after the building was renovated to become living quarters for his family. The trees, which he obtained from the state nursery in 1962, were so small, the family worried they would not survive, but those trees grew into the towering cedars that line the front walkway of the building today. (Courtesy of the author.)

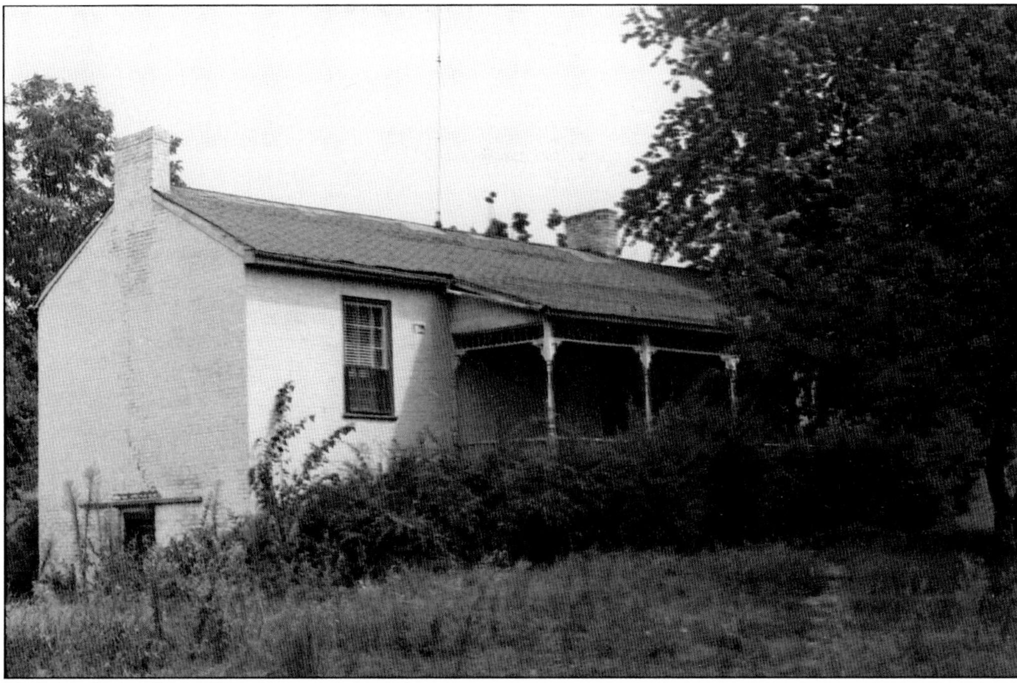

Dr. Matthew Hall arrived in Arrow Rock in 1845 and built this home in 1846. For a dozen years, Hall was one of Arrow Rock's most influential citizens, but he was dismayed by the prevalence of drinking, gambling, and carousing in the growing town. In 1857, he moved his family to the country to spare his children from "the evil influence of a river town." The Hall House was given new life in 1962 when the Arrow Rock State Park embarked on a major restoration effort. The home served as state headquarters for the Daughters of the American Revolution and later as office space for the park. The property is maintained by the Missouri Department of Natural Resources. (Images courtesy of the Missouri Department of Natural Resources.)

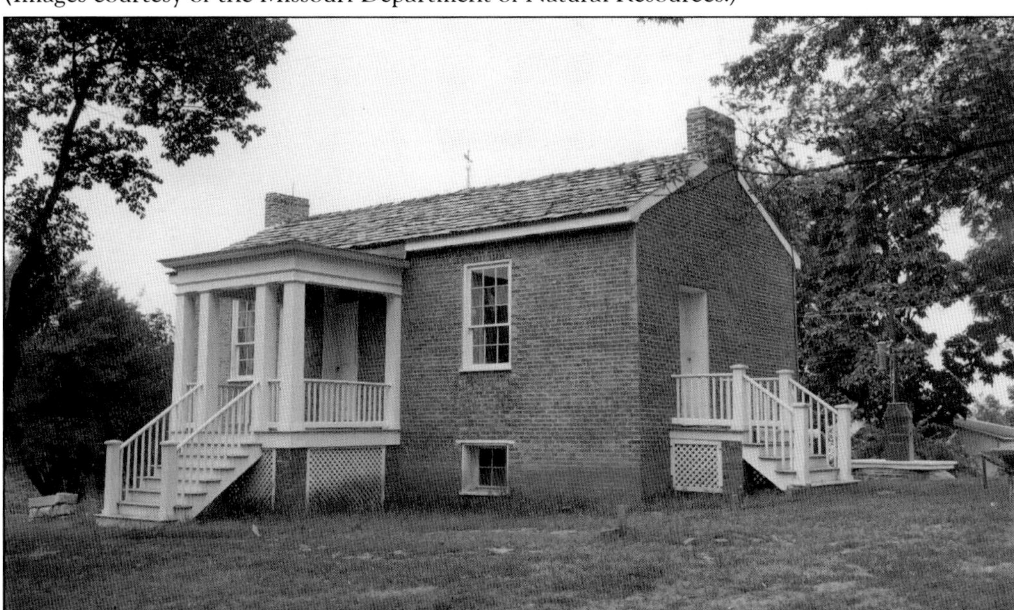

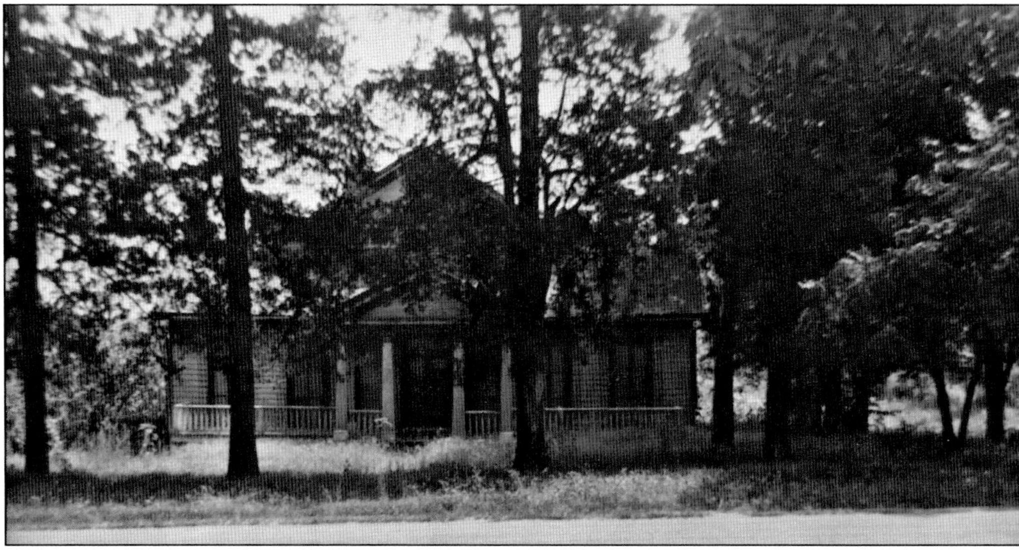

It took true visionaries to see potential in the Miller-Bradford House as it looked in 1956, when Bill and Cora Lee Miller saw a for-sale sign on the property. They rejected the owner's asking price of $14,000 with good reason. Just five years earlier, an appraiser had said, "Under most favorable conditions, there would be practically no market for such a property in Arrow Rock, and I feel safe in saying it would be difficult to sell the property as it stands for $2,000." The Millers stepped away from the negotiation, and a year later, the homeowner reconsidered his asking price and the two parties made a deal. That marked the beginning of a comprehensive and exhausting restoration project that breathed new life into Arrow Rock's preservation movement. (Images courtesy of Friends of Arrow Rock.)

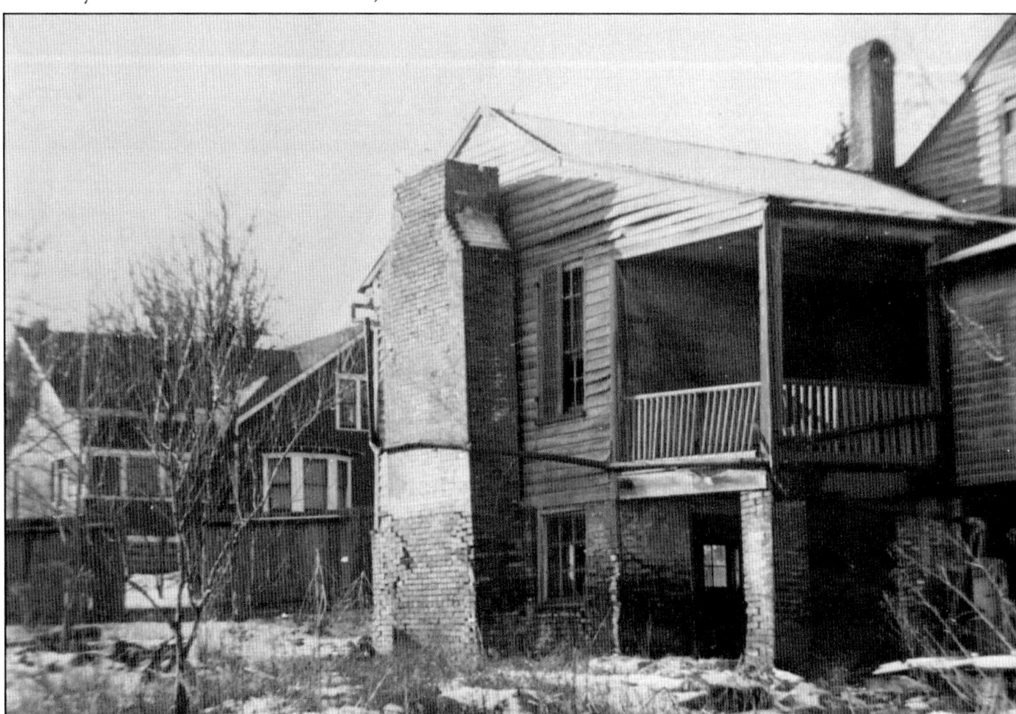

During their restoration of the Miller-Bradford House, owners Bill and Cora Lee Miller set up temporary living quarters in the former slave kitchen located in the basement of the home's back ell. The couple did almost all the work on the restoration themselves. They were able to preserve the original walnut siding and many original interior details of the house. (Courtesy of Friends of Arrow Rock.)

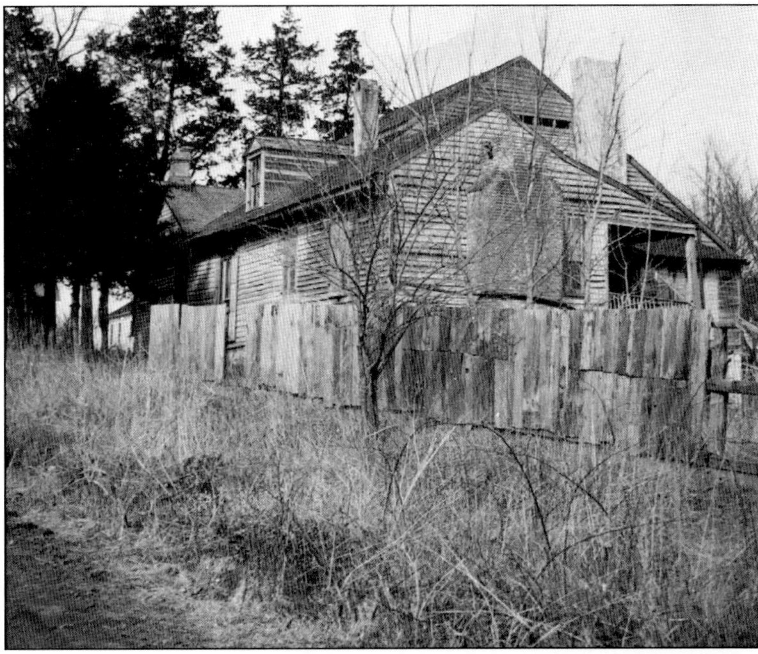

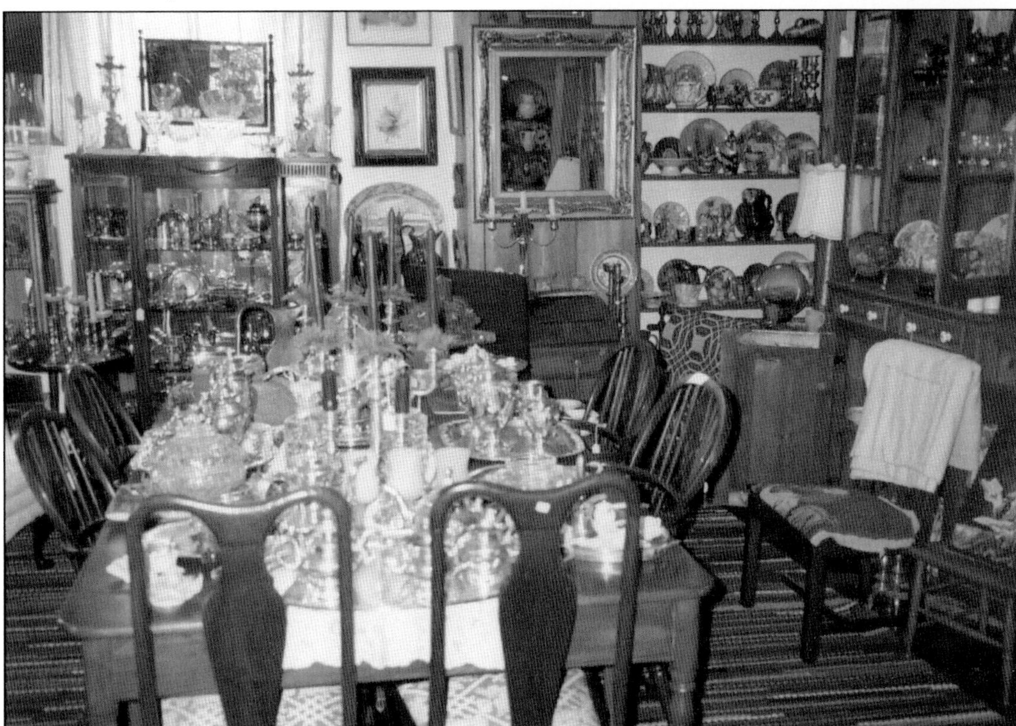

When a passerby asked Cora Lee Miller if there was anywhere in town to buy antiques, the Millers set out a card table and went into the antiques business. Soon, their beautifully restored home doubled as one of the premier antique stores in the Midwest. The Millers passed away in 1994 (Bill in February, Cora Lee in May), leaving their home and antiques to the Friends of Arrow Rock, Inc. (Courtesy of Friends of Arrow Rock.)

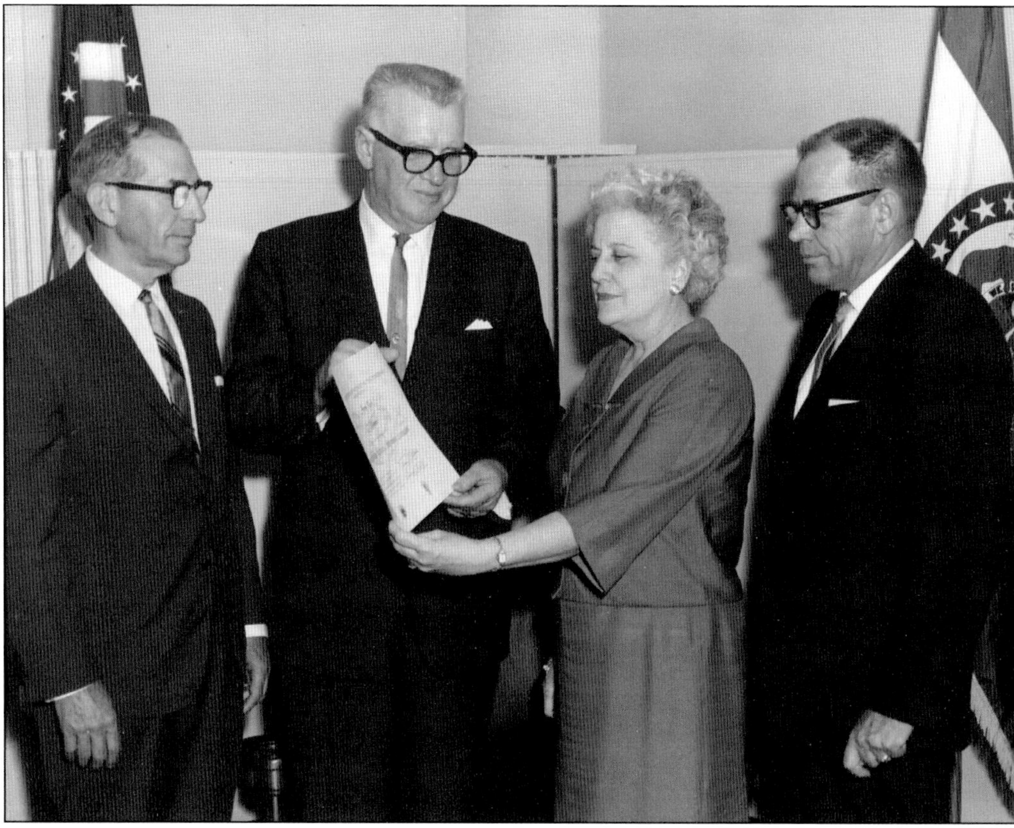

Arrow Rock claims the proud distinction of two National Historic Landmark designations. In 1963, the US Department of the Interior National Parks Service gave that designation to the entire village in recognition of the town's important role in Westward Expansion and its significant place near the head of the Santa Fe Trail. Town board chairman Sallie Hailey received the official certificate. (Courtesy of Friends of Arrow Rock.)

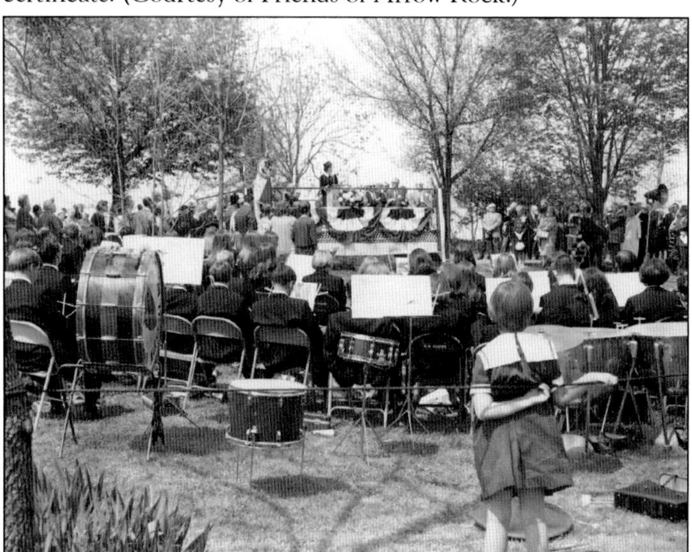

In 1965, the home of artist George Caleb Bingham earned its own National Historic Landmark status in honor of the painter's importance to the history of American art. Missouri first lady Betty Hearnes was the guest speaker at the 1966 ceremony marking the honor. (Courtesy of Friends of Arrow Rock.)

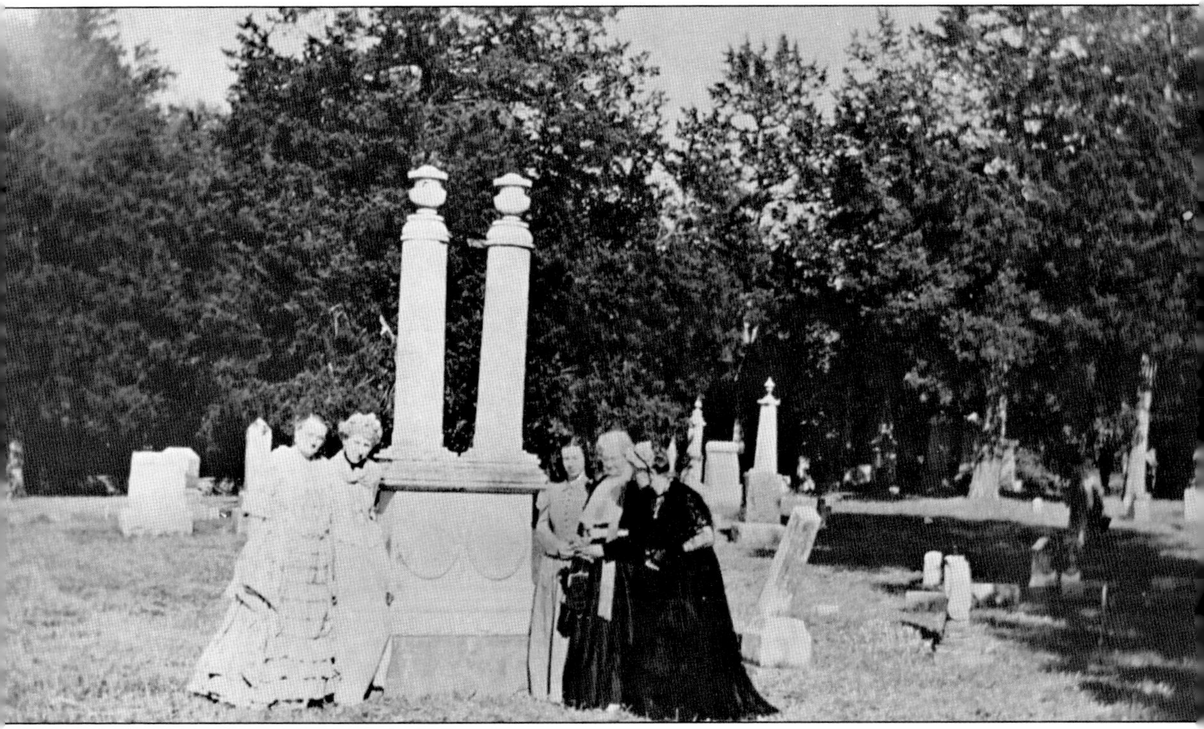

The Arrow Rock Chapter of the Daughters of the American Revolution led a tour of the Sappington Cemetery in 1954. The cemetery is the final resting place of 110 members of the Sappington family, including Missouri governors Claiborne Fox Jackson and Meredith Miles Marmaduke. Dr. John Sappington, "Quinine Doctor" and patriarch of the Sappington family, is laid to rest beneath a stone sarcophagus inscribed with these words: "A Truly Honest Man is the Noblest Work of God. He lay like a warrior taking his rest." His wife, Jane, is buried beside him, also beneath a stone sarcophagus, but one with the much less aggrandized sentiment of "Consort to Dr. John Sappington." The cemetery, located west of Arrow Rock, is now maintained by the Missouri Department of Natural Resources as Sappington Cemetery State Historic Site. (Courtesy of Missouri Department of Natural Resources.)

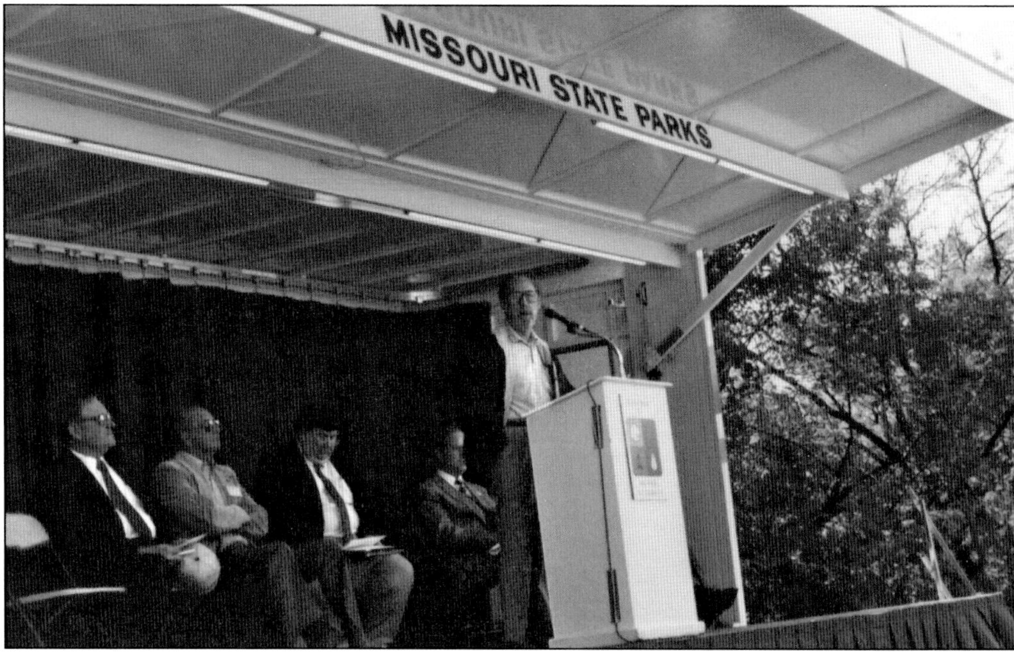

In September 1991, the State of Missouri held a ribbon cutting for the Arrow Rock State Historic Site's new visitors' center. The million-dollar project provided modern, properly controlled archival storage for important artifacts and incorporated a state-of-the-art museum to showcase treasures from the region's past, including Indian relics, tools used in early settlement, and original George Caleb Bingham paintings. Above, Former Arrow Rock State Historic Site administrator Richard Forry, who still lives in the village, speaks at the dedication ceremony. Below, Michael Dickey, site administrator since 1995, welcomes guests into the visitors' center for a first look. Dickey has become the preeminent authority on Arrow Rock history; his book *Arrow Rock: Crossroads of the Missouri Frontier* is an in-depth historical account of the region. (Above, courtesy of Missouri Department of Natural Resources; below, courtesy of Friends of Arrow Rock.)

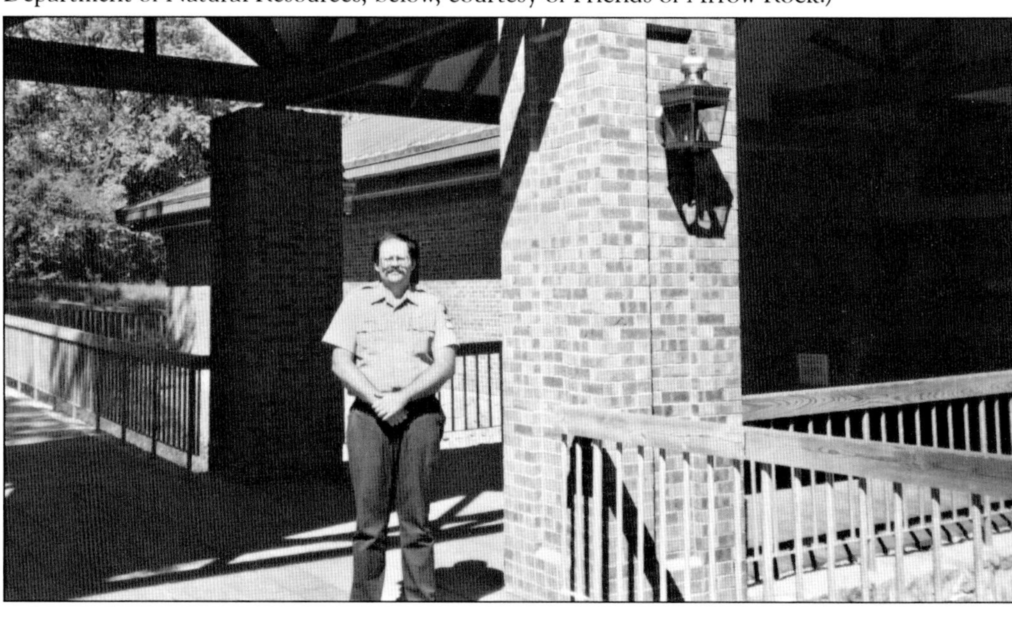

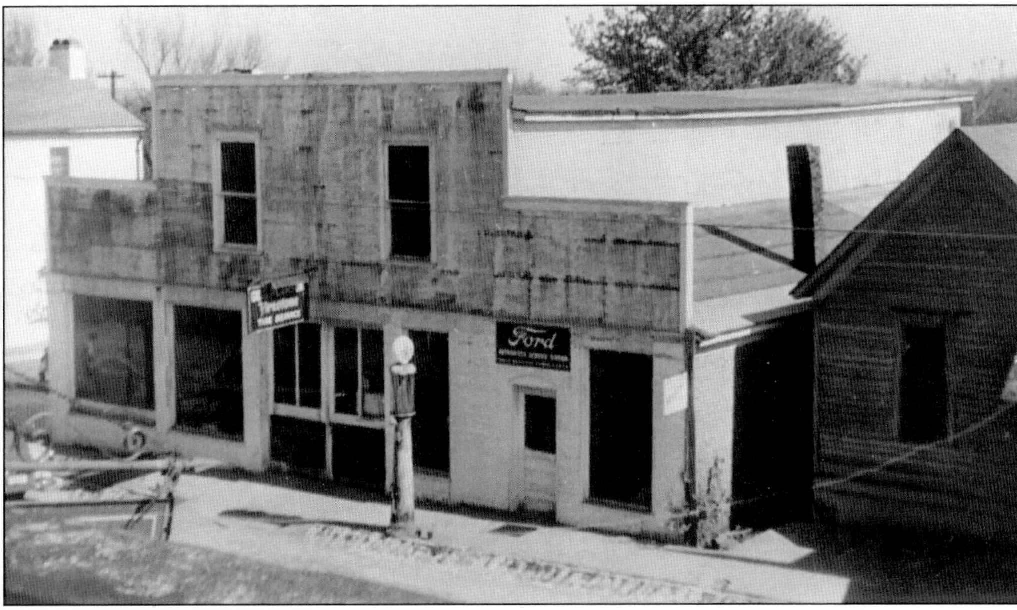

In 1958, the State of Missouri purchased the building that had contained the Pearson Garage, plus three other houses occupying land adjacent to the Arrow Rock Tavern. The structures were torn down, and the area was landscaped. Today, the Tavern Lawn is used as a site for outdoor events, including an annual Easter egg hunt for children. (Courtesy of Friends of Arrow Rock.)

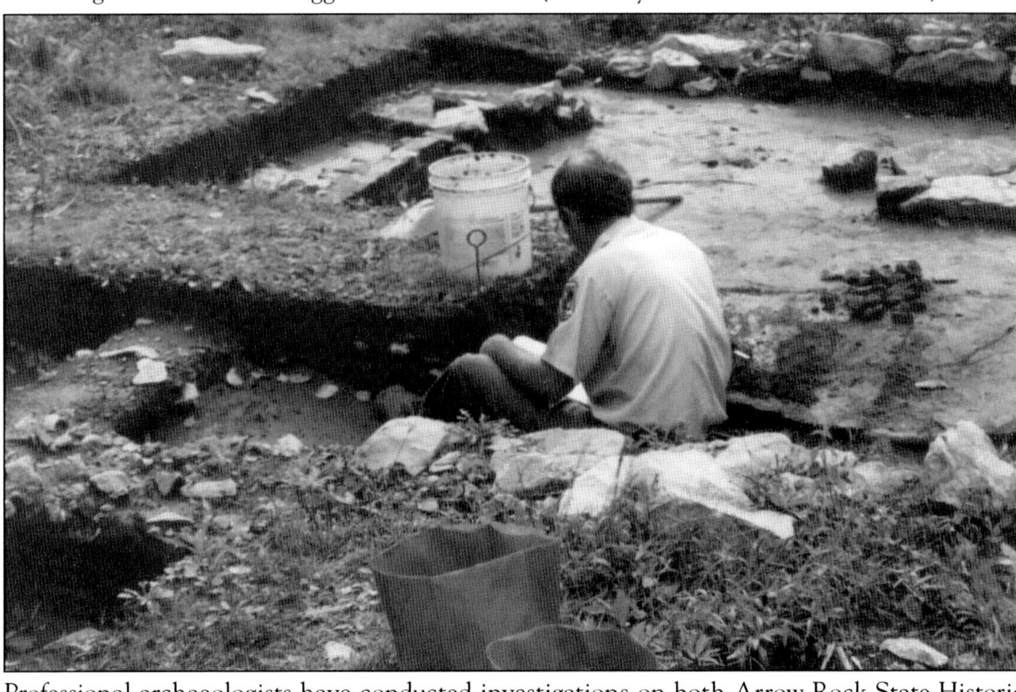

Professional archaeologists have conducted investigations on both Arrow Rock State Historic Site and Friends of Arrow Rock properties. In 1991, state parks archaeologist Larry Grantham conducted an excavation of this early mercantile store on the corner of Fourth and Van Buren Streets near the Arrow Rock State Historic Site Visitors' Center. (Courtesy of Missouri Department of Natural Resources.)

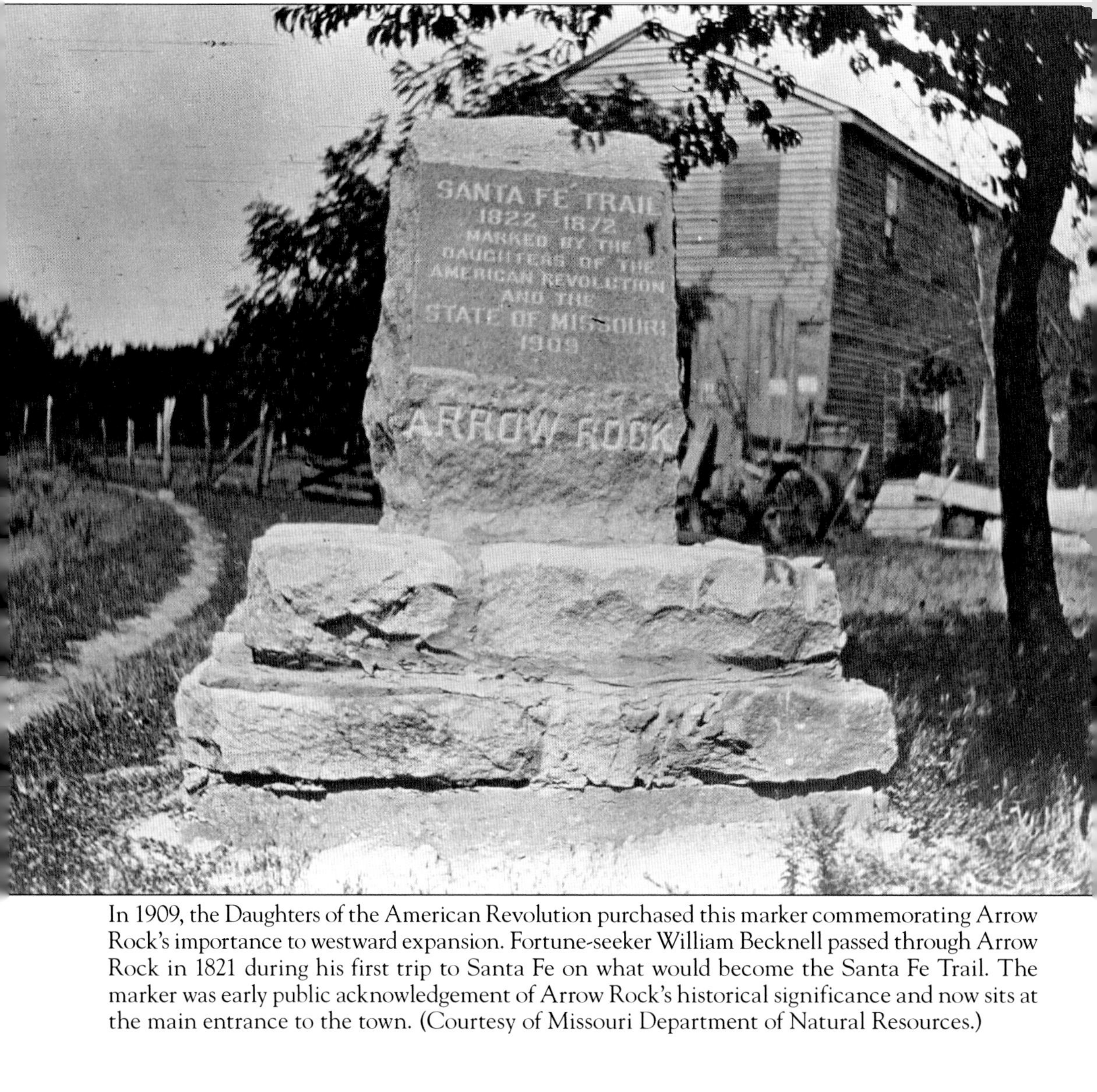

In 1909, the Daughters of the American Revolution purchased this marker commemorating Arrow Rock's importance to westward expansion. Fortune-seeker William Becknell passed through Arrow Rock in 1821 during his first trip to Santa Fe on what would become the Santa Fe Trail. The marker was early public acknowledgement of Arrow Rock's historical significance and now sits at the main entrance to the town. (Courtesy of Missouri Department of Natural Resources.)

Three

Making Friends

The success of the Miller-Bradford House restoration was the catalyst for a preservation movement that swept through Arrow Rock. Private homes began to receive some much needed attention. But what could be done about the other unloved properties in Arrow Rock? They needed a friend.

The Friends of Arrow Rock was established in 1959. Its first project—the restoration of the old courthouse building—was such a success that the group kept up its good work. It grew, and the more it thrived, the more properties it could purchase and restore. Fundraising has been central to the evolution of the organization. Home tours and annual auctions were among the group's first efforts, but as it has grown, it has sought and received major grants, created an endowment, and recently completed a million-dollar capital campaign.

Today, the organization owns and maintains 12 historic properties and one modern building in Arrow Rock, including the Sites Gun Shop and adjacent home, the Masonic and Odd Fellows Lodges, Brown's Chapel and Brown Lodge, the Christian Church, and the property that inspired it all, the Miller-Bradford House.

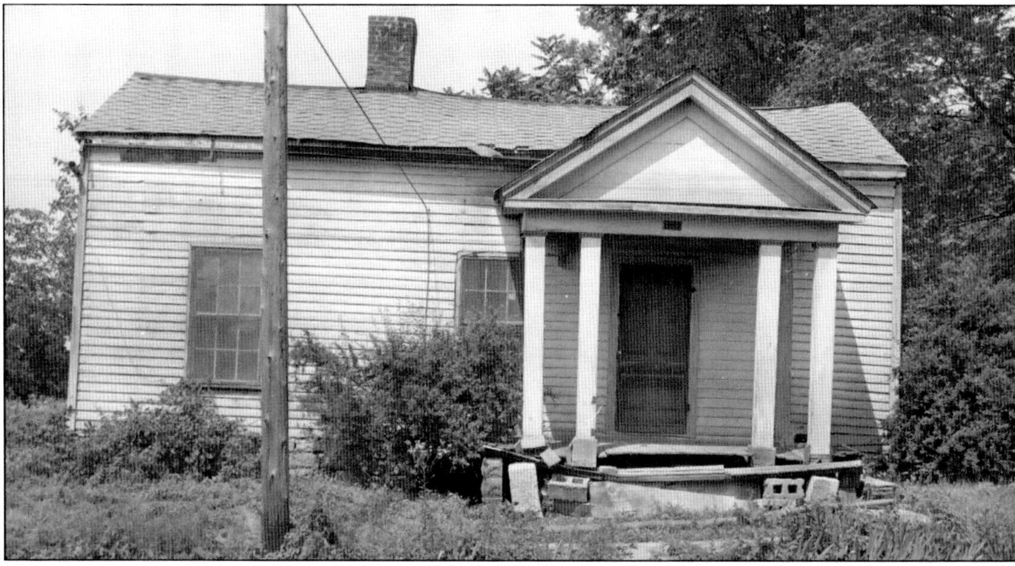

Arrow Rock enjoyed a one-year stint as the Saline County seat from 1839 to 1840. Although the building does not match the description found in an 1881 county history, oral tradition has identified this 1835 log structure as the Saline County courthouse. By the 1950s, the courthouse building had deteriorated and was at risk for demolition. (Courtesy of Friends of Arrow Rock.)

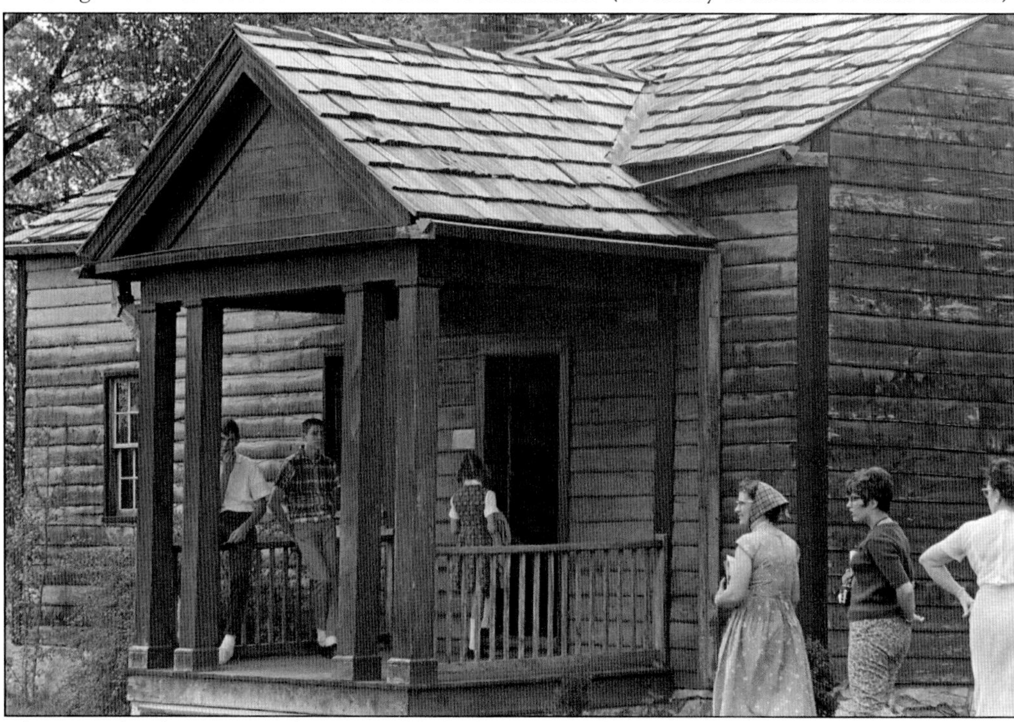

The Friends of Arrow Rock was established in 1959. The newly formed organization took on the restoration of the Saline County Courthouse as its first project. The Friends purchased the dilapidated building and financed its restoration, then called on former director of the Missouri Historical Society Charles Van Ravenswaay to guide the project. Soon after, the building was opened for public tours. (Courtesy of Friends of Arrow Rock.)

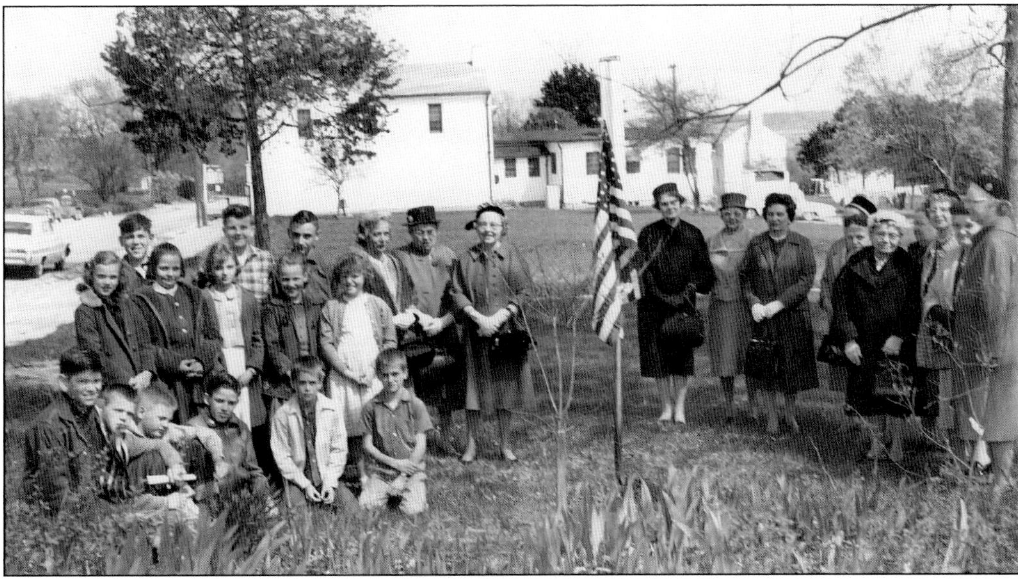

After completing a careful restoration of the courthouse building, the Friends of Arrow Rock donated the building to the State of Missouri in 1962. In 1963, the Marshall, Missouri, chapter of the Daughters of the American Revolution, along with a group of local schoolchildren, planted a dogwood tree to beautify the courthouse lawn. (Courtesy of Friends of Arrow Rock.)

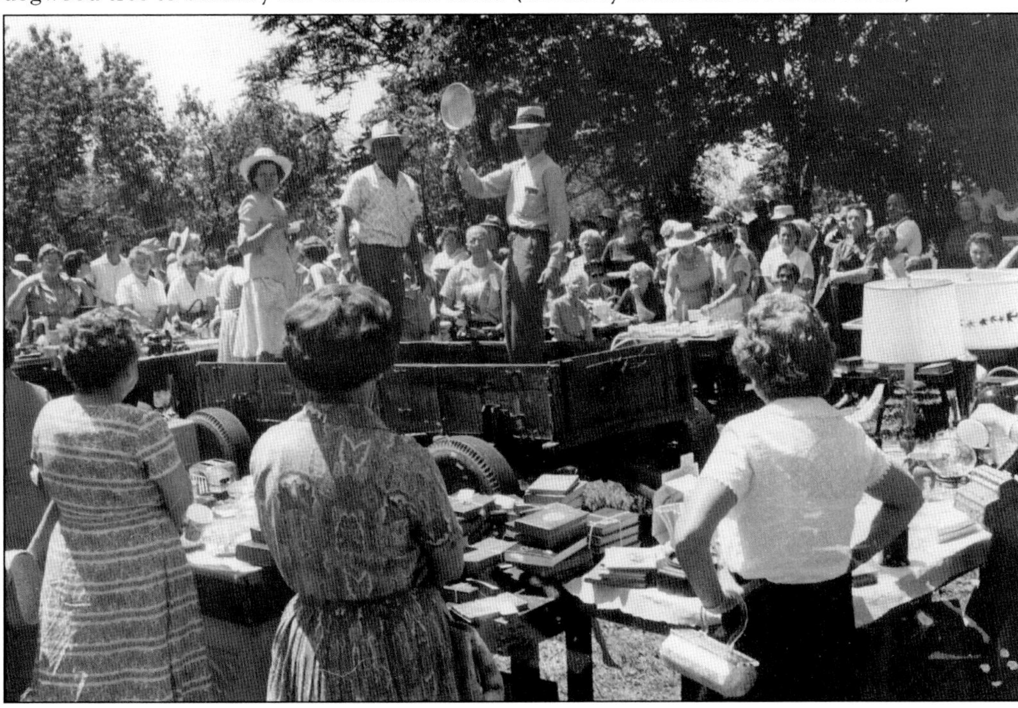

To help fund its early restoration projects, the Friends of Arrow Rock held annual auctions that drew hundreds of bidders and spectators to the village. The first auction in 1960 raised $1,960. That amount, when combined with thousands of dollars worth of volunteer labor, went a long way toward completing the Friends' restoration of the Saline County Courthouse. (Courtesy of Friends of Arrow Rock.)

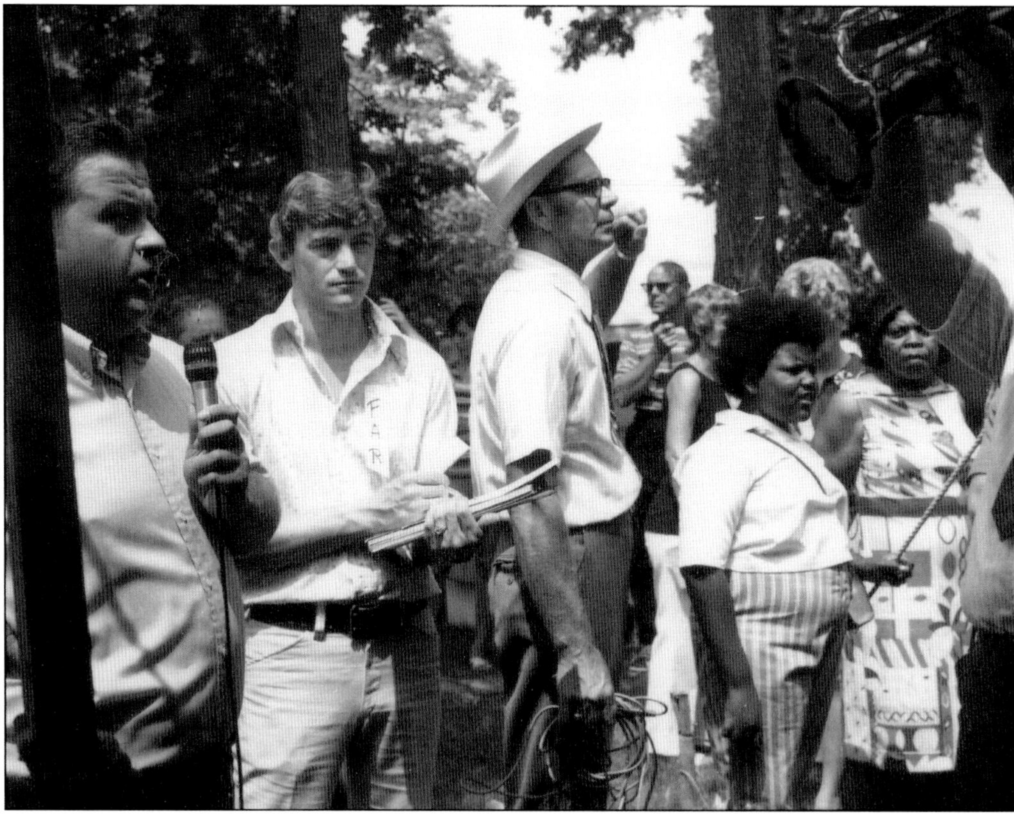

The Friends of Arrow Rock relied on donated items for its annual auctions. Donations included precious antiques and the occasional car or boat, but many of the items up for sale were small household items, like this oscillating fan being auctioned off in 1974. The auctions continued until 1977. (Courtesy of Friends of Arrow Rock.)

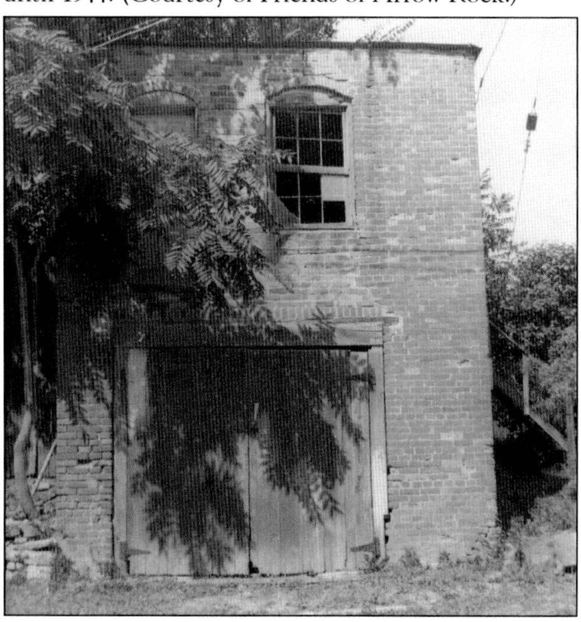

Virginia-born Johnny Sites learned the art of gunsmithing from his father. The young gunsmith moved to Arrow Rock in 1844 and set up shop on Main Street, where he earned a reputation as one of the region's premier gunsmiths. Following the Civil War, he moved his shop to this building. In time, manufacturing replaced gunsmithing, and the building was converted for other uses. (Courtesy of Thomas B. Hall III.)

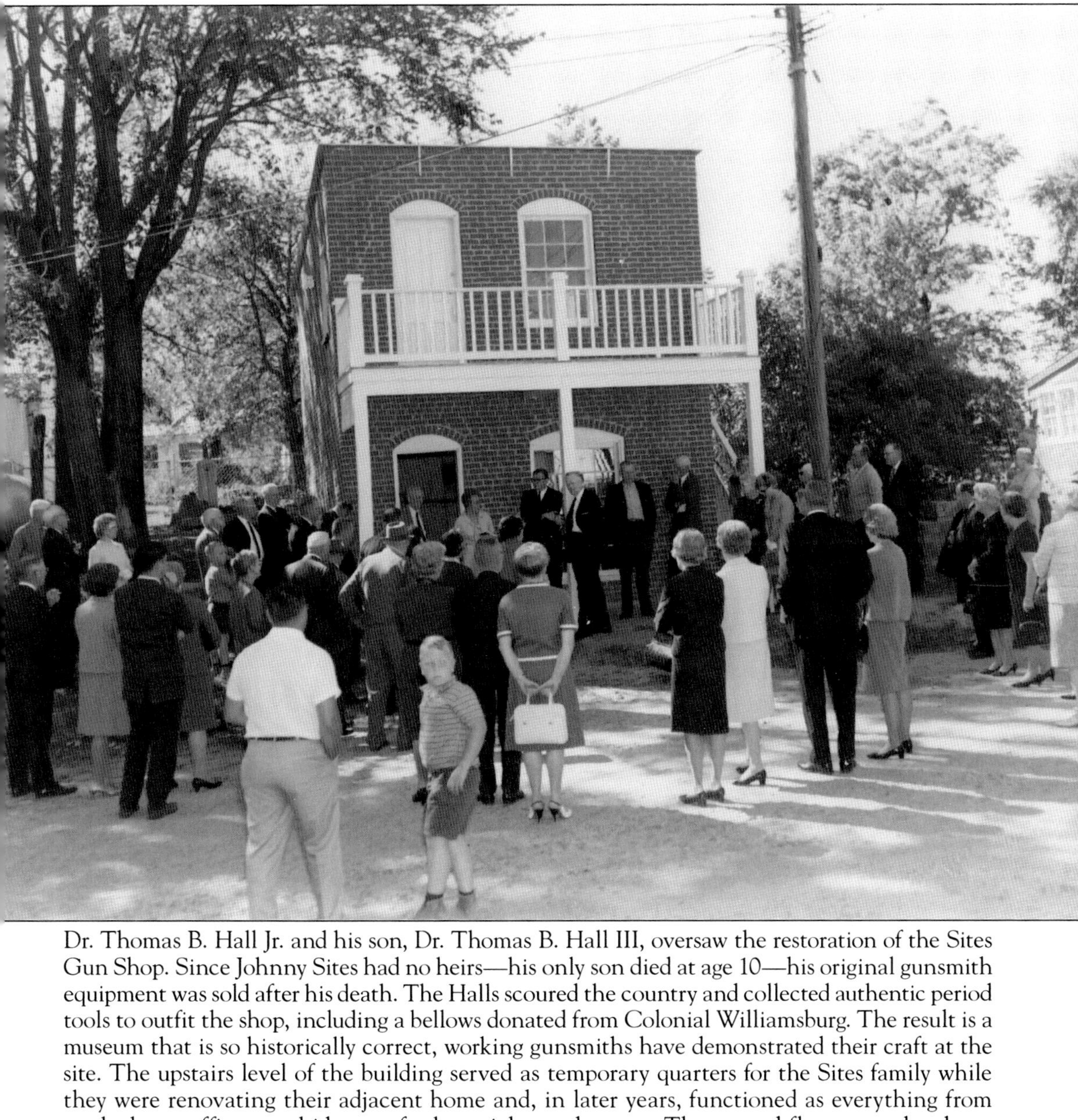

Dr. Thomas B. Hall Jr. and his son, Dr. Thomas B. Hall III, oversaw the restoration of the Sites Gun Shop. Since Johnny Sites had no heirs—his only son died at age 10—his original gunsmith equipment was sold after his death. The Halls scoured the country and collected authentic period tools to outfit the shop, including a bellows donated from Colonial Williamsburg. The result is a museum that is so historically correct, working gunsmiths have demonstrated their craft at the site. The upstairs level of the building served as temporary quarters for the Sites family while they were renovating their adjacent home and, in later years, functioned as everything from a telephone office to a hideaway for late-night card games. The second-floor space has been converted into an educational display area where visitors can see actual rifles made by Johnny Sites. The restored building was dedicated at this ceremony in September 1967. (Courtesy of Friends of Arrow Rock.)

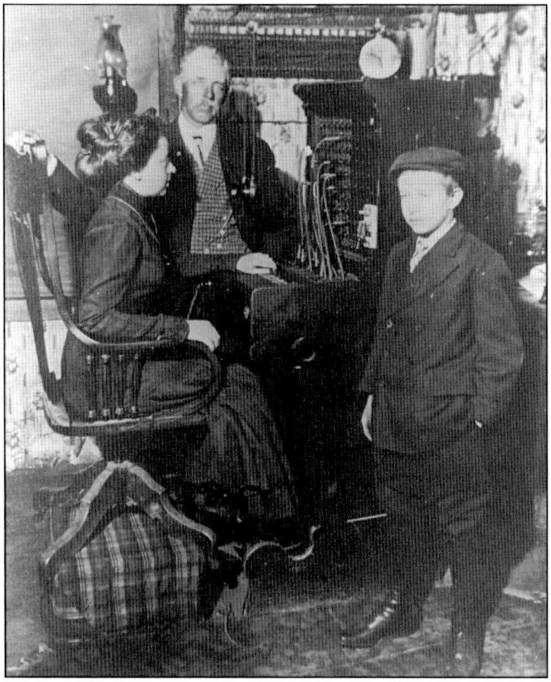

As a gunsmith's art was falling out of vogue, new technology was sweeping the nation. In 1907, the second story of the former Sites Gun Shop housed the town's telephone office. Henry Edwards oversaw the business. Perhaps it was Henry who devised the clever, if precarious, elevated chair for his daughter, who worked as the switchboard operator. (Courtesy of Friends of Arrow Rock.)

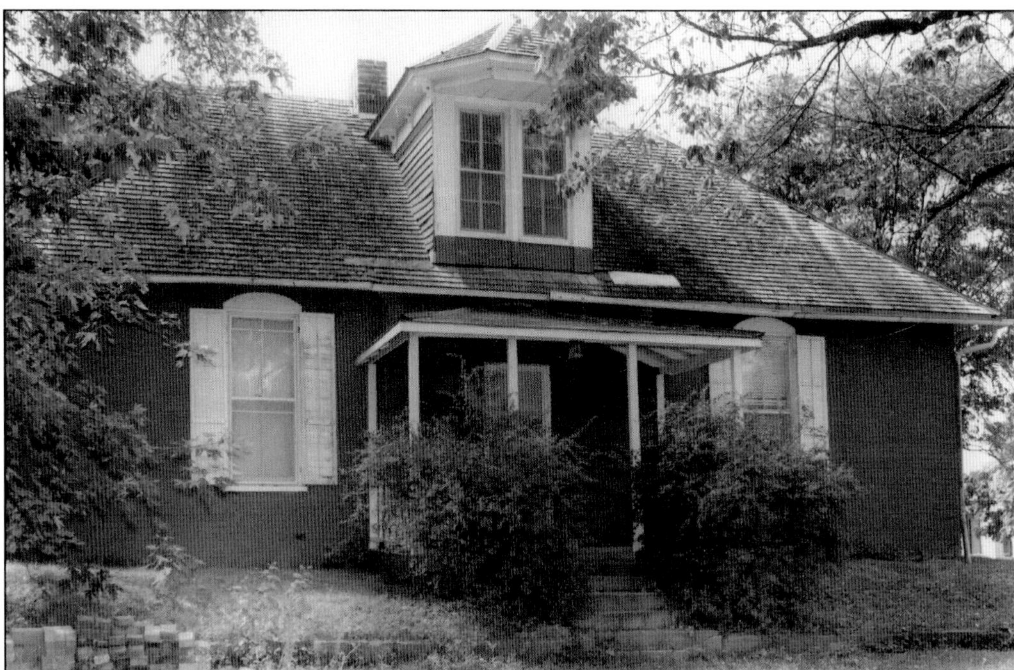

Friends of Arrow Rock president Dr. Thomas B. Hall III has conducted extensive research on historic American gunsmith shops and concluded that Arrow Rock is the only place in the United States with a restored gunsmith's shop and adjacent home in their original locations. Johnny Sites and his wife, Nannie, purchased the 1830s cottage in 1866 and expanded it in 1875. Johnny's affection for Nannie is found in the home's details, including a small door that allowed her to retrieve firewood without stepping outside. (Courtesy of Missouri Department of Natural Resources.)

Although the home had been stripped of much of its Victorian decoration over the years, the Friends of Arrow Rock set out to restore it to its Sites-era glory. Restoration work included the recreation of an enclosed front porch and upstairs balcony. Jean Hamilton (front) and Louise Bagby welcome guests to the restored home's dedication in 1973. (Courtesy of Missouri Department of Natural Resources.)

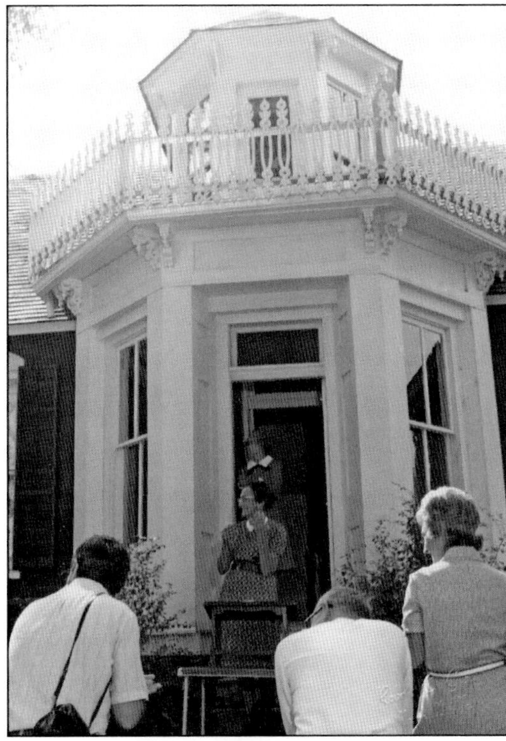

Friends of Arrow Rock trustees and members gather in front of the Odd Fellows Lodge Hall before a home tour fundraiser in September 1974. They are, from left to right, George Bagby, William Miller, Cora Lee Miller, Jean Hamilton, Sallie Hailey, Louise Bagby, Lynn Burge, and two unidentified Odd Fellows representatives, who presented the Friends with a check for $400. (Courtesy of Friends of Arrow Rock.)

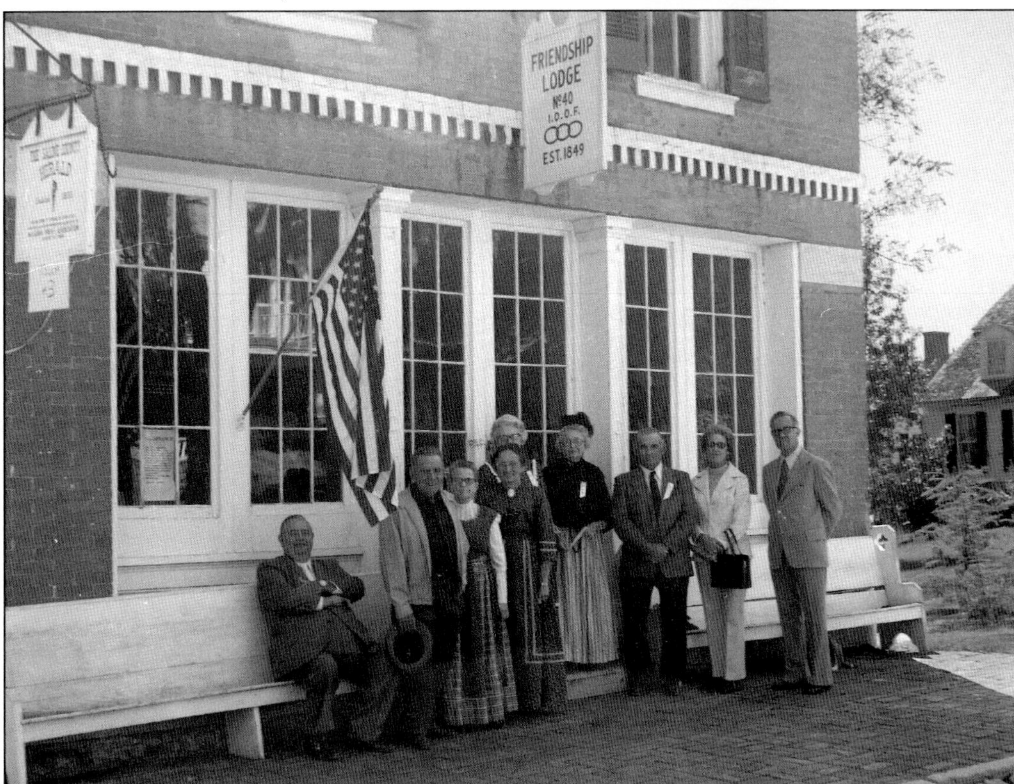

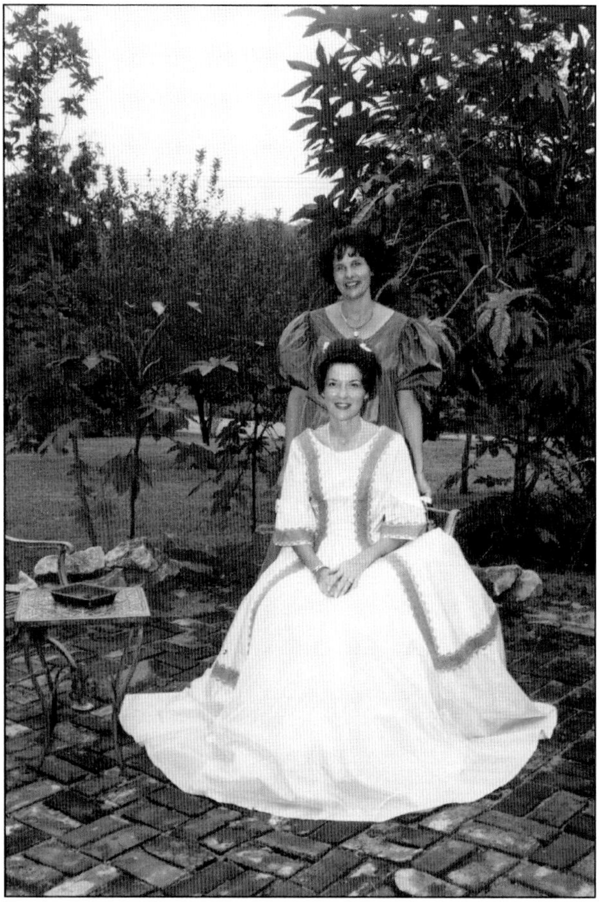

The Friends of Arrow Rock's home tour fundraisers of the 1960s evoked the gentility of an earlier age, thanks to hostesses like these who dressed for the occasion in elegant period attire. Betty Sue O'Dell (now Simonson, seated) still lives in Arrow Rock and Marshall resident Donna Huston is now vice president of the Friends of Arrow Rock Board of Trustees. (Courtesy of Friends of Arrow Rock.)

A group of 47 citizens formed a new Disciples of Christ congregation named the Church of Christ at Arrow Rock in April 1872. The church remained an active house of worship until the 1920s. After a brief reemergence in the 1940s when this photograph was taken, Arrow Rock's Christian Church folded into the Federated Church in 1950. (Courtesy of Department of Natural Resources.)

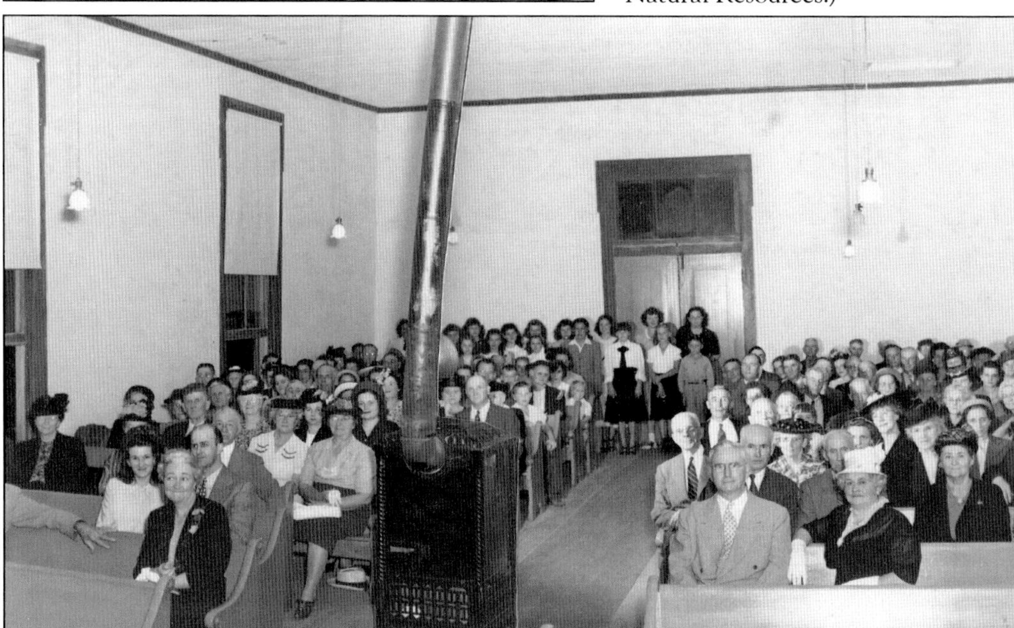

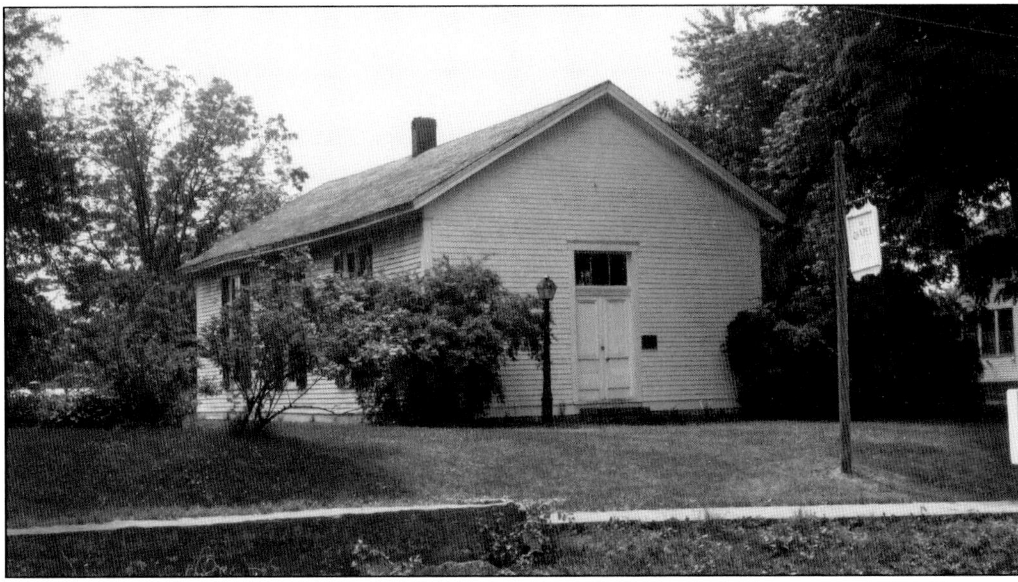

The Friends of Arrow Rock, along with the Arrow Rock Craft Club, restored the Christian Church in the 1960s. It remains open for tours, weddings and other gatherings, and has been used twice as a movie location. Once a year, it comes back to life as a house of worship when townspeople gather for an old-fashioned service during the Heritage Craft Festival. (Courtesy of Friends of Arrow Rock.)

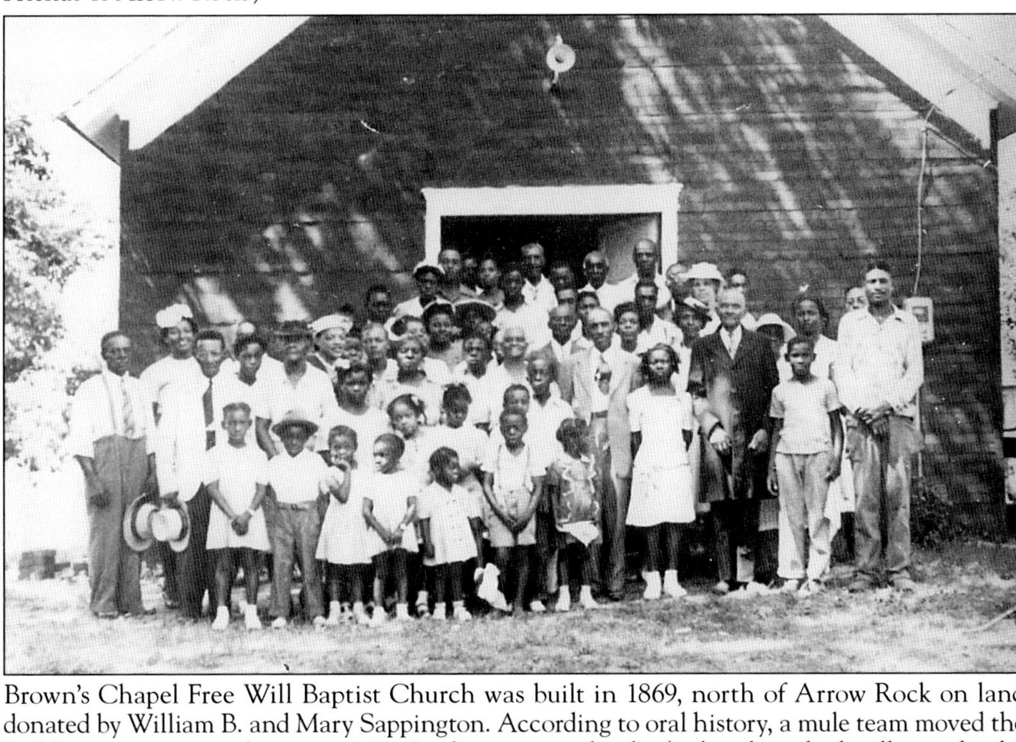

Brown's Chapel Free Will Baptist Church was built in 1869, north of Arrow Rock on land donated by William B. and Mary Sappington. According to oral history, a mule team moved the building to its present location in 1883, where it served as both church and schoolhouse for the emancipated black population. At its height, the church boasted Sunday School enrollment of 192. (Courtesy of Friends of Arrow Rock.)

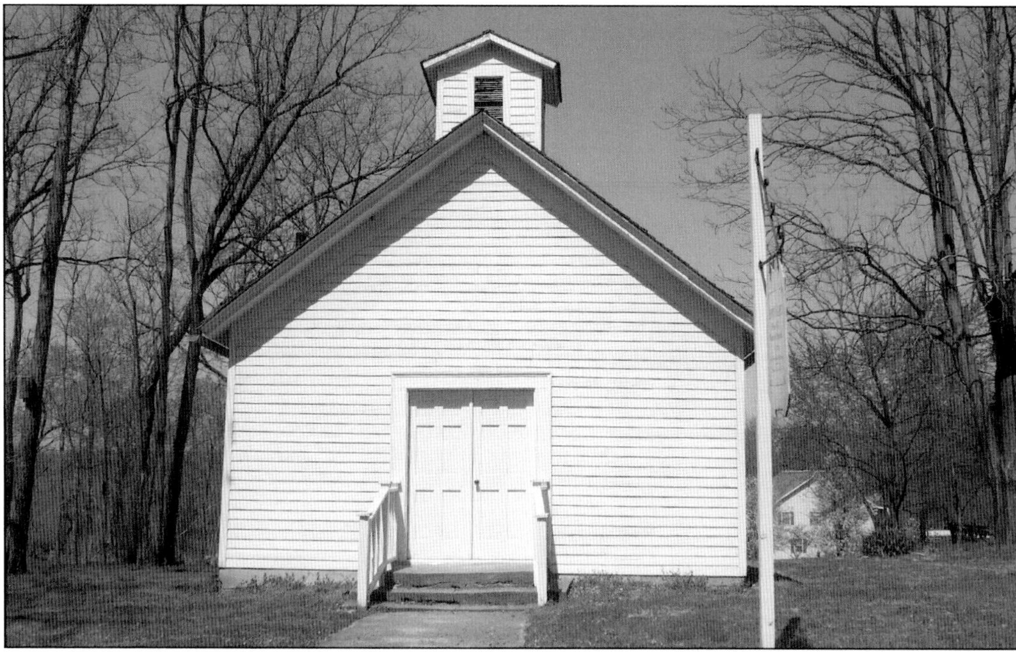

Brown's Chapel closed in 1988. Arrow Rock residents Ted and Virginia Fisher purchased the building and, in 1996, donated it to the Friends of Arrow Rock on the condition it be restored and used to teach Arrow Rock's black history. After a conscientious restoration, the building was rededicated with a homecoming celebration in 1998. Today, Brown's Chapel is available for events and weddings. (Courtesy of the author.)

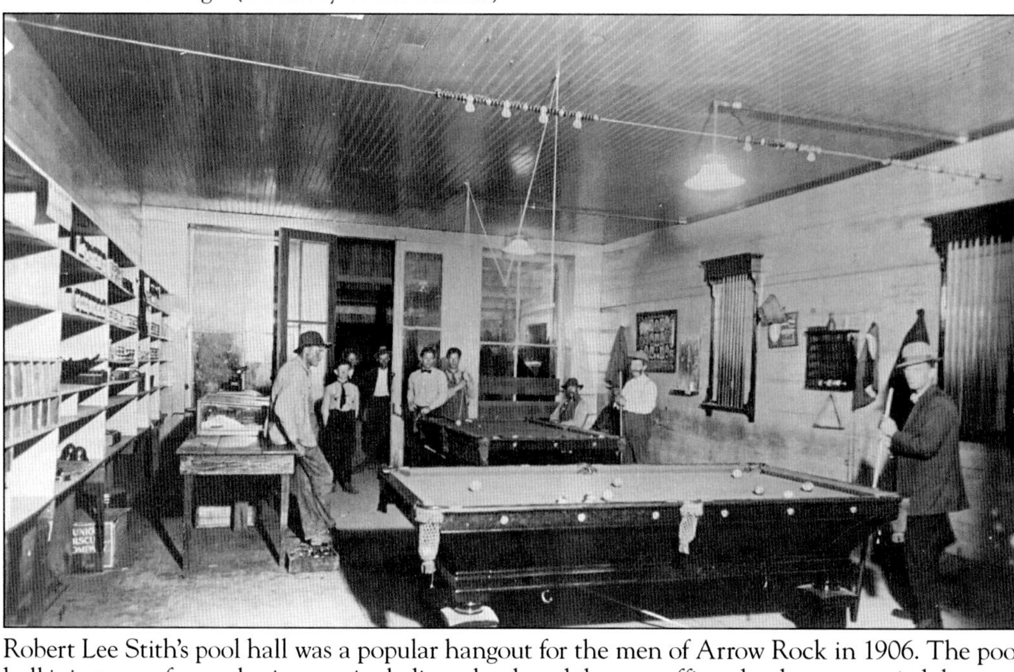

Robert Lee Stith's pool hall was a popular hangout for the men of Arrow Rock in 1906. The pool hall is just one of many businesses, including a bank and the post office, that have occupied that spot on the boardwalk over the years. The building currently houses the offices of the Friends of Arrow Rock, where Stith's granddaughter Elaine works as a tour guide. (Courtesy of Elaine Breshears.)

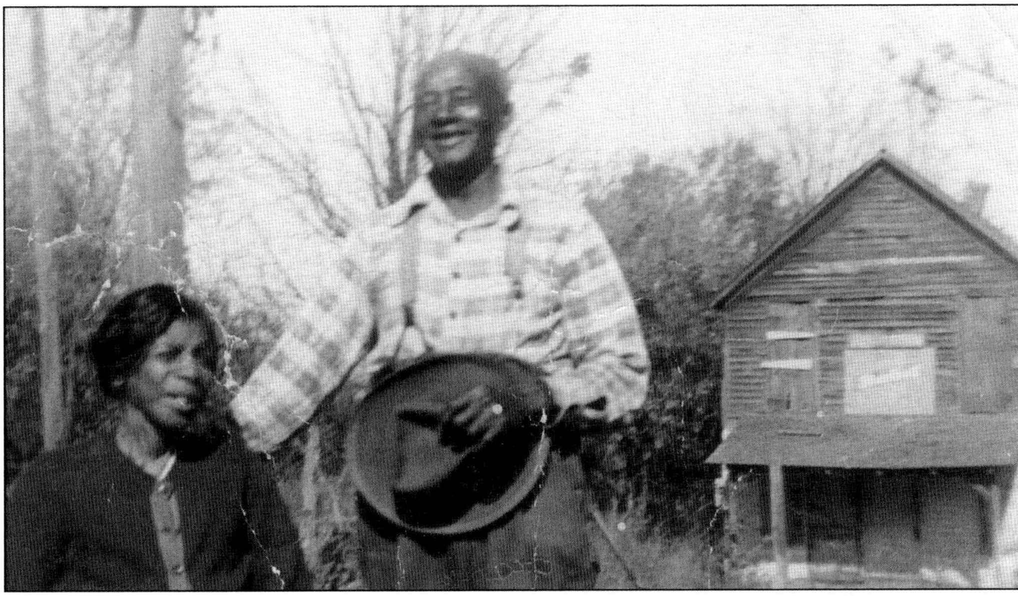

The building constructed by Brown Lodge No. 22 of the Free and Accepted Masons was one of three African American lodges built in Arrow Rock in the 1800s. By the 1950s, when Bettie and Dennis Banks were among a dwindling number of African Americans living in Arrow Rock, the lodge building had fallen into disrepair. (Courtesy of Friends of Arrow Rock.)

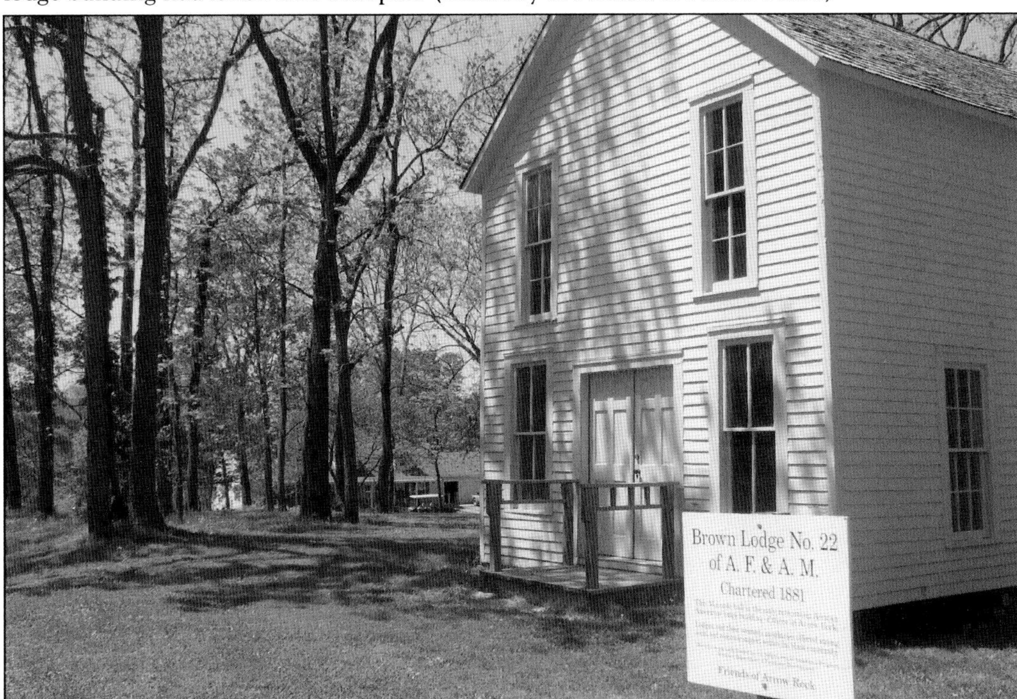

In 1996, local residents Ted and Virginia Fisher donated the Brown Lodge building to the Friends of Arrow Rock. Following an extensive stabilization and restoration effort that began in 1999, the building was converted to a museum that documents the history of Arrow Rock's African American community. (Courtesy of the author.)

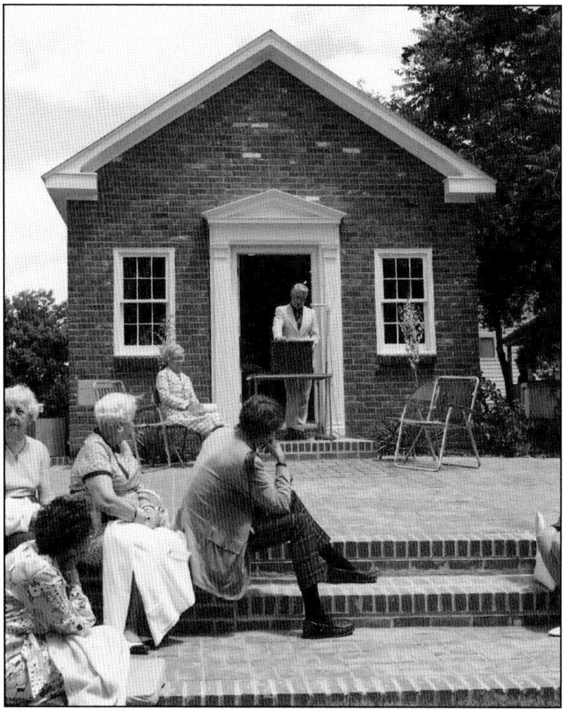

The Sappington Museum building is the only modern structure among the 13 properties owned by the Friends of Arrow Rock. It was completed and dedicated at this ceremony in 1974. The museum celebrates the life and work of Dr. John Sappington, who popularized the use of quinine as a treatment for malaria. The museum was updated with new displays and reopened in 2012. (Courtesy of Friends of Arrow Rock.)

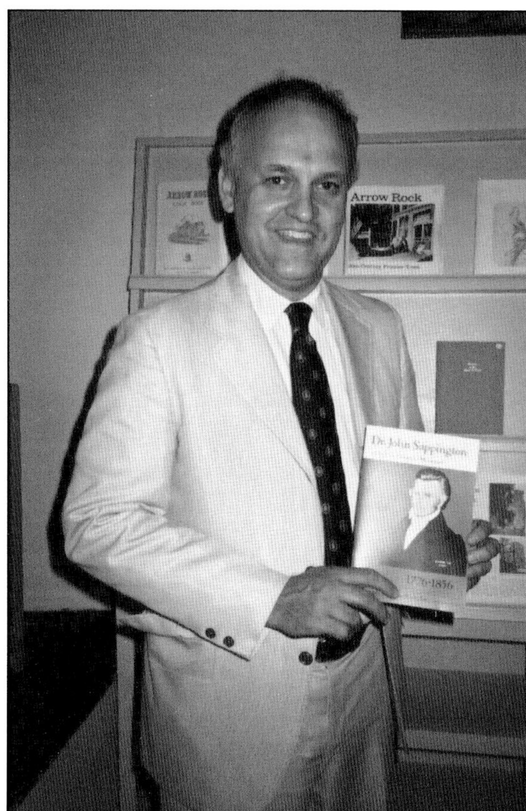

Dr. Thomas B. Hall Jr. was an avid student of the groundbreaking career of Dr. John Sappington and authored several publications on pioneer-era medicine, including the 1971 *Medicine on the Santa Fe Trail*. His 1974 book, *Dr. John Sappington of Saline County, Missouri*, is shown here held by his son, Dr. Thomas B. Hall III, who is the current Friends of Arrow Rock president. (Courtesy of Friends of Arrow Rock.)

The old log cabin on Main Street is the only building owned by the Friends of Arrow Rock that is not original to the town. The 1838 structure was moved to the village from its original site near Marshall, Missouri. It was reconstructed log-by-log and clad with walnut siding. Ninety-year-old J. Logan Buntin did much of the meticulous work of reconstruction himself. From 1976 to 1998, the building housed a medical museum filled with items collected by Dr. John Lawrence (shown at right in 1979). In 1998, the contents of the museum were divided between Fitzgibbon Hospital in Marshall, which received the 20th-century items, and the Sappington Museum, a Friends of Arrow Rock property devoted to frontier medicine. (Images courtesy of Friends of Arrow Rock.)

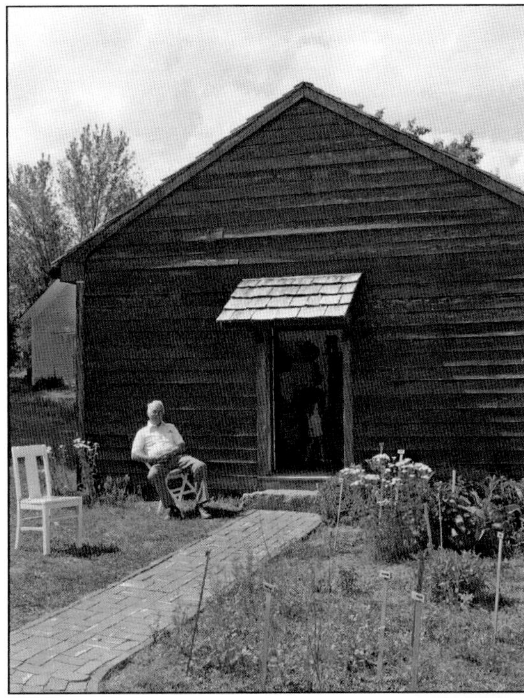

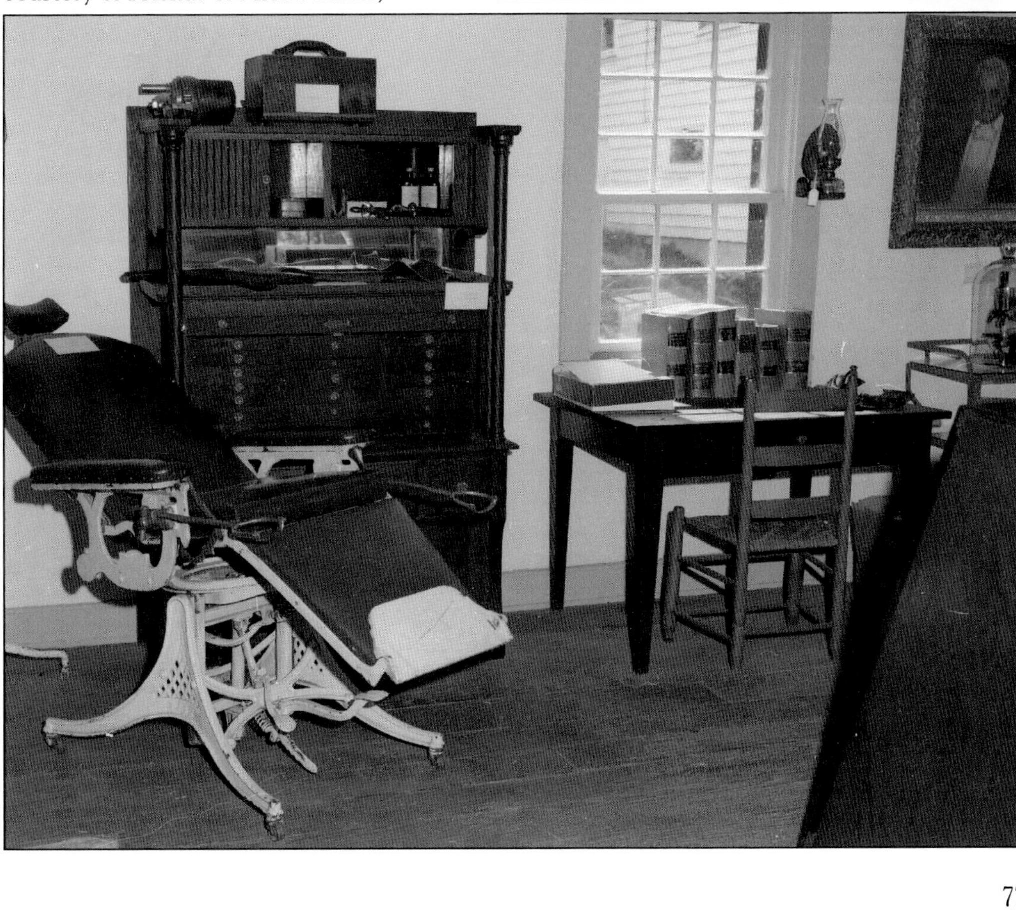

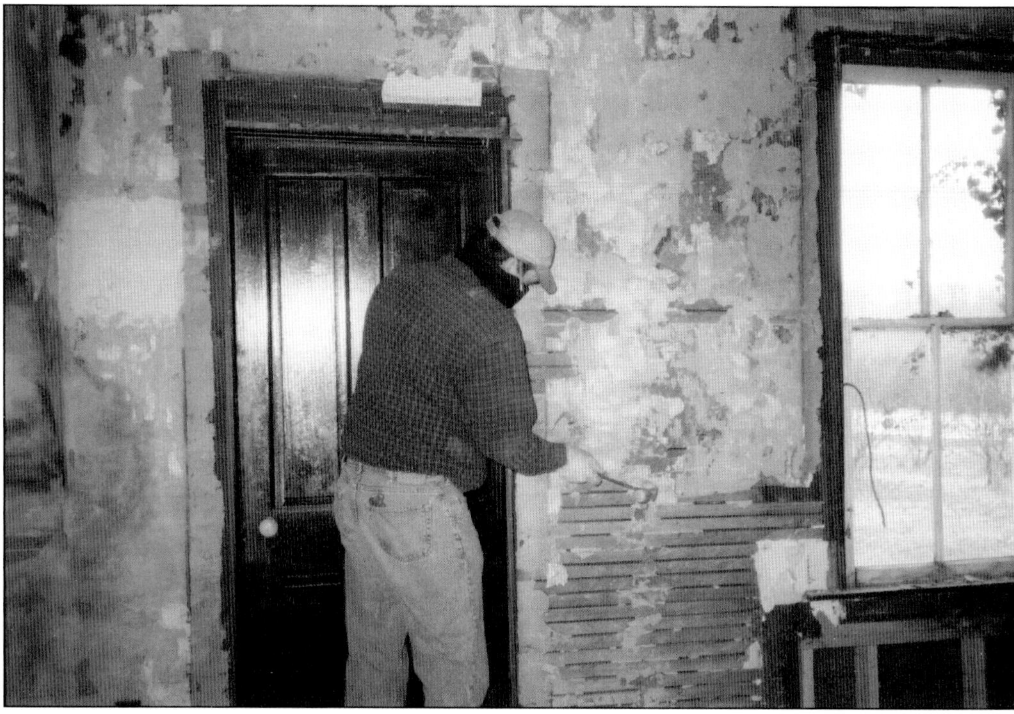

Gladys Thomas, a descendant of the Lawless family, gave the Friends of Arrow Rock a gift of more than $100,000 to restore her family homestead. The home and the property on which it sits are owned by the Missouri Department of Natural Resources, but under the provisions of a long-term lease, the Friends of Arrow Rock maintains the property. The extensive restoration effort took the home down to its bare bones and turned back the architectural clock to 1903, when the lovely Queen Anne–style farmhouse was new. Care was taken to decorate the home with wallpaper, paint colors, and furnishings that were authentic to the period. (Above, courtesy of Missouri Department of Natural Resources; below, courtesy of Friends of Arrow Rock.)

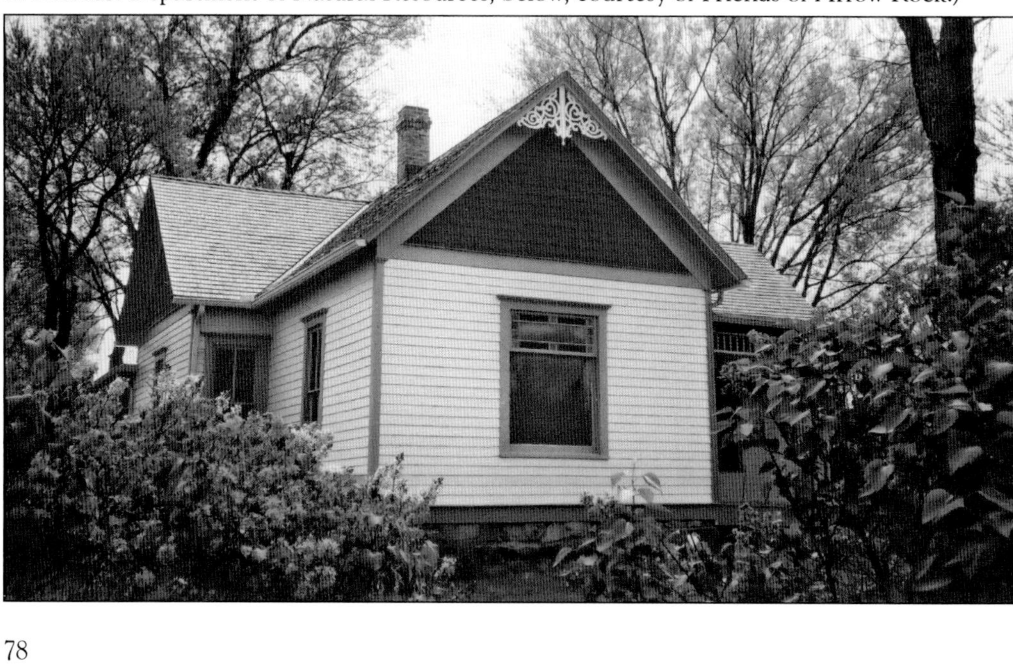

The Friends of Arrow Rock took a big step forward in its development as an organization when it established an endowment in 1984. The endowment was celebrated and supported with a $1,000-per-person gala at the Prairie Park estate near Arrow Rock. From left to right, Whitney Kerr, R. Crosby Kemper, and Bebe Kemper were among the attendees at the elegant event. (Courtesy of Friends of Arrow Rock.)

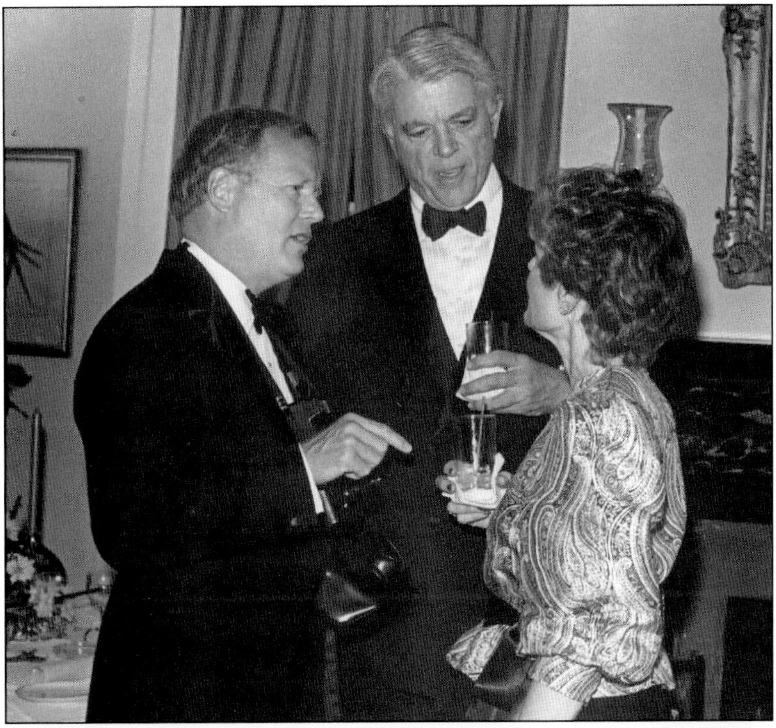

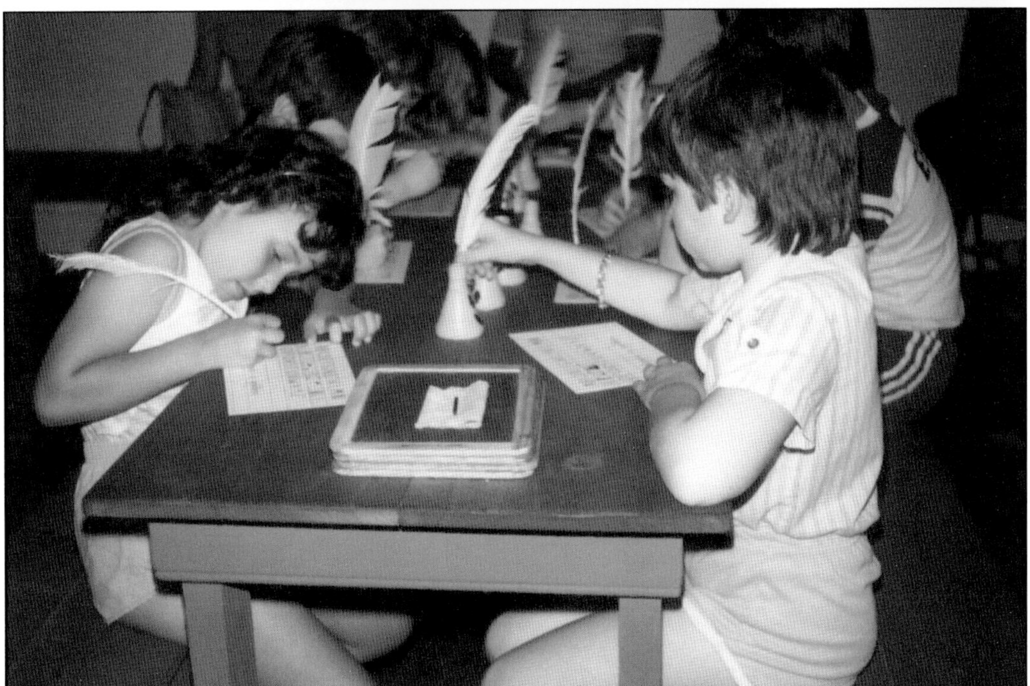

Education is a key component of the Friends of Arrow Rock mission, and the organization frequently hosts school groups that come to see real-life examples of life in 19th-century America. The lesson on writing with quill pens is always a crowd-pleaser with children, like those who visited the village in 1985. (Courtesy of Friends of Arrow Rock.)

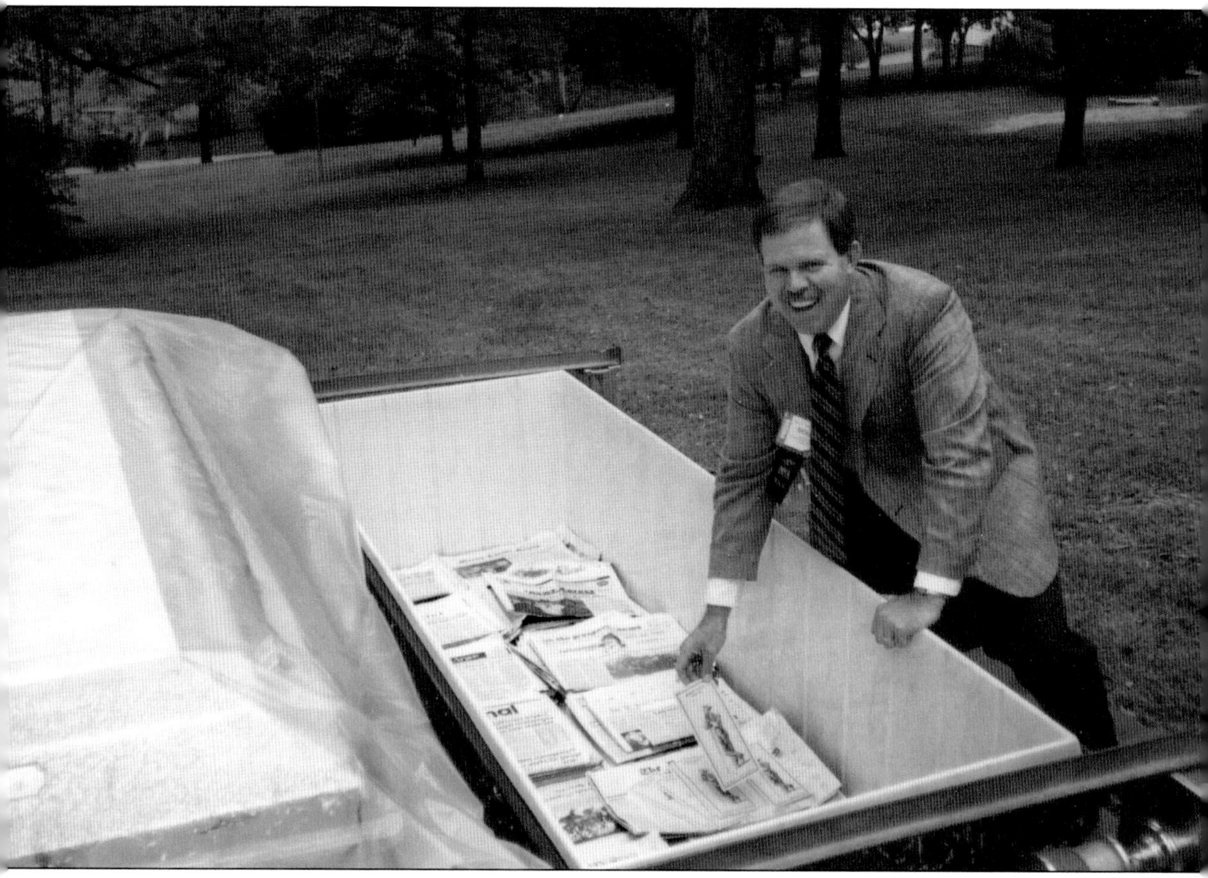

In 1966, to commemorate its centennial, the Missouri Press Association established a museum on the lower level of the IOOF Lodge in space once occupied by the *Arrow Rock Statesman* newspaper. The museum houses authentic presses and other equipment. In 1991, Missouri Press Association executive director Doug Crews led the 125th-anniversary celebration by filling a time capsule with newspapers from around the state. (Courtesy of Friends of Arrow Rock.)

Four

The Arts in Arrow Rock

Perhaps the spirit of great American artist George Caleb Bingham still lingers in Arrow Rock or maybe the town that inspired Bingham is still inspiring artists today. Whatever the reason, Arrow Rock is a haven for artists.

The Arrow Rock Lyceum Theatre and the Arrow Rock Craft Club both sprang to life in 1961. The craft club operation has changed little in 50 years. Members still bring in their handcrafted items to sell in the club's shop on the lower level of the Masonic Lodge, and those items still include perennial favorites such as jellies, quilts, and toys.

The Arrow Rock Lyceum Theatre, on the other hand, has seen sweeping changes over the same period. The budgets have grown, the productions are bigger, and most significantly, the theater itself has blossomed from a tiny stage in a sweltering old church to a modern, 408-seat auditorium.

The arts and crafts of Bingham's day get their due each October at the Heritage Craft Festival. The event, sponsored by the Historic Arrow Rock Council, brings dozens of artisans and thousands of visitors to the village for a back-in-time festival that features everything from rug hooking to blacksmithing.

Throughout the year, artists come to the village for weaving lessons, quilt camps, watercolor workshops, or just to draw on the inspiration the town has been providing since 1829.

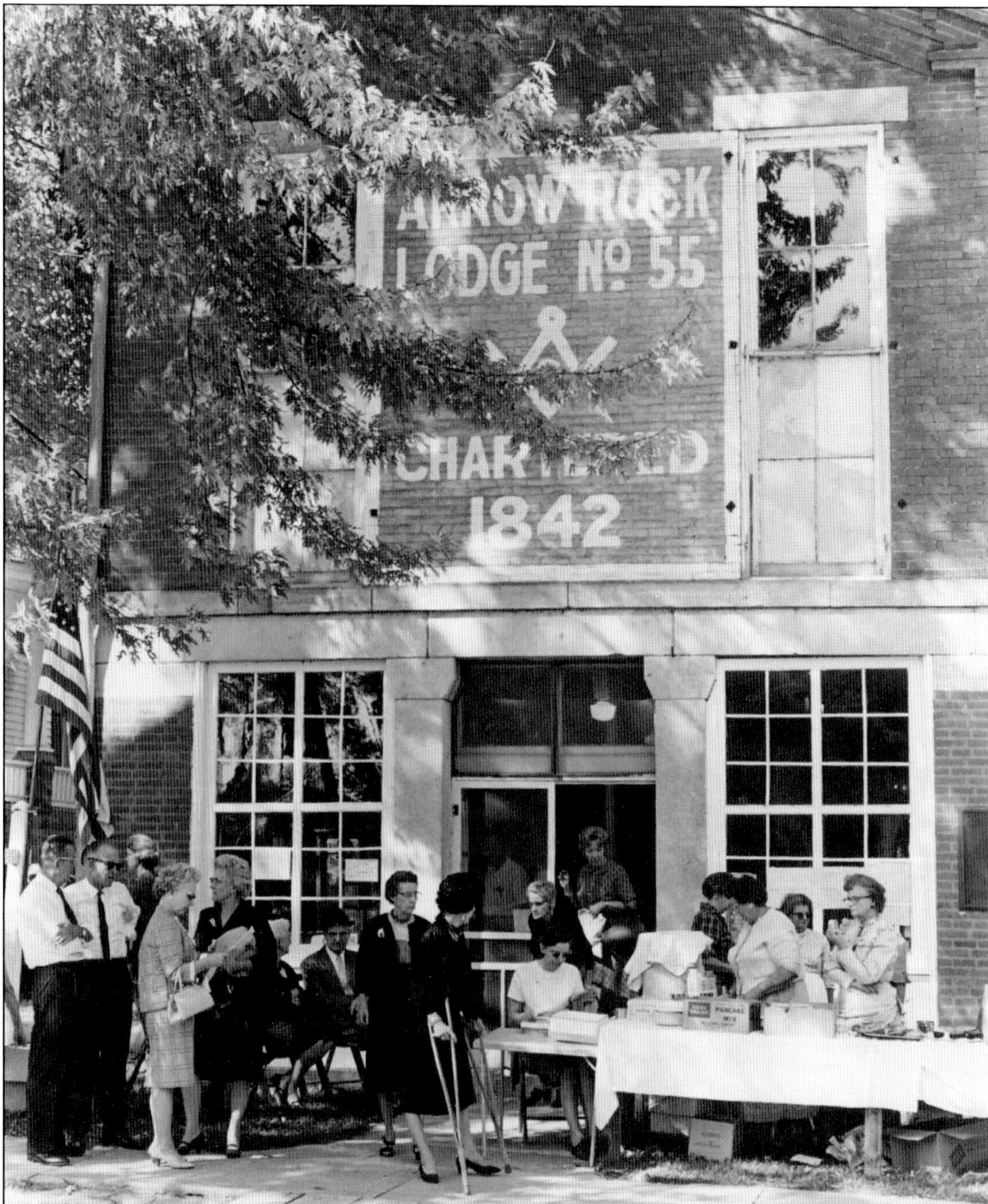

A handwritten note records the birth of the Arrow Rock Craft Club: "On November 14th, [1960], a group of ladies gathered at the home of Mrs. Nelle Thompson and Miss Amy Harris for an all day meeting. The purpose of said meeting was to organize a craft club to be called the Arrow Rock Craft Club to promote Arrow Rock and make and sell homemade articles of any kind you would think would interest a stranger coming into our town." The note went on to say the group hoped to find a suitable building as a permanent home for the club. Fortunately, many of the charter craft club members were wives of Masons, and in 1961, they persuaded their husbands to lease them the vacant ground-floor space of the Masonic Lodge. The club, which still operates out of its original location, recently celebrated its 50th anniversary. (Courtesy of Friends of Arrow Rock.)

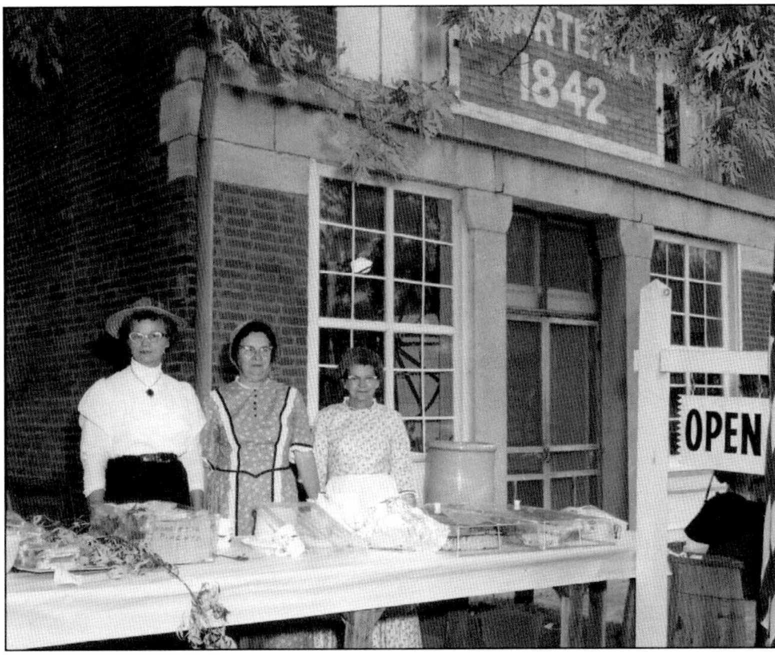

Early Arrow Rock Craft Club members, including, from left to right, Tracy Thomas, Maude Leimkuhler, and Susie Templeton, held a luncheon to raise money for the organization's start-up expenses and necessary building repairs. Then as now, Arrow Rock Craft Club members took turns manning the shop. (Courtesy of Missouri Department of Natural Resources.)

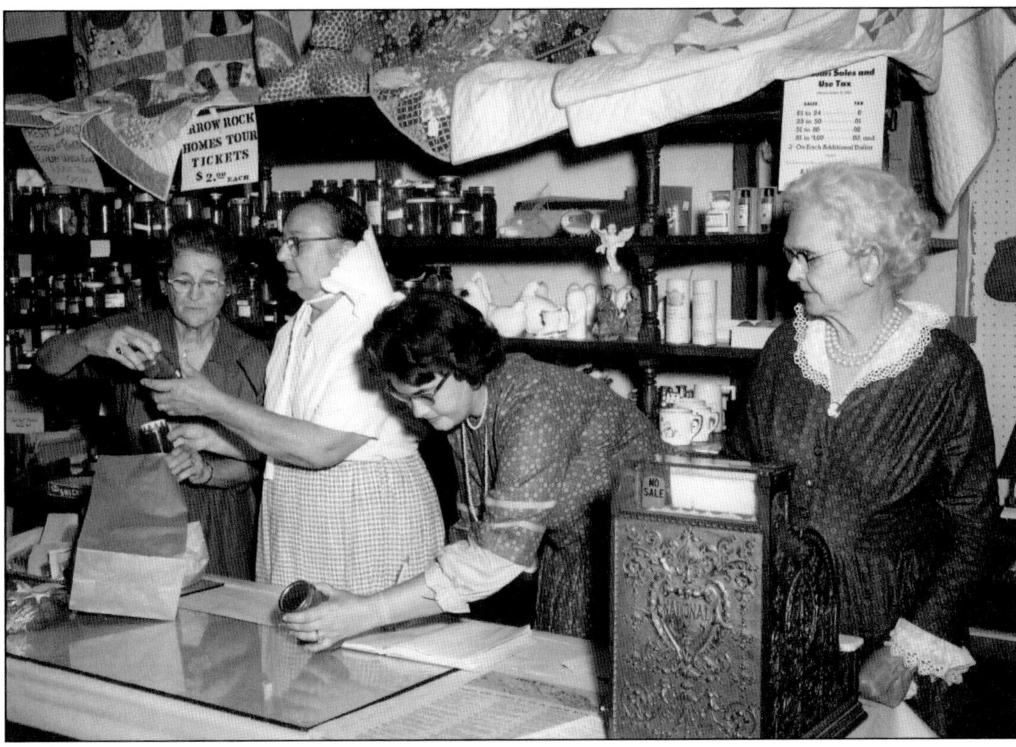

Homemade food items have always sold well at the Arrow Rock Craft Club, but members fill the shop with a variety of items. A 1962 story in the *Missouri Farmer* described items for sale, including dolls, quilts, and lace handkerchiefs. At the time, members were surprised by the popularity of one product: 50¢ bags of sheep manure tourists took home to spread on gardens. (Courtesy of Friends of Arrow Rock.)

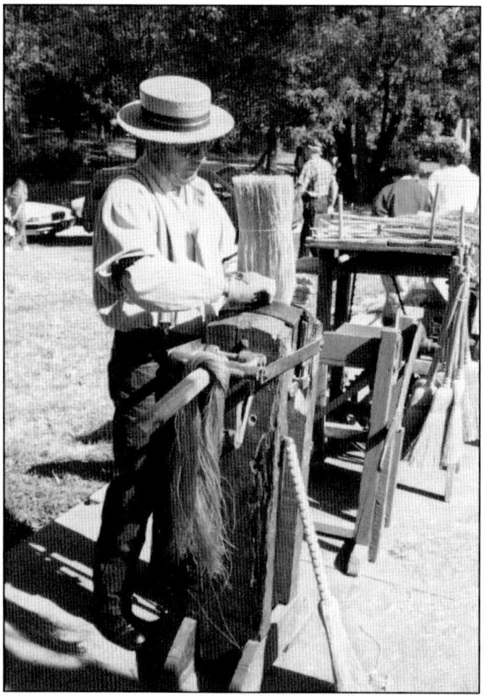

Arrow Rock launched its annual Heritage Craft Festival in 1968 to showcase the 19th-century arts and crafts that were once essential to daily living. Broom maker Tom Beamer and his wife, Mary, first came to Arrow Rock as participants in the craft festival in 1986 but became full-time residents of the village in 1992. (Courtesy of Friends of Arrow Rock.)

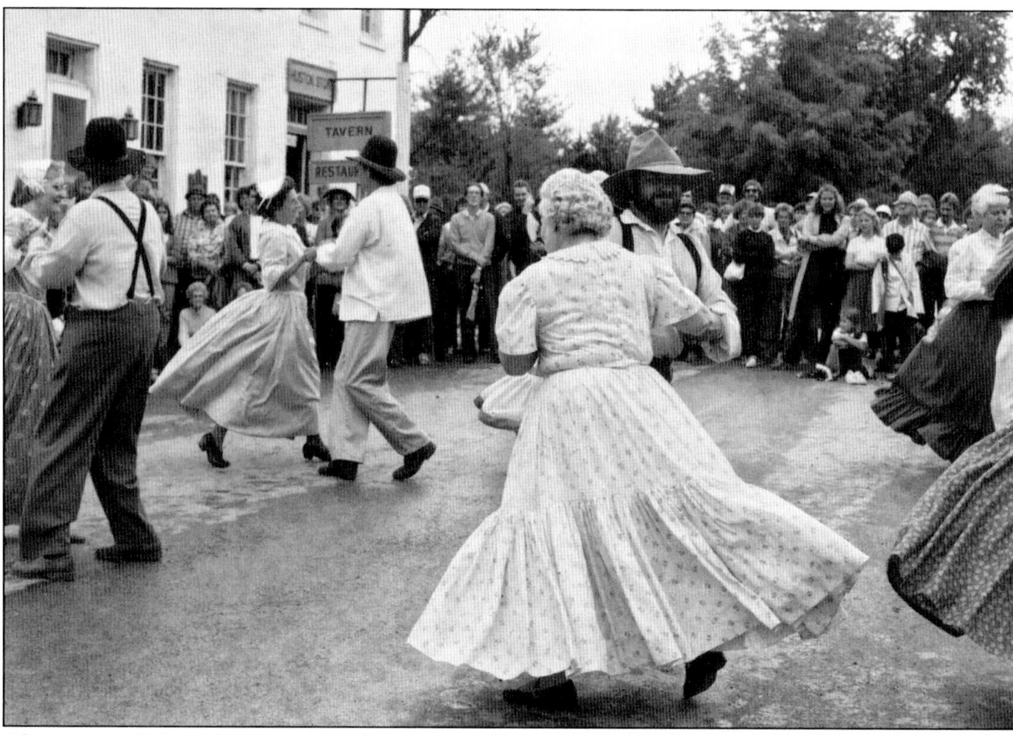

The Missouri Town Dancers have been a popular attraction for Heritage Craft Festival attendees for decades. The group, accompanied by a live band playing old-time tunes, brings 1850s-era dances to life for the crowd and sometimes even invites willing bystanders to go for a spin. (Courtesy of Friends of Arrow Rock.)

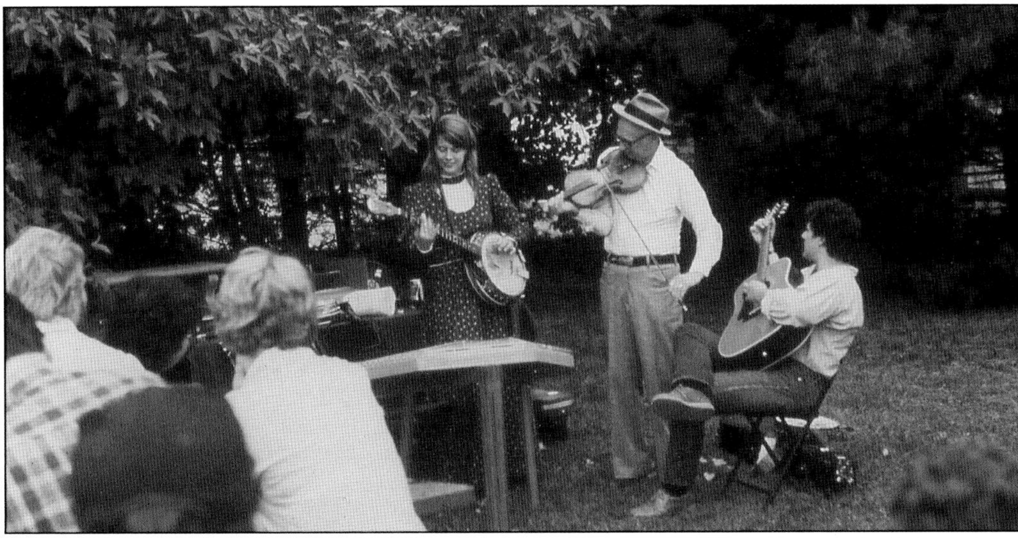

Arrow Rock quickly recognized the talent of young folk musicians Cathy Barton (with banjo) and Dave Para (seated). The duo from Boonville, Missouri, performed at the Heritage Craft Festival during the 1980s. Although they now enjoy an international following, Barton and Para return to Arrow Rock every December for the Christmas Folk Sing at the Federated Church. (Courtesy of Friends of Arrow Rock.)

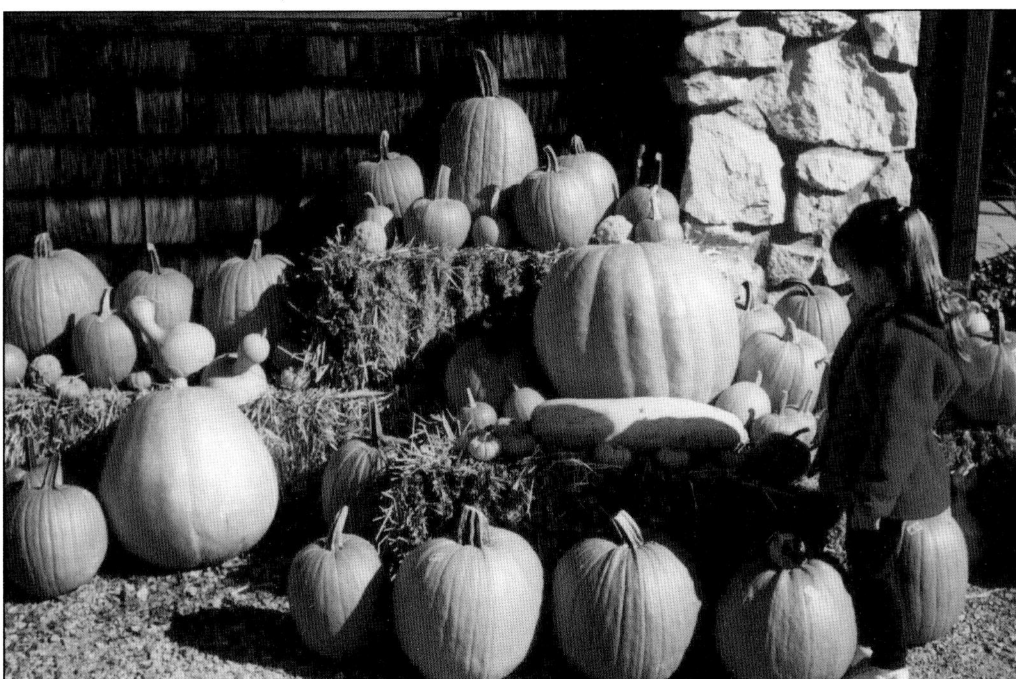

The crafts aren't the only colorful thing in Arrow Rock on Heritage Craft Festival weekend. Autumn color is everywhere, from the changing leaves to the pumpkins stacked up in front of the Arrow Rock Station. The former service station sitting at the entrance of the town has been transformed into a combination restaurant/bed and breakfast. (Courtesy of Missouri Department of Natural Resources.)

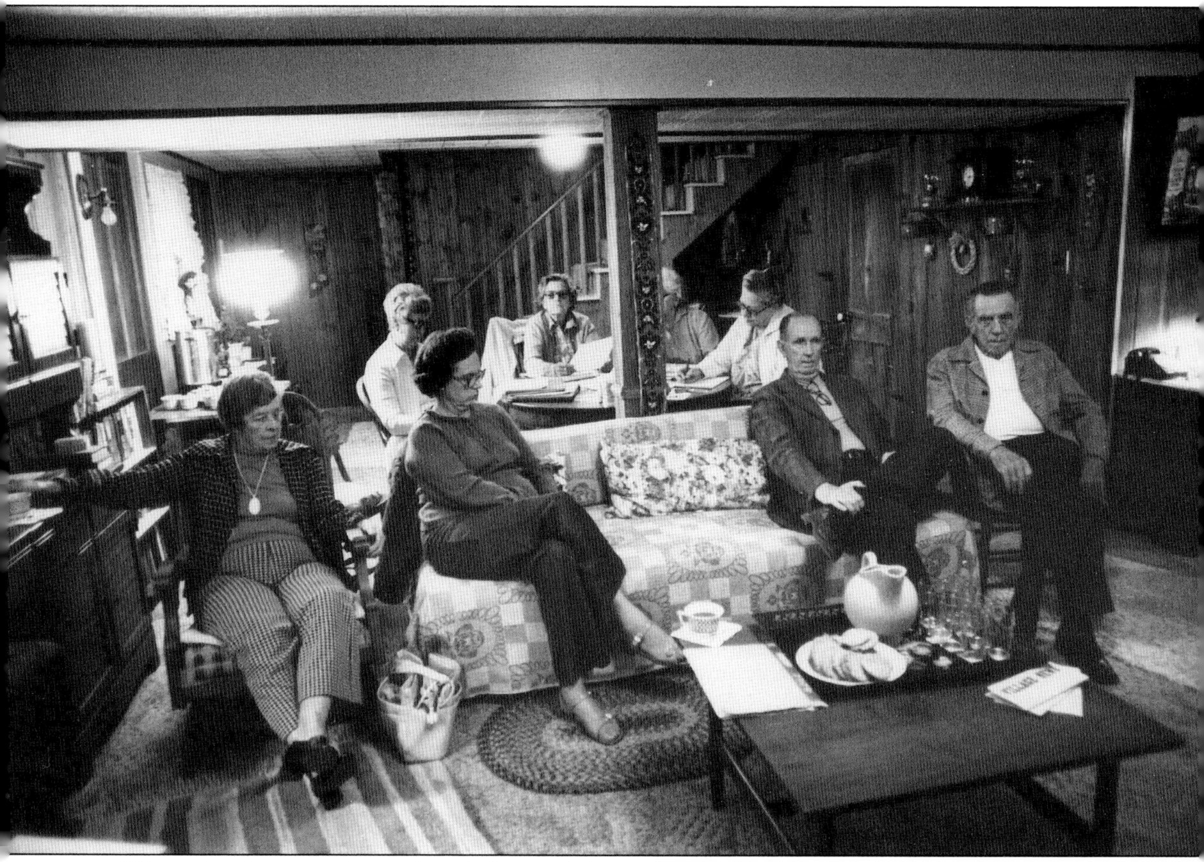

When the Historic Arrow Rock Council formed in 1974, its mission was to bring together representatives from all community organizations to work together for common goals. Over the years, it has evolved into an events- and arts-driven organization. Today, the organization is responsible for some of Arrow Rock's most popular events, including the Heritage Craft Festival, which draws thousands to the village on the second weekend of October, and the Spring Garden Show. Sisters and early Historic Arrow Rock Council members Buena Stolberg and Corinne Jackson purchased the Old Schoolhouse and later donated it to the organization. The building functions as a community center and serves as a rehearsal hall for the Arrow Rock Lyceum Theatre. Attendees at this 1980 meeting of the Historic Arrow Rock Council include, from left to right, Ginner Emmerson, Thelma VanArsdale, Helen McDaniel, Cora Lee Miller, Sallie Hailey, Ginny Fisher, Johnny McDaniel, and Bill Miller. (Courtesy of Friends of Arrow Rock.)

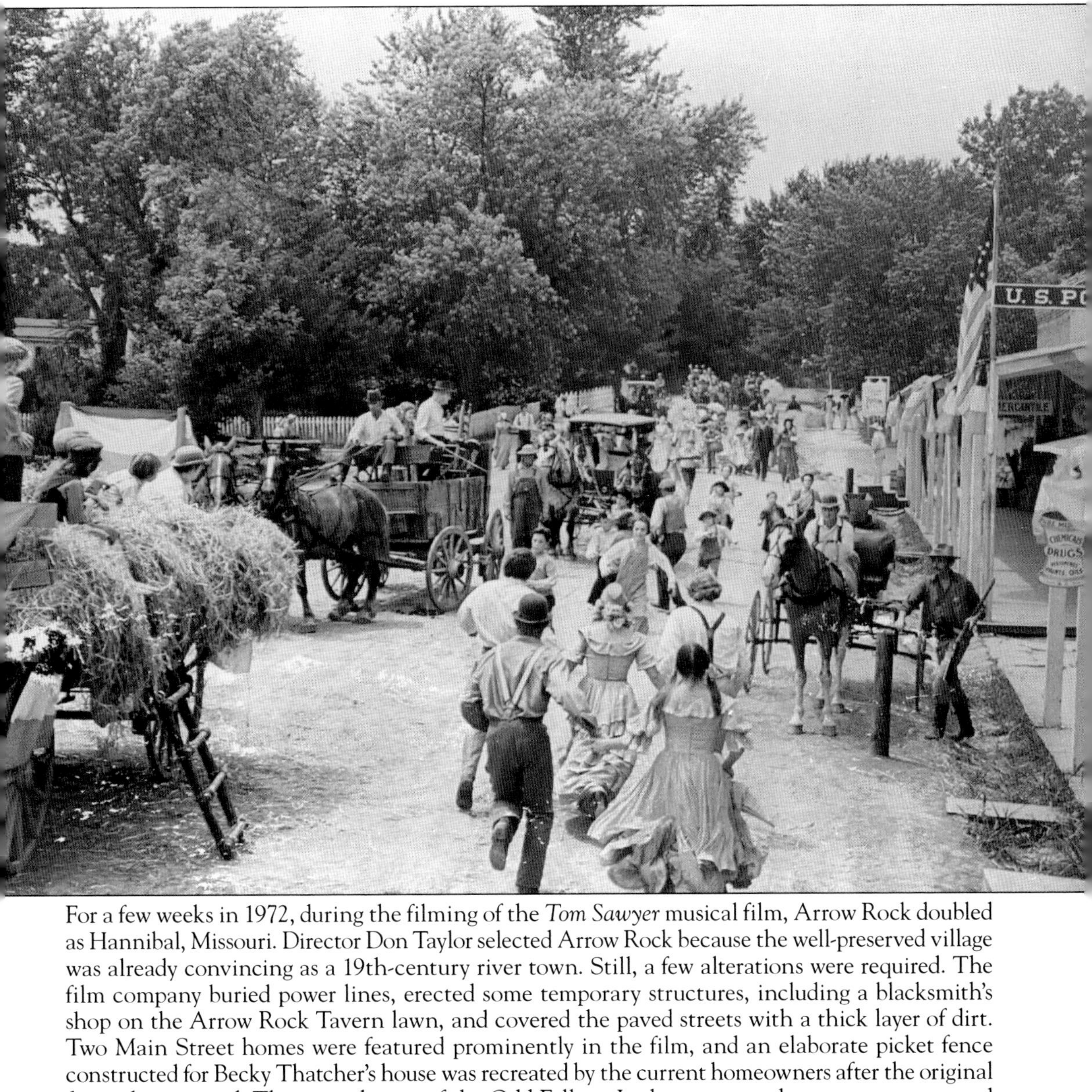

For a few weeks in 1972, during the filming of the *Tom Sawyer* musical film, Arrow Rock doubled as Hannibal, Missouri. Director Don Taylor selected Arrow Rock because the well-preserved village was already convincing as a 19th-century river town. Still, a few alterations were required. The film company buried power lines, erected some temporary structures, including a blacksmith's shop on the Arrow Rock Tavern lawn, and covered the paved streets with a thick layer of dirt. Two Main Street homes were featured prominently in the film, and an elaborate picket fence constructed for Becky Thatcher's house was recreated by the current homeowners after the original fence deteriorated. The second story of the Odd Fellows Lodge was remade as a courtroom, and the Christian Church was filled with actors playing mourners for Tom and Huck's premature funeral. The town picnic scene called for a crowd of extras to gather on Main Street for some make-believe merriment. Locals who worked as extras during the film earned a wage of $2.50 an hour. (Courtesy of the Friends of Arrow Rock.)

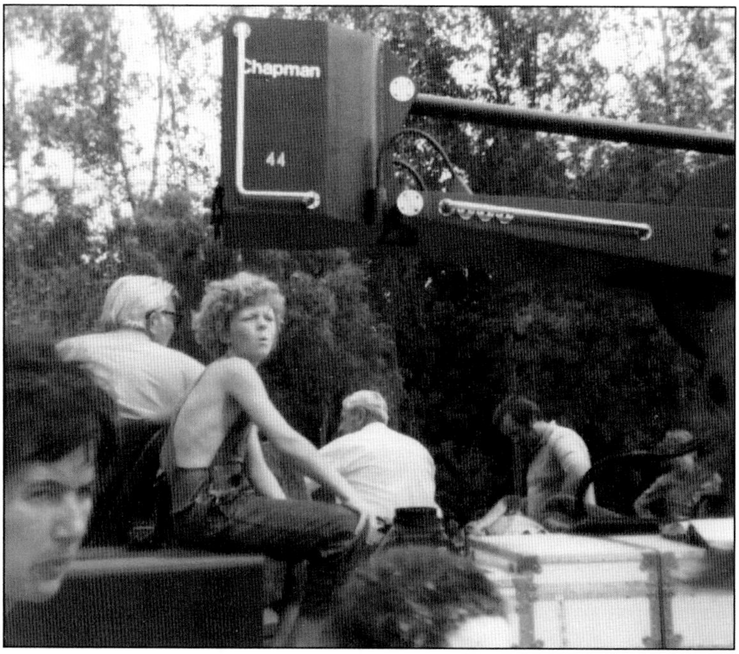

Child star Johnny Whitaker was reluctant to accept the title role in *Tom Sawyer*. He preferred instead to attend Boy Scout camp and sold greeting cards door-to-door to raise the money to pay his camp fee. After some tough negotiations with his parents and the director, he was allowed to attend camp for four days before reporting to Arrow Rock to begin filming. (Courtesy of Missouri Department of Natural Resources.)

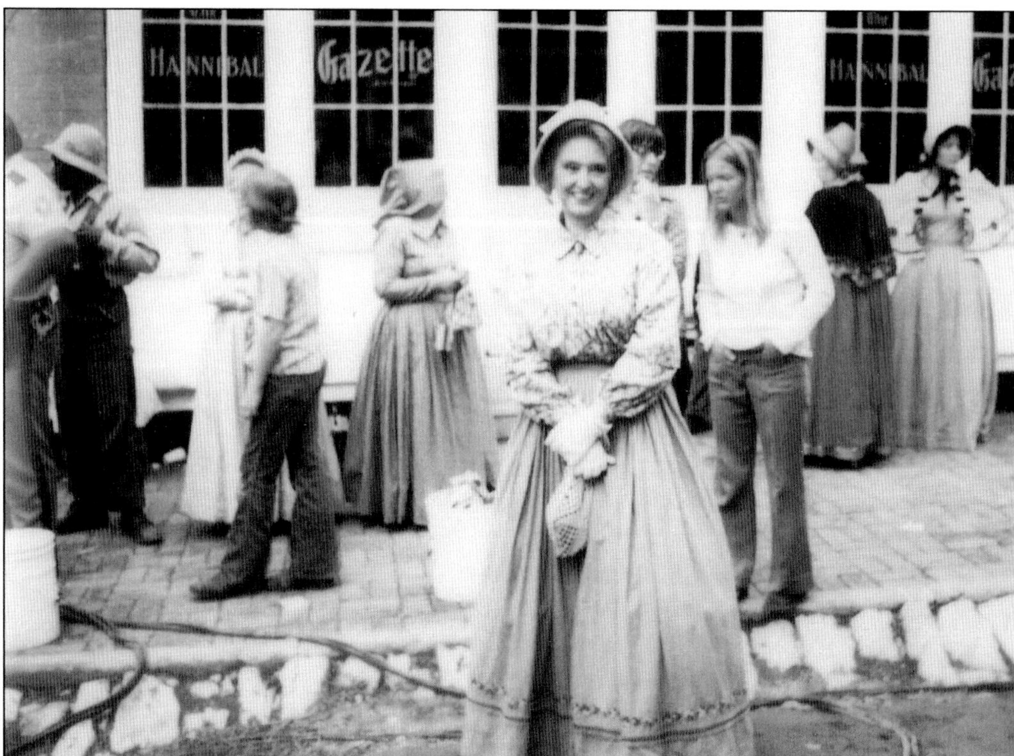

Celeste Holm, shown here on the movie set, was among the *Tom Sawyer* stars who returned to Arrow Rock in 2008 for the 35th anniversary of the film's release. "Arrow Rock has a sense of history," she said during her return visit. "It knows who it is and how it got there. That's as nice in places as it is in people." (Courtesy of Missouri Department of Natural Resources.)

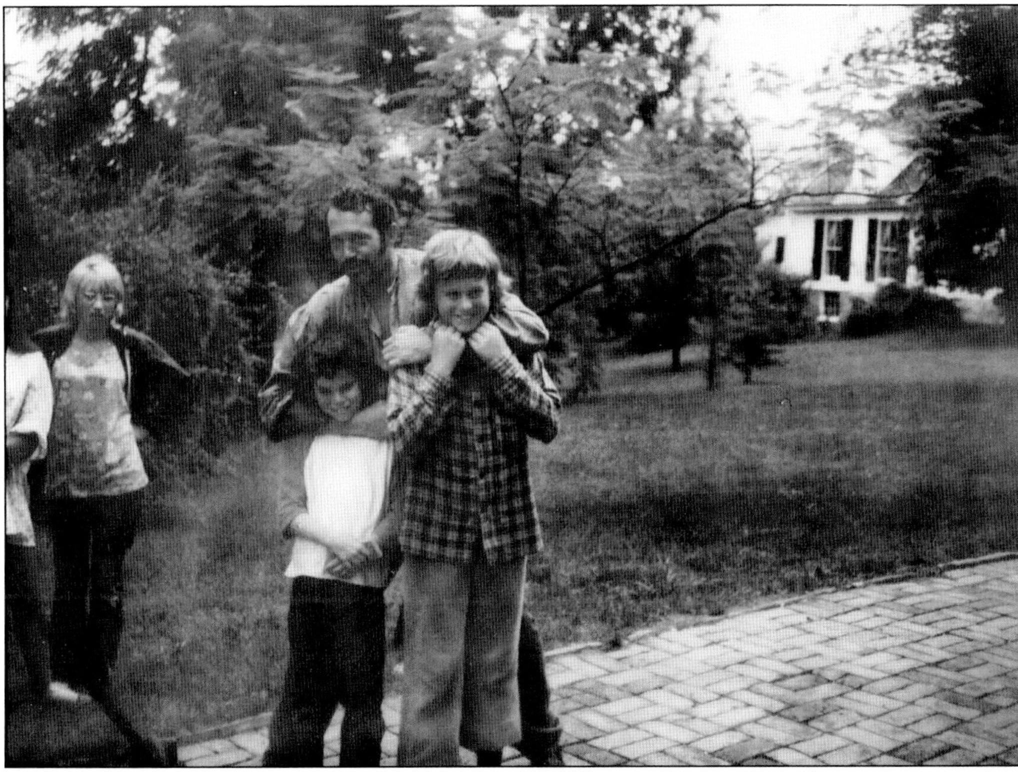

Many members of the *Tom Sawyer* cast and crew brought their families with them for the summertime shoot, including Warren Oates (center), who invited his son Tim (left). Oates won plenty of friends among the locals, including Huck Finn stand-in David Martin (right) and area farmer Bill Burge, who served as both stand-in and fishing buddy for Oates. (Courtesy of Missouri Department of Natural Resources.)

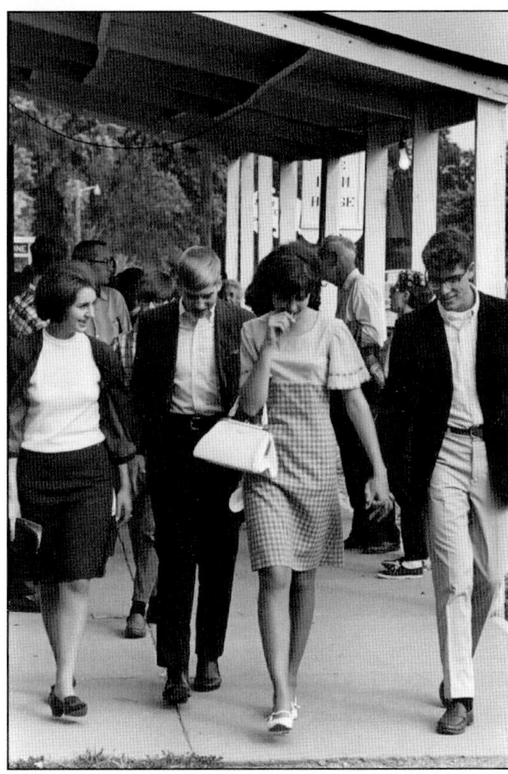

By the 1960s, the wooden planks of Arrow Rock's historical boardwalk had been replaced by utilitarian concrete sidewalks. The *Tom Sawyer* movie crew recreated the boardwalk, and the town's merchants liked it so much, they decided to keep it. The boardwalk continues to add to the charm of the shopping experience in the village. (Courtesy of Friends of Arrow Rock.)

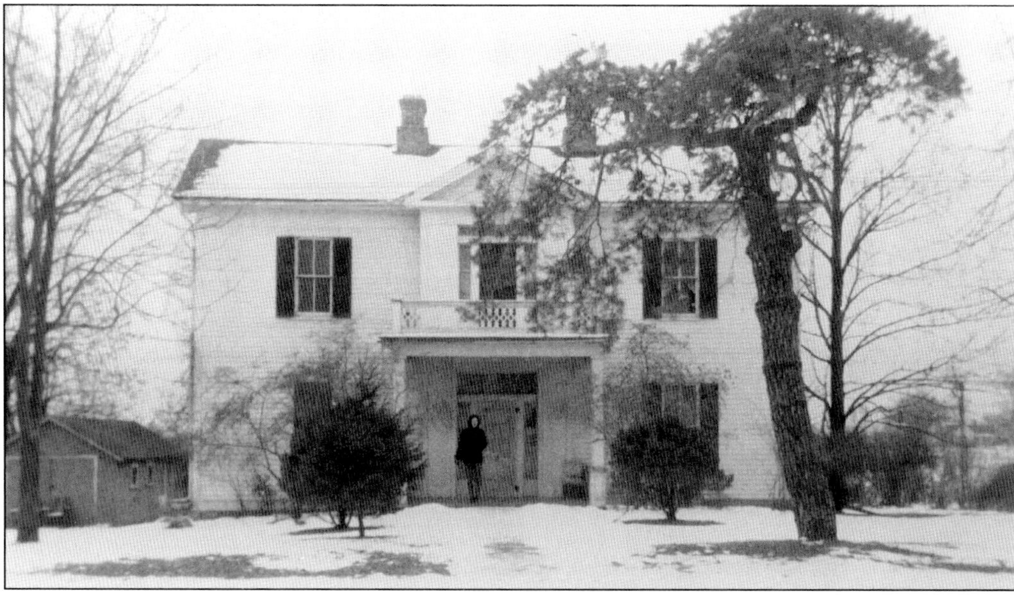

The 1840s Main Street home owned by Page Williams (pictured above) had once been an office for Dr. William Price, one of Arrow Rock's first physicians. The interior and exterior of the home was used as Aunt Polly's house for the *Tom Sawyer* film. The home was destroyed by fire shortly after filming completed. (Courtesy of Missouri Department of Natural Resources.)

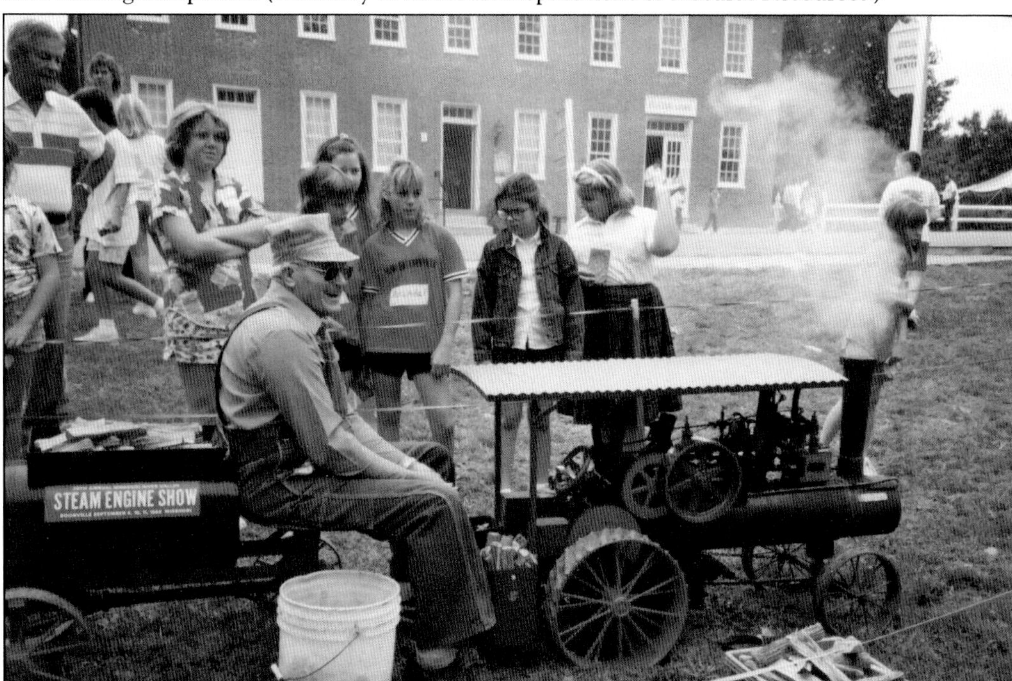

The Friends of Arrow Rock believes the best way to teach history to children is to bring history to life. The organization accomplishes its education mission through interactive learning experiences, including the Children's Craft Festival. In 1988, festival attendees learned about steam power from Leonard Stroup, owner of this miniature steam engine. (Courtesy of Friends of Arrow Rock.)

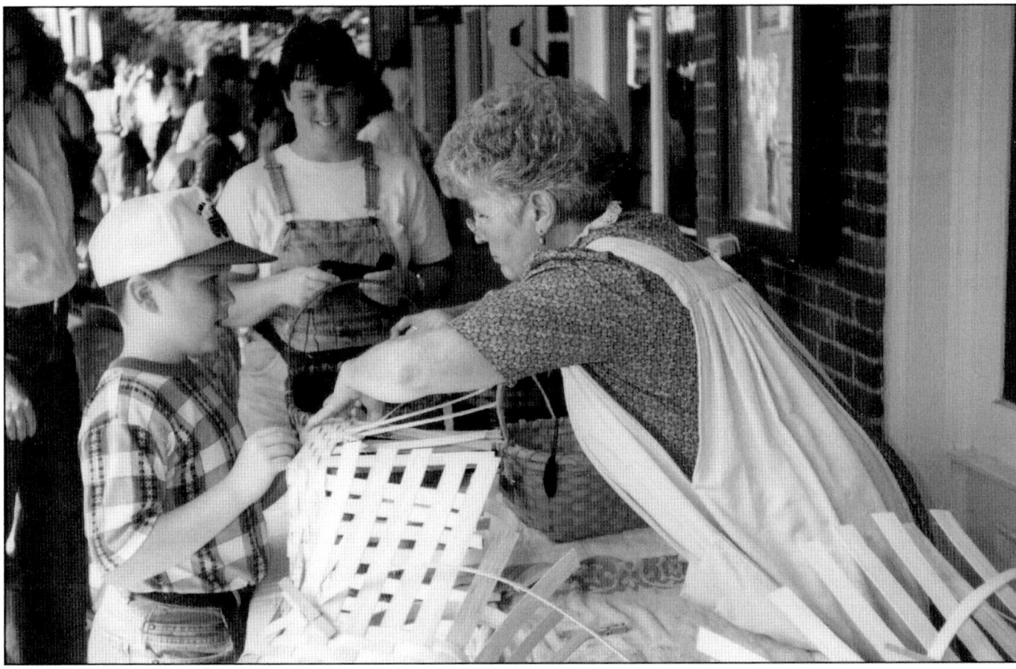

The Friends of Arrow Rock and the Arrow Rock State Historic Site established the biennial Children's Craft Festival in 1984. The event educates hundreds of area schoolchildren about life in the 19th century by letting them see and experience games and crafts that have been lost to time. Arrow Rock resident and merchant Mary Beamer demonstrates the basics of basket making. (Courtesy of Missouri Department of Natural Resources.)

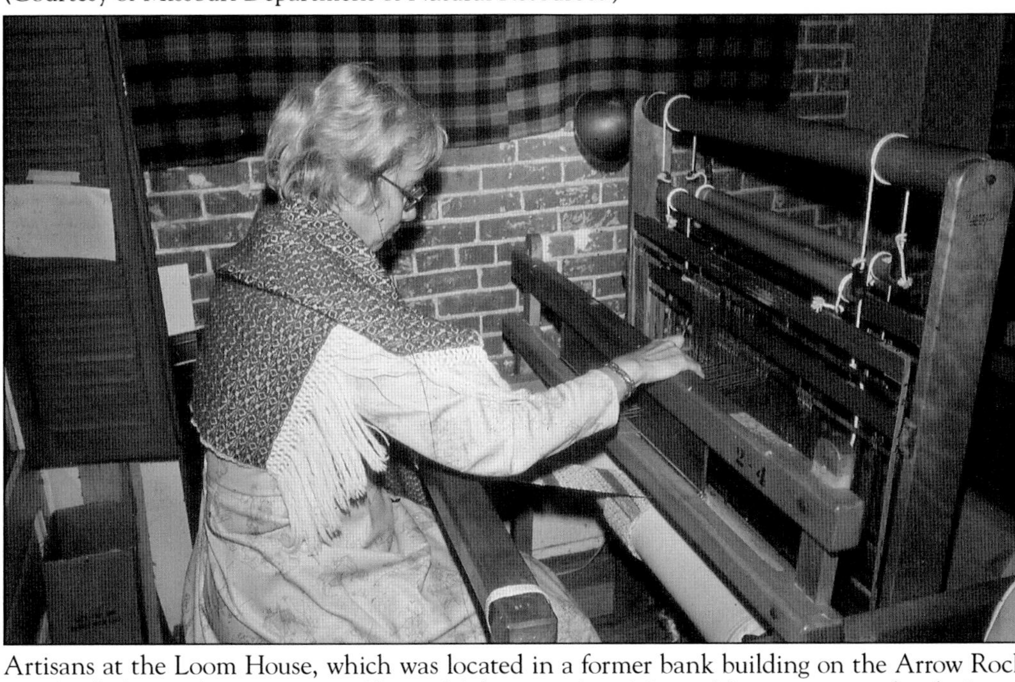

Artisans at the Loom House, which was located in a former bank building on the Arrow Rock boardwalk during the 1970s, created beautiful, functional art. Many of the pieces created at the Loom House still can be found on display in area homes today. (Courtesy of Friends of Arrow Rock.)

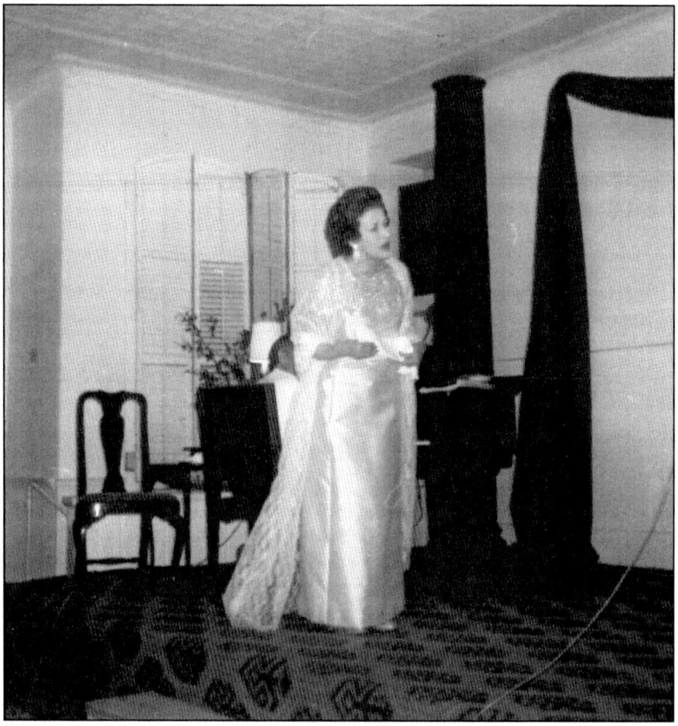

Jane Froman, star of television, film, and the Broadway stage and a successful recording artist, retired from performing in 1961. She moved home to her native Columbia, Missouri. A few years later, she helped establish the Jane Froman Music Center at the Old Schoolhouse in Arrow Rock. From 1969 to 1972, she served as a music consultant for various productions at the center and used her influence as a celebrity to attract international artists to perform with the students. She is shown here in 1969, participating in a Labor Day weekend benefit for the center. (Images courtesy of the Historic Arrow Rock Council.)

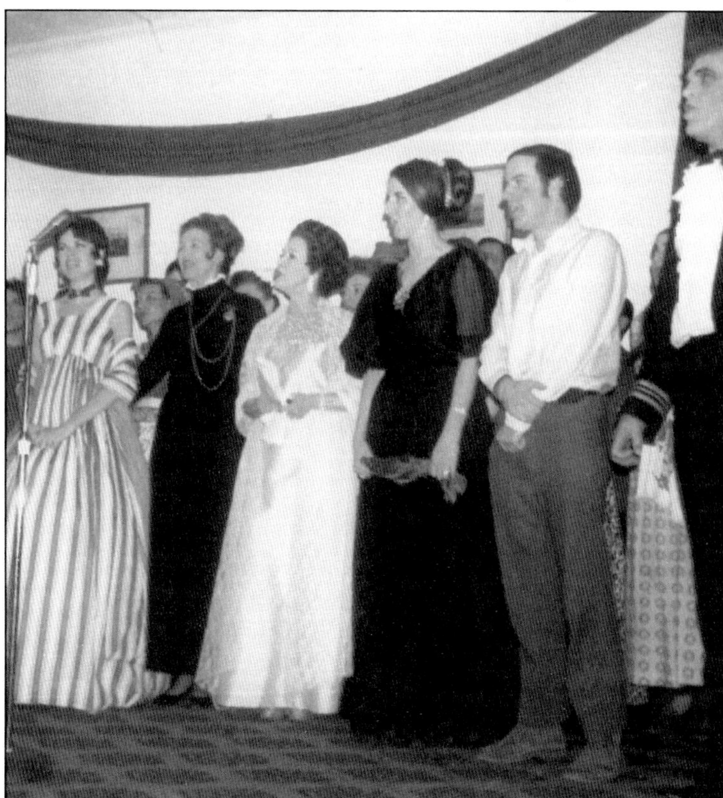

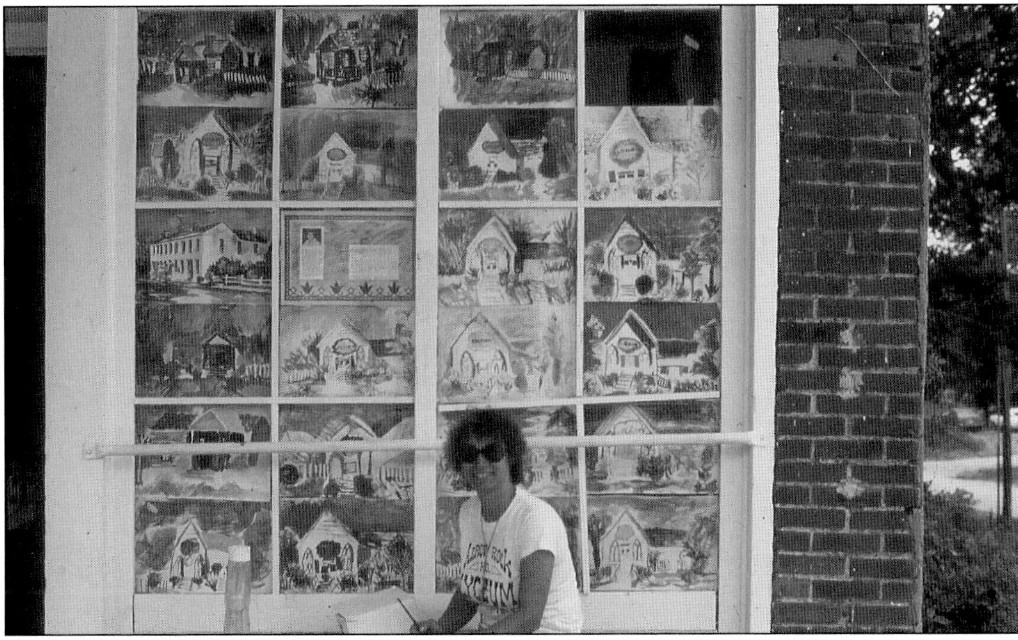

Missouri watercolorist Marilynne Bradley has been holding her summer watercolor workshops in Arrow Rock since 1978. Hundreds of students have honed their painting technique with guidance from Bradley. Arrow Rock landmarks, including the Lyceum Theatre and the Arrow Rock Tavern, are popular subjects for student paintings. (Courtesy of Friends of Arrow Rock.)

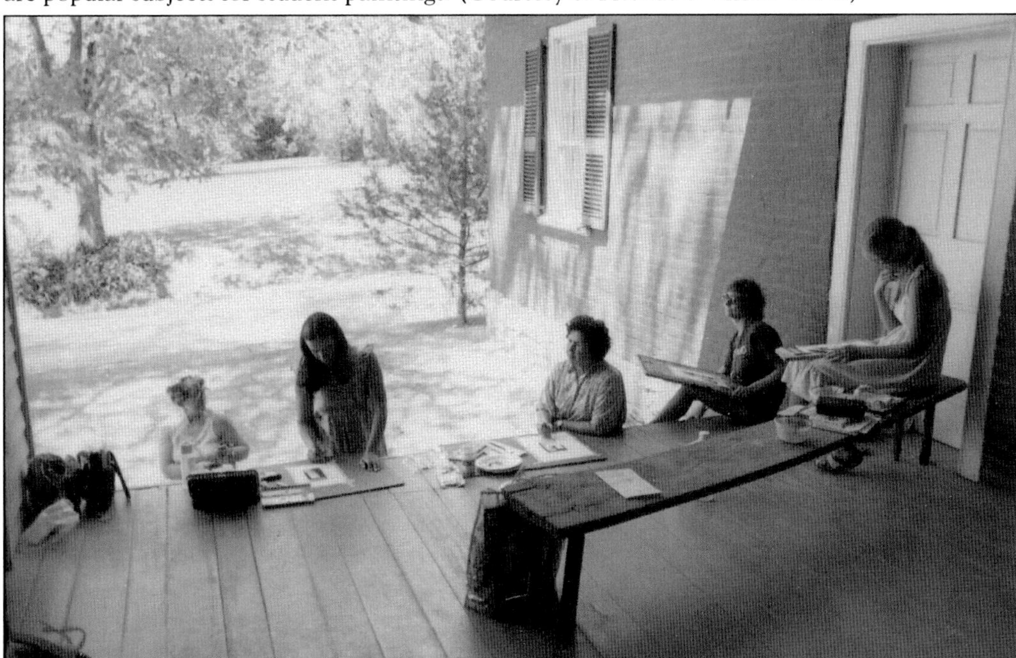

Participants of the annual Arrow Rock Watercolor Workshop enjoy the camaraderie and often form close friendships. Many of the same students return for the workshop year after year. This group enjoys both the view and the companionship from their impromptu studio in the George Caleb Bingham house dogtrot. (Courtesy of Missouri Department of Natural Resources.)

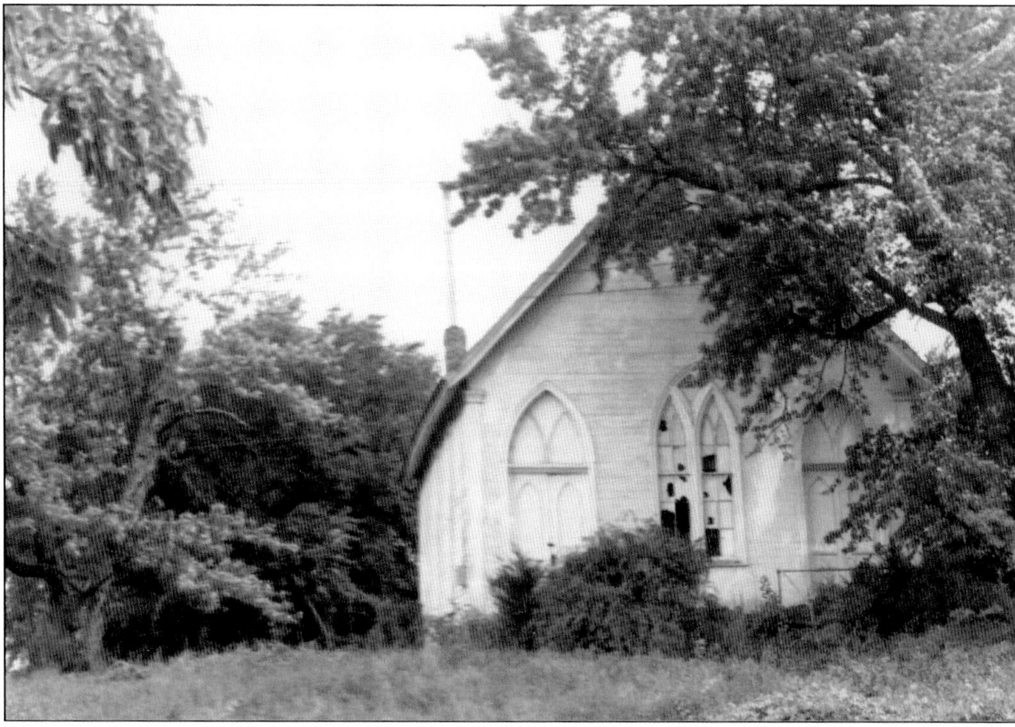

Two couples, John and Marianna Lawrence and Fletcher C. "Red" and Lucia Argubright, owned the old Baptist Church building in Arrow Rock. By 1960, the vacant building had become an eyesore and was in desperate need of repair. The couples decided to donate the building for use as a theater. (Courtesy of Missouri Department of Natural Resources.)

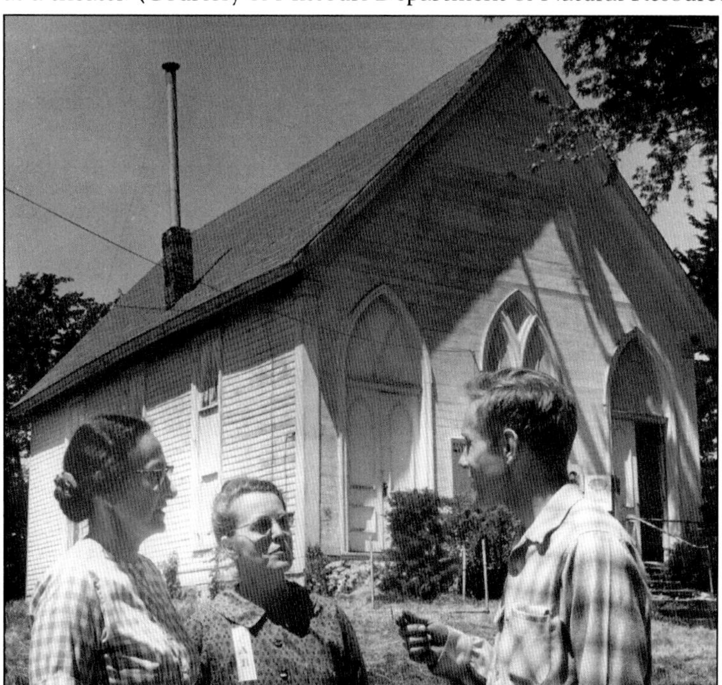

Jean Hamilton (left) and Cora Lee Miller welcome the Arrow Rock Lyceum Theatre's first artistic director, Henry Swanson. Swanson produced the theater's 1961 inaugural season on a budget of $3,500. The season opened on a stormy night, and power went out shortly after the curtain rose on *The Importance of Being Earnest*. An actor entertained the crowd with banjo music until electricity was restored. (Courtesy of Friends of Arrow Rock.)

On opening day in 1961, leading lady and future soap opera star Susan Flannery decided to beautify the Arrow Rock Lyceum Theatre grounds by clearing away an unsightly vine that had grown around the bell tower. The vine was poison ivy, and the actress was in misery, but knowing the show must go on, she performed through the discomfort. (Courtesy of Friends of Arrow Rock.)

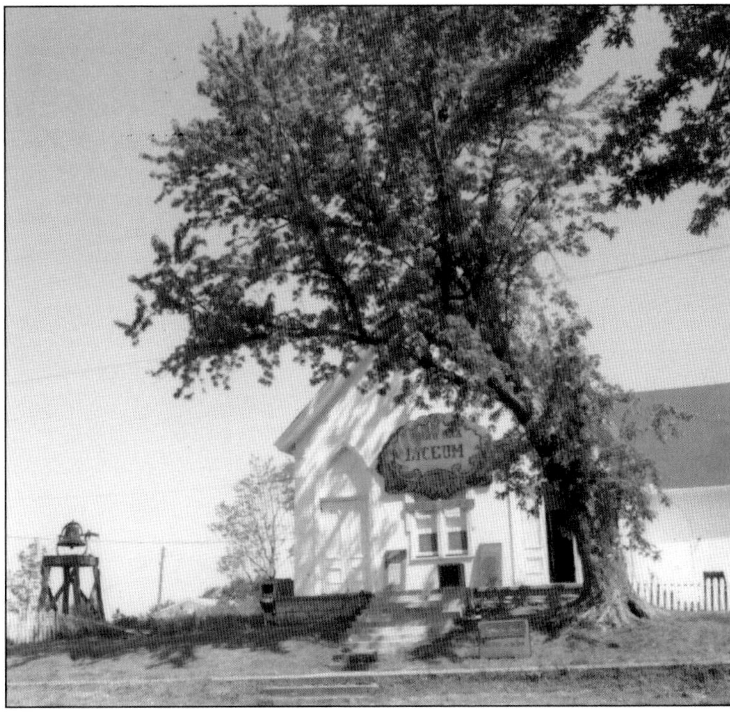

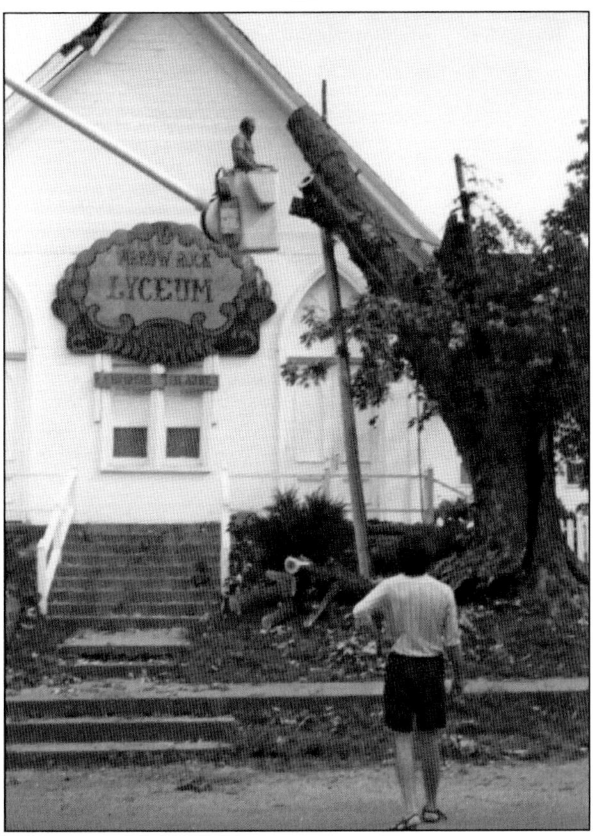

Shortly before the 1975 season began, a severe thunderstorm took out the old tree on the front lawn and the old tree took out a chunk of the Arrow Rock Lyceum Theatre roof. A curious onlooker watches as the remnants of the tree are removed. (Courtesy of the McGlaughlin family.)

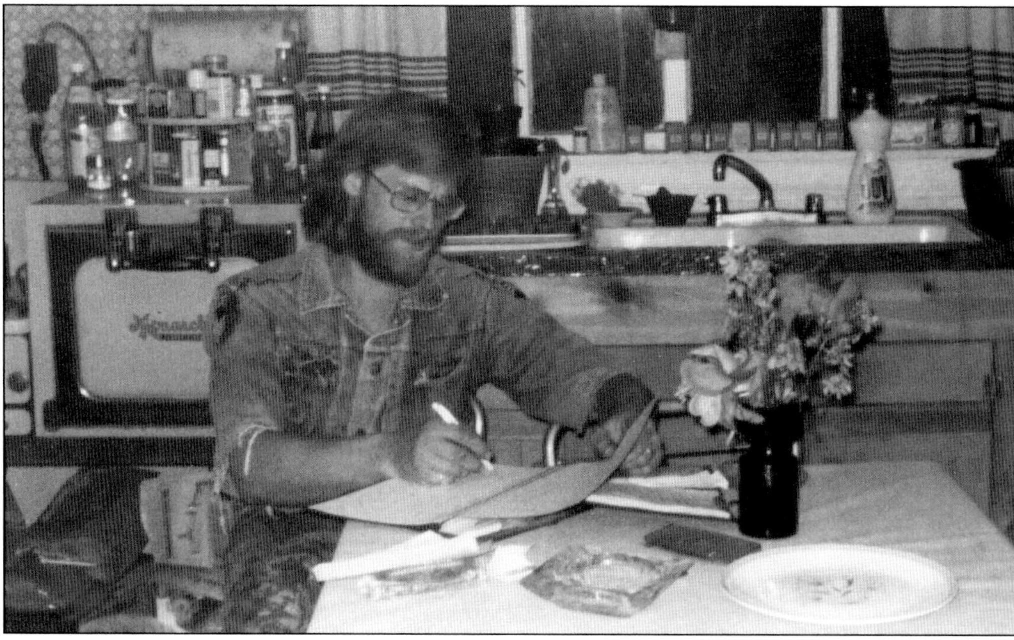

Bruce McGlaughlin first came to town in 1970 to work as an actor and set designer for the Arrow Rock Lyceum Theatre. He married his college sweetheart, Tempe Marsh, in 1975 and Tempe made her Lyceum acting debut that same year. The couple moved to California to follow their Hollywood dreams in 1976, but the simplicity and wholesome values of small-town living pulled them back to Arrow Rock in 1984 to raise their family. Today, Bruce uses his considerable skills as a woodworker and carpenter on projects throughout town. Tempe is Arrow Rock's postmaster and unofficial concierge for travelers coming to town for the first time. (Courtesy of the McGlaughlin family.)

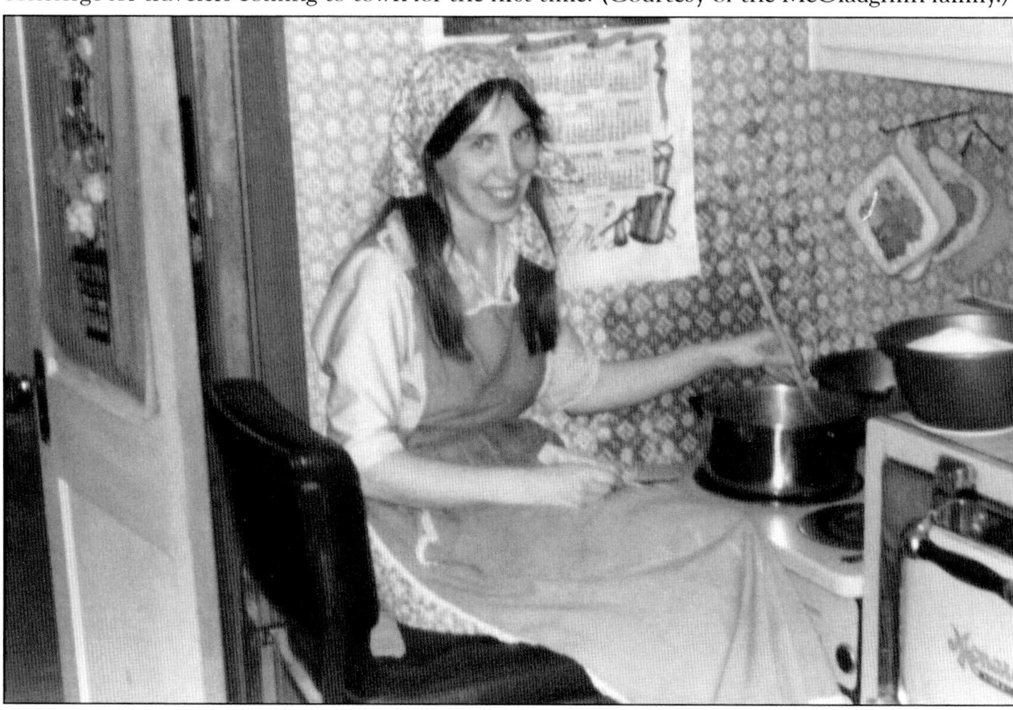

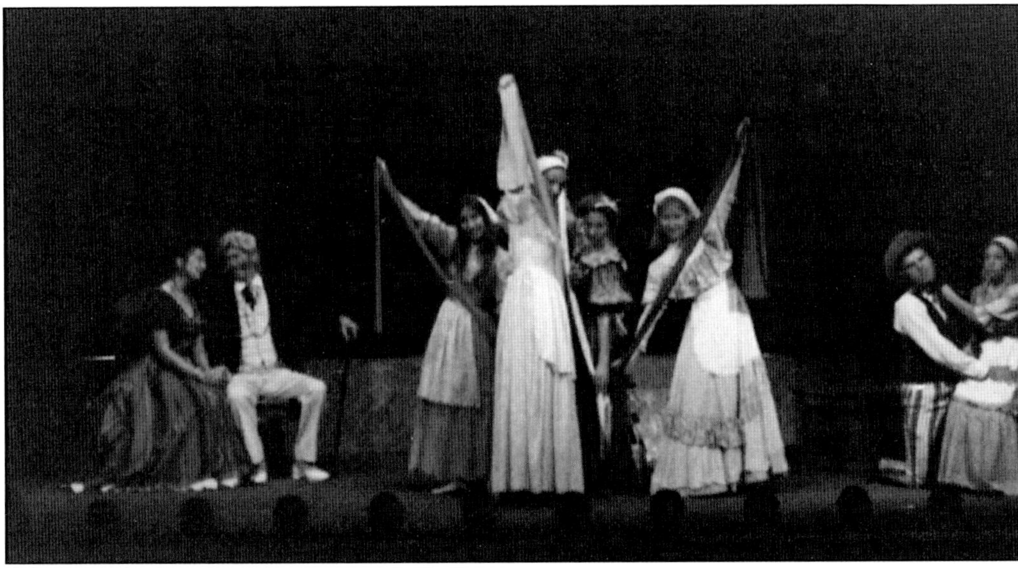

In its early years, most of the plays produced by the Arrow Rock Lyceum Theatre were old classics or British farces, such as *Lady Audley's Secret* in 1975. As the theater's reputation and budget grew, so did the scale of its productions. Within a few years, it would be staging well-known plays and musicals. (Courtesy of the McGlaughlin family.)

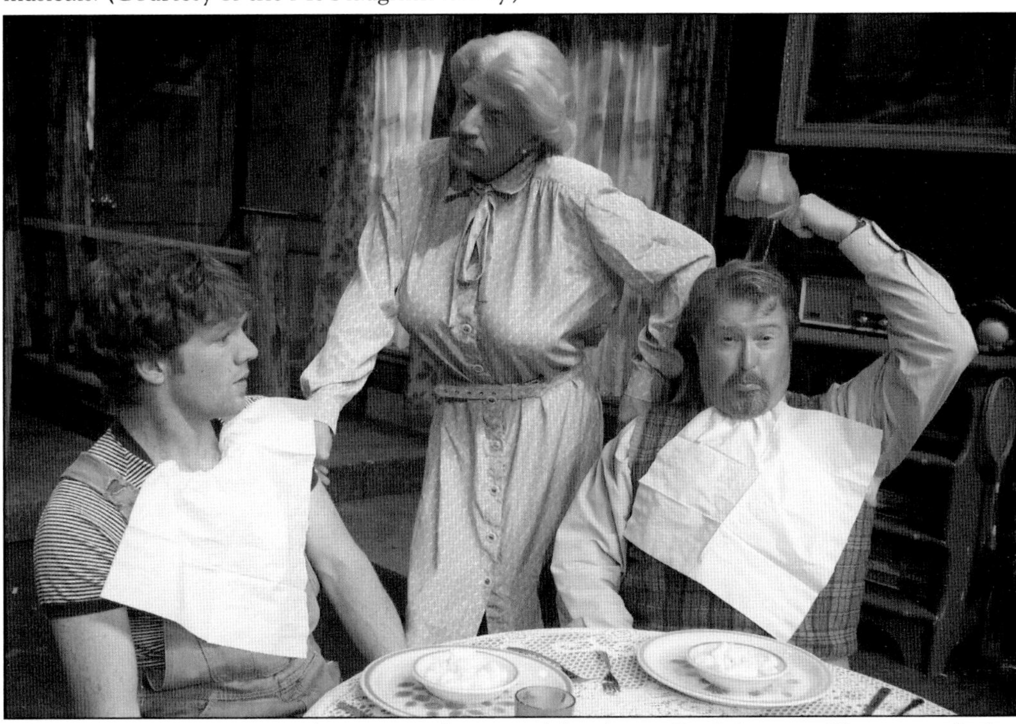

After Henry Swanson retired as artistic director of the Arrow Rock Lyceum Theatre in the late 1970s, Michael Bollinger was hired. During his 25-year tenure, Bollinger boosted the organization's success by adding 20th-century musicals to the repertoire and gathering support for a major expansion. Bollinger, on the right, shared the stage with assistant director Philip Coffield (center) during 1990's *The Foreigner.* (Courtesy of Arrow Rock Lyceum Theatre.)

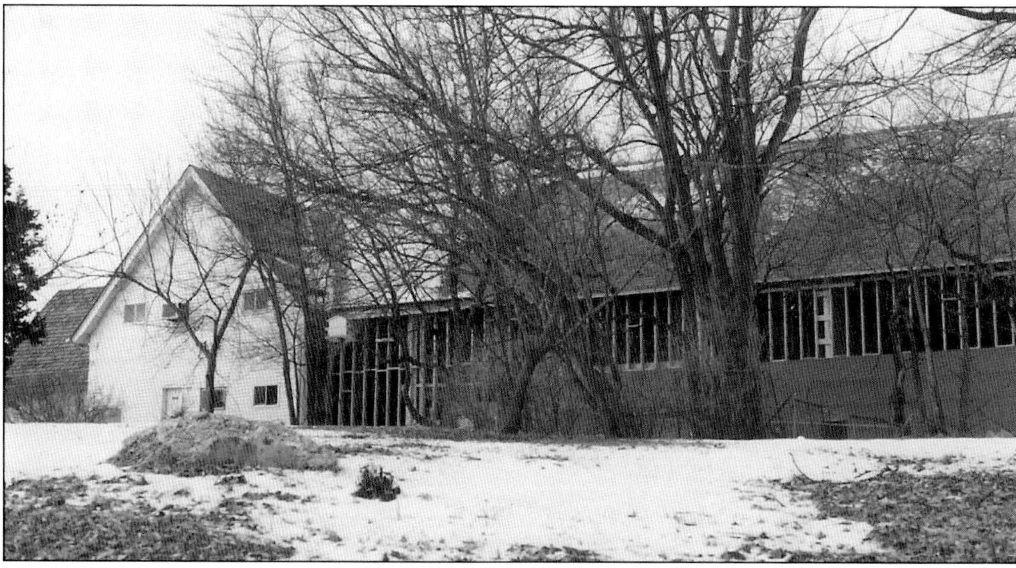

By 1993, the Arrow Rock Lyceum Theatre had outgrown its space. With tax credits from the Missouri Neighborhood Assistance Program and support from generous patrons, the theater embarked on a million-dollar expansion project. The result was an up-to-date, 408-seat theater attached to the rear of the historic church building, which was converted into lobby space. (Courtesy of Arrow Rock Lyceum Theatre.)

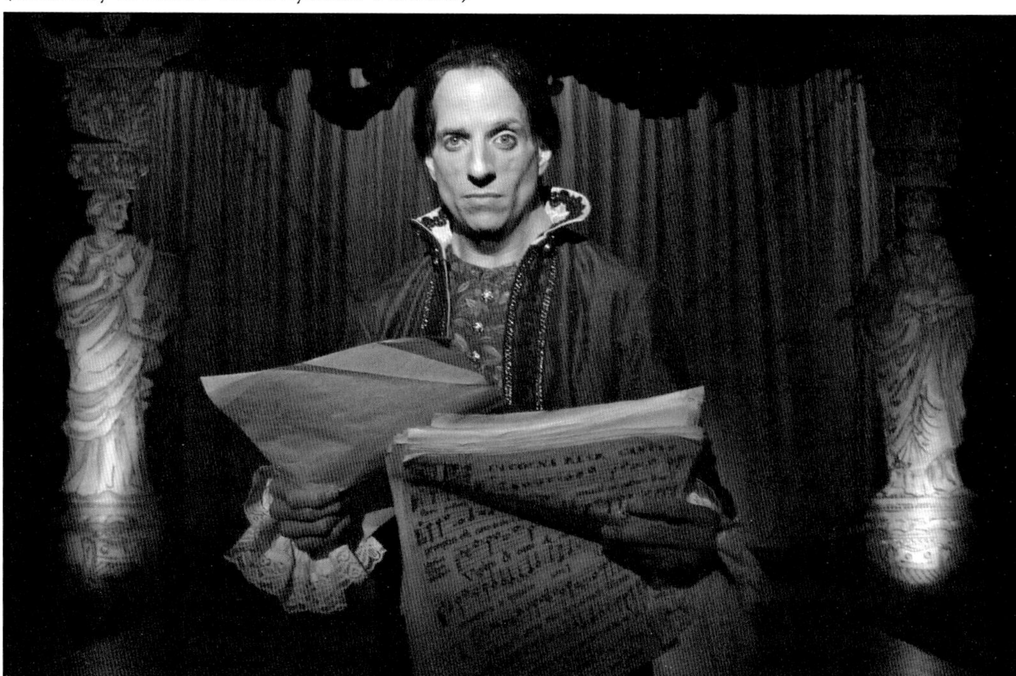

Philip Coffield joined the Arrow Rock Lyceum Theatre staff in 1989. He began his Lyceum career as assistant artistic director and appeared in many productions, including *Amadeus* in 2003. When long-time artistic director Michael Bollinger resigned in 2004, Coffield was tapped for the job. Sadly, his career and life were cut short by illness. Coffield died in 2006. (Courtesy of Arrow Rock Lyceum Theatre.)

Fire destroyed the Arrow Rock Lyceum Theatre's dormitory in 2004. The townspeople rallied around the theater and provided housing for the cast for the next three seasons until money was raised to construct a new dorm. Many of the actors and their hosts forged deep friendships that have continued long after the housing crisis was resolved. (Courtesy of Arrow Rock Lyceum Theatre.)

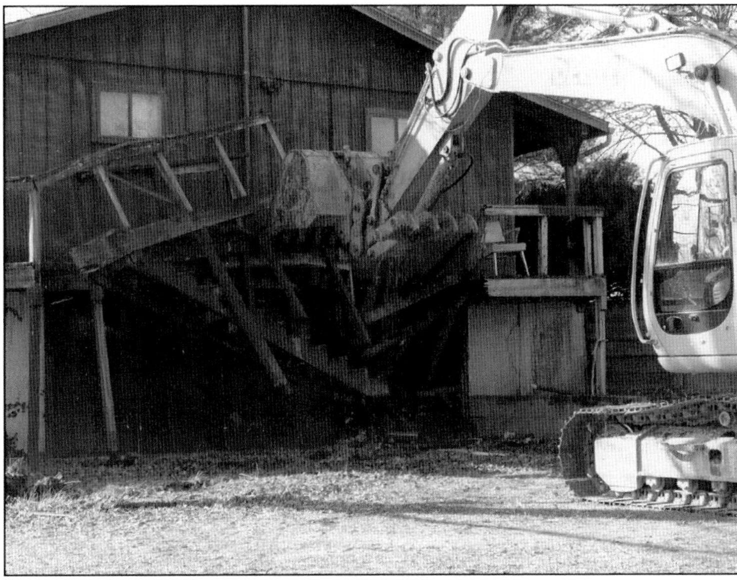

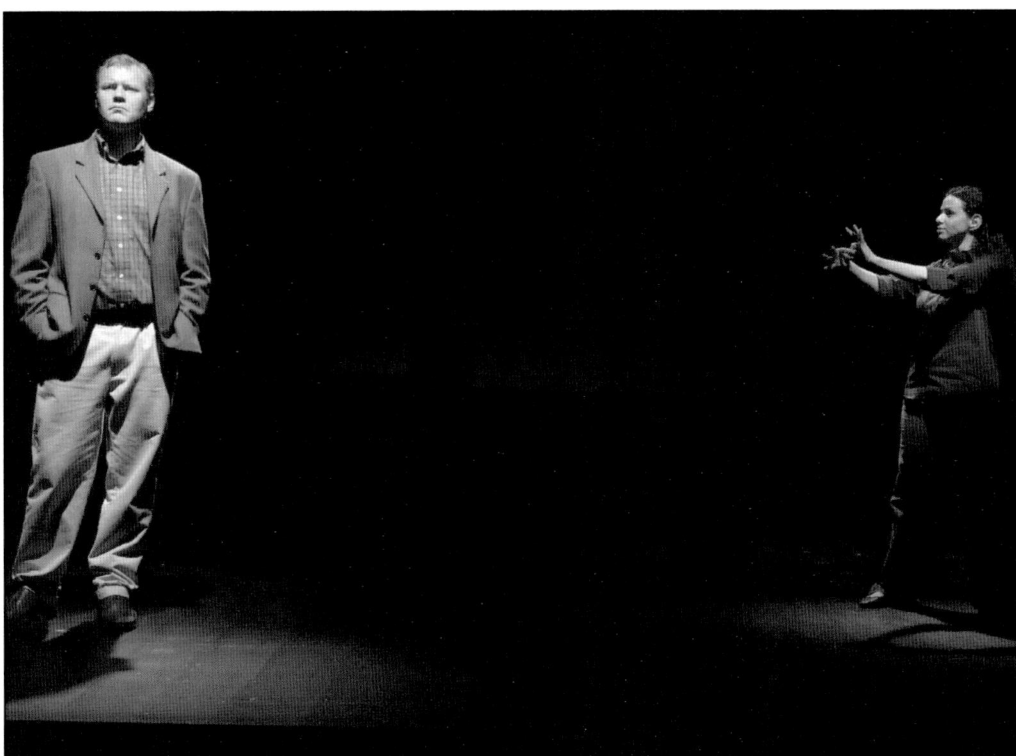

Quin Gresham became artistic director of the Arrow Rock Lyceum Theatre in 2005 and, along with managing director Steve Bertani, continued to build on the organization's success with ambitious productions and steadily increasing ticket sales. Like his predecessors, Gresham is gifted as both an actor and director. He has appeared in many productions, including 2007's *Children of a Lesser God*. (Courtesy of Arrow Rock Lyceum Theatre.)

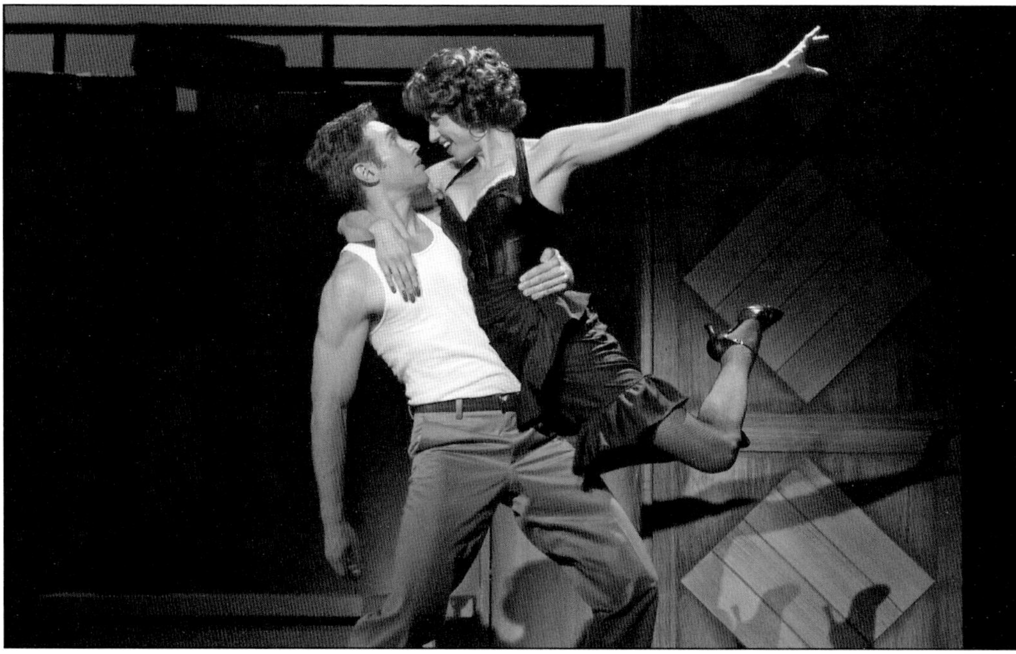

After the 2005 season, the Arrow Rock Lyceum Theatre discontinued running a portion of its season in repertory, which allowed for more elaborate sets and staging. The theater's reputation for exceptional quality helps it attract top talent from across the United States. Many Lyceum actors have Broadway credentials on their resumes. (Courtesy of Arrow Rock Lyceum Theatre.)

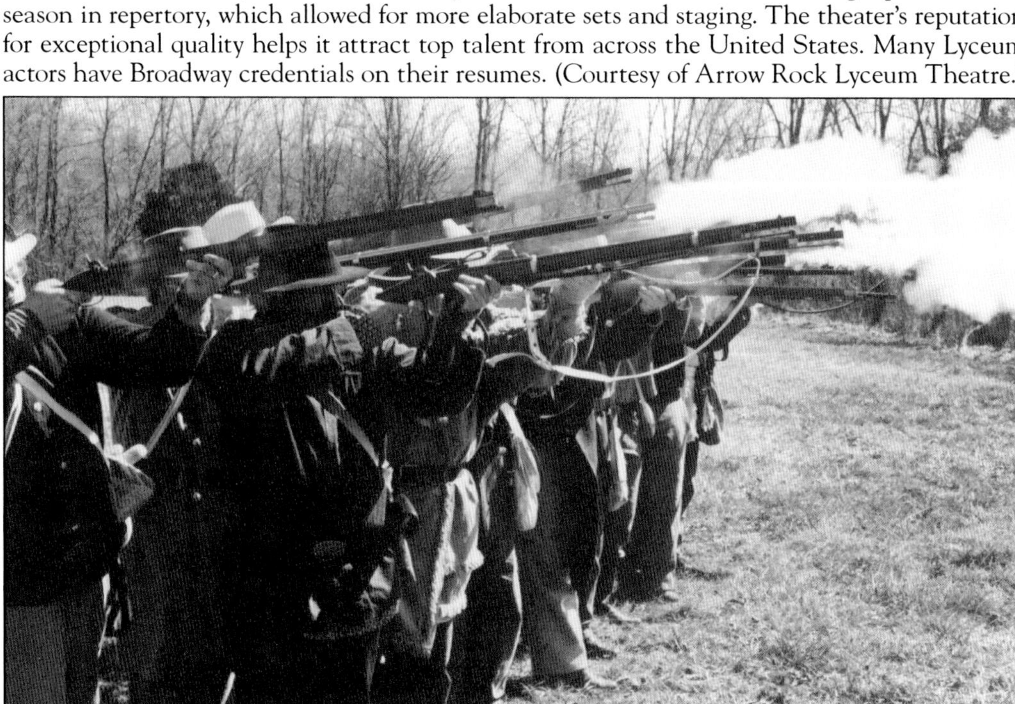

Arrow Rock escaped the Civil War without becoming a battlefield, but it did experience the terrors of guerrilla warfare and other violent episodes. Reenactors, like the militia that visited Arrow Rock in 1991, often seek out the authentic surroundings of this 19th-century village for their encampments. (Courtesy of the Duncan family.)

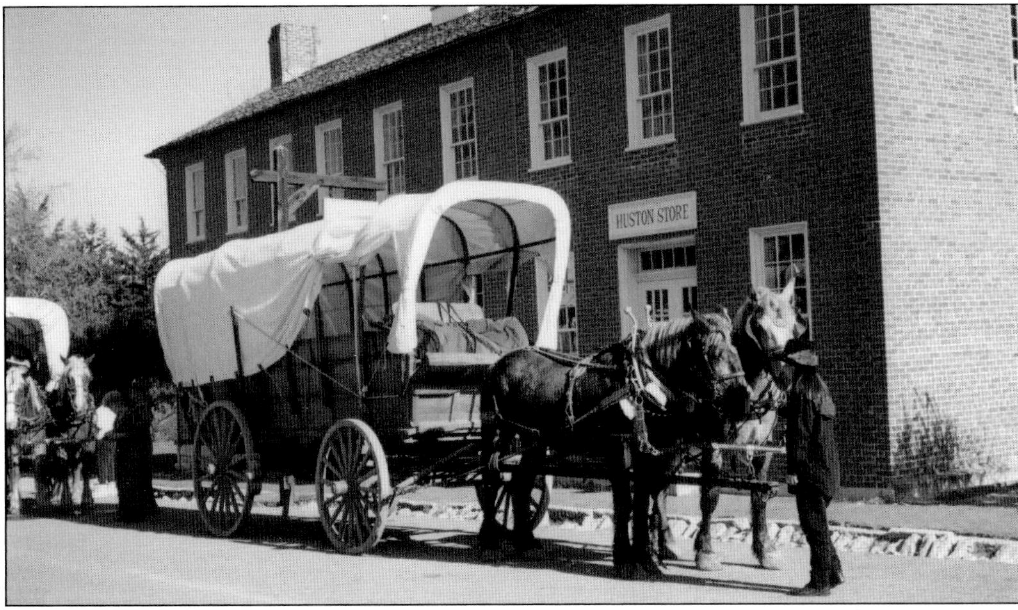

In 1999, the Official California Trail Gold Rush Wagon Train of the 49ers was on a mission to recreate the 2,300-mile trek from St. Charles, Missouri, to Sacramento, California. The wagon train passed through Arrow Rock near the start of its five-month journey in April. In addition to the personal challenge the journey presented to its participants, it had a greater mission to educate people along the way about historic trail preservation and the obstacles faced by American pioneers. When possible, the wagons traveled the exact route used 150 years earlier and organizers spent many months prior to the event contacting private landowners for permission to cross through their property. (Images courtesy of Missouri Department of Natural Resources.)

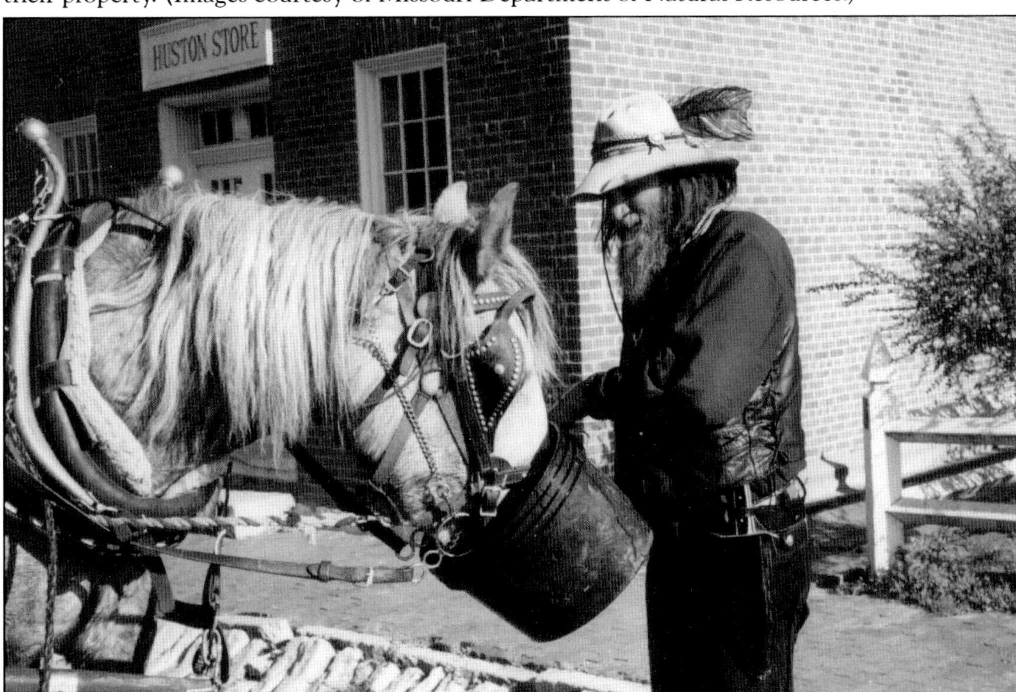

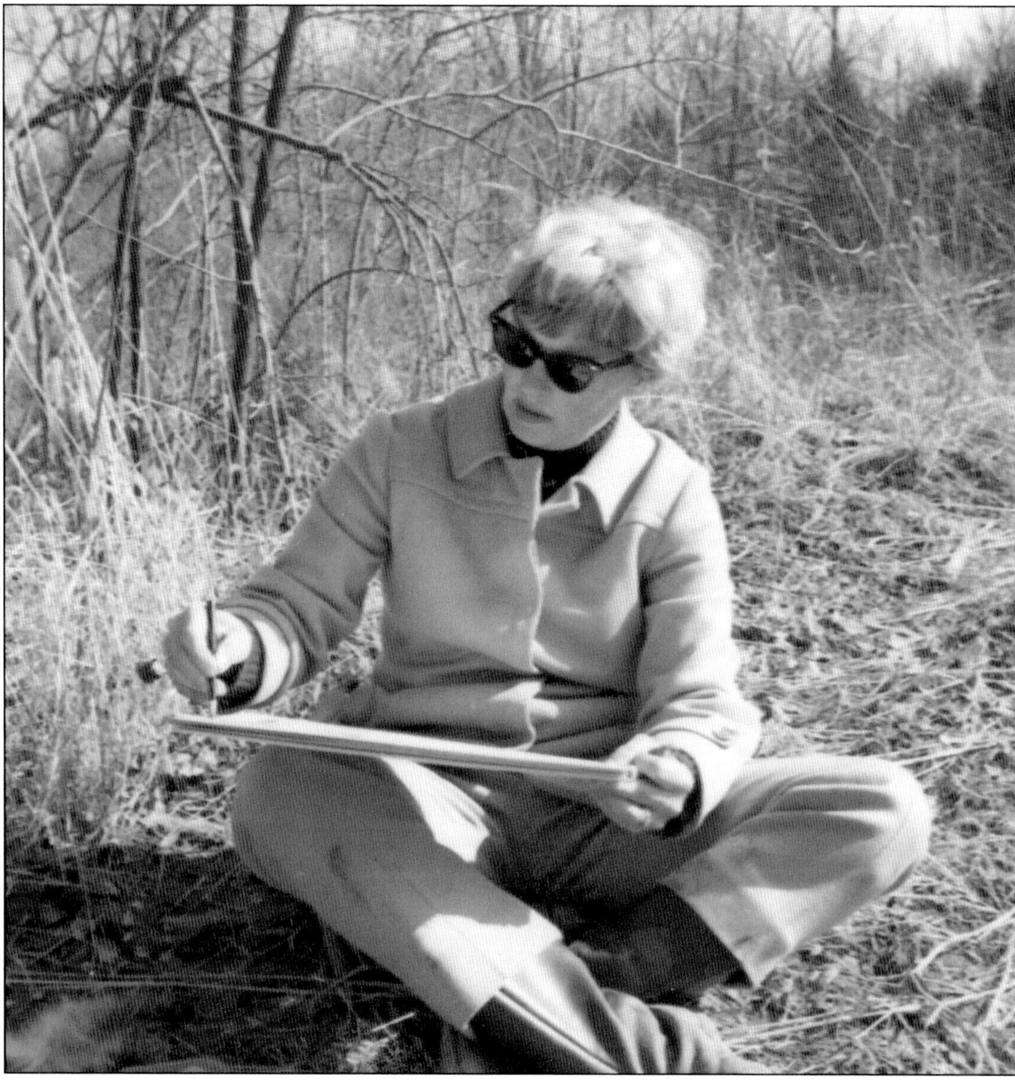

Artists do not need a workshop or a special event to find inspiration in Arrow Rock. Many, like Anna Mae Hodge, simply come to town on a pretty day, choose one of the many scenic spots in the village, set up their sketchpads or easels, and begin to create. (Courtesy of Anna Mae Hodge.)

Five

A Living Village

For all its historical significance, Arrow Rock would be nothing but a collection of soulless old buildings if it were not for the people who live in the town and bring it to life. The village has been—and still is—home to great thinkers, bold adventurers, acclaimed artists and innovative entrepreneurs. It has also been—and still is—home to eccentrics, goofballs, and lovable characters. That is what makes it such a wonderful place to call home.

It is the kind of place where extraordinary happenings are part of the ordinary course of things. Arrow Rockers have seen Oscar-winning actresses stroll down Main Street. They have entertained powerful politicos and regularly attend first-class theatrical productions.

People who live in such a place might lose sight of wholesome, small-town values, but not the people of Arrow Rock. They are down-to-earth folks who put on a charmingly haphazard parade on Independence Day, swap stories about an audacious pair of peacocks, worship together at church, and jockey for position at the potluck dessert table for a piece of Rosemary Kelly's pecan pie.

Arrow Rock, once home to 1,000 citizens, is now home to only 56, but it has not died, nor does it sleep. Arrow Rock is awake and alive and writing fascinating new chapters in its history every day.

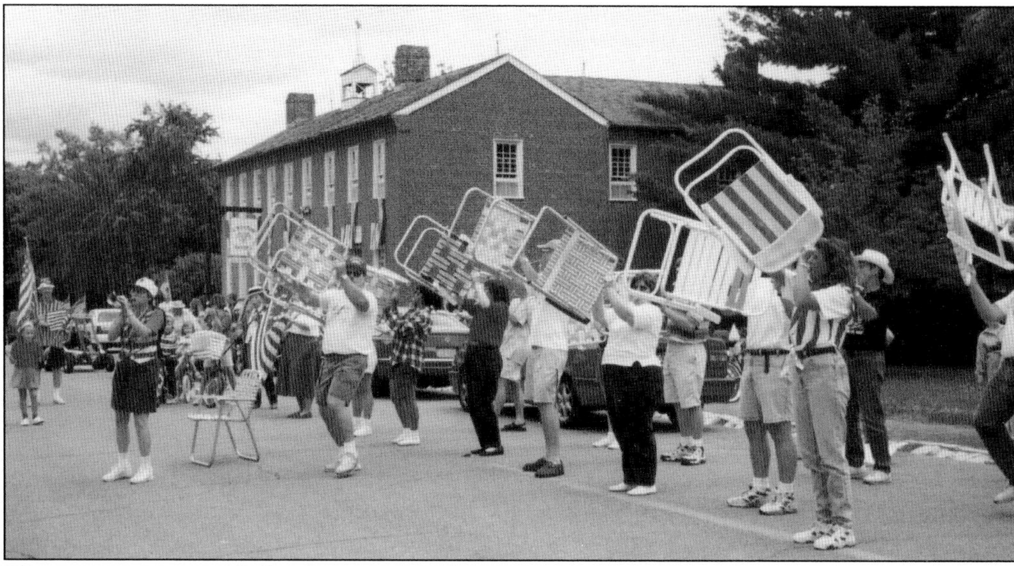

The Impromptu Parade has been a Fourth of July tradition since the mid-1980s. As the name implies, there is little in the way of organization, and anyone who wishes to participate is welcome. One consistent highlight is the kazoo band, which performs patriotic tunes as it marches down Main Street. In the 1990s, the band doubled as the Lawn Chair Brigade and entertained spectators with choreographed routines. (Courtesy of Anna Mae Hodge.)

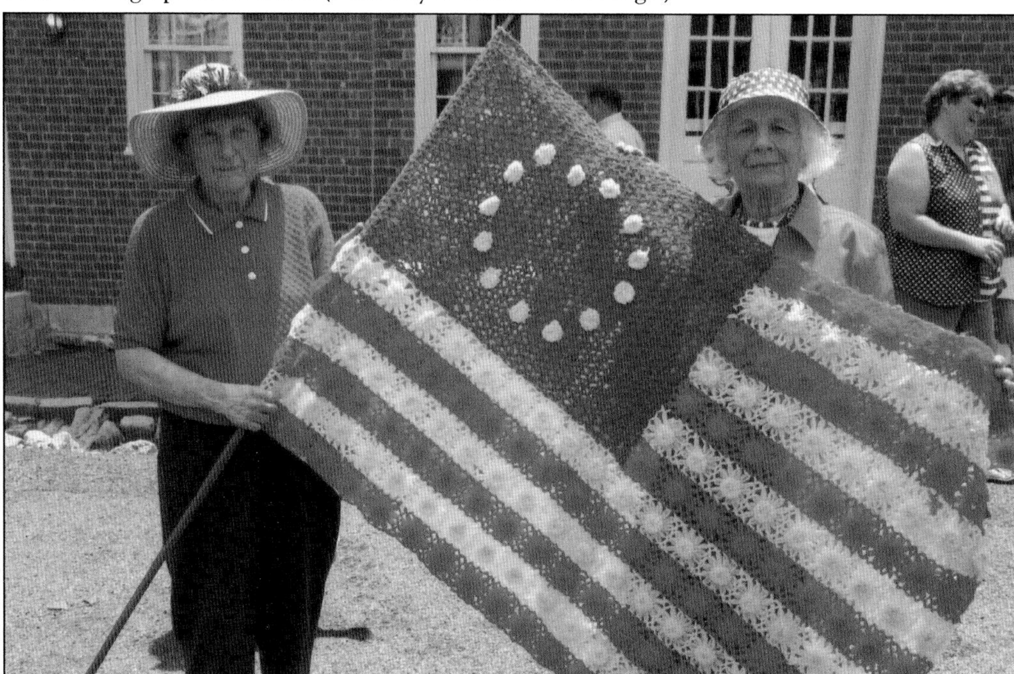

Rosemary Kelly (left) and Mary Burge, members of the Arrow Rock chapter of the Daughters of the American Revolution, are the flag bearers leading off the annual Fourth of July Impromptu Parade. In the 1950s, every Arrow Rock DAR member crocheted four squares, which were combined to create the flag. This community treasure is stored safely away until needed for parades or other special occasions. (Courtesy of Mary Burge.)

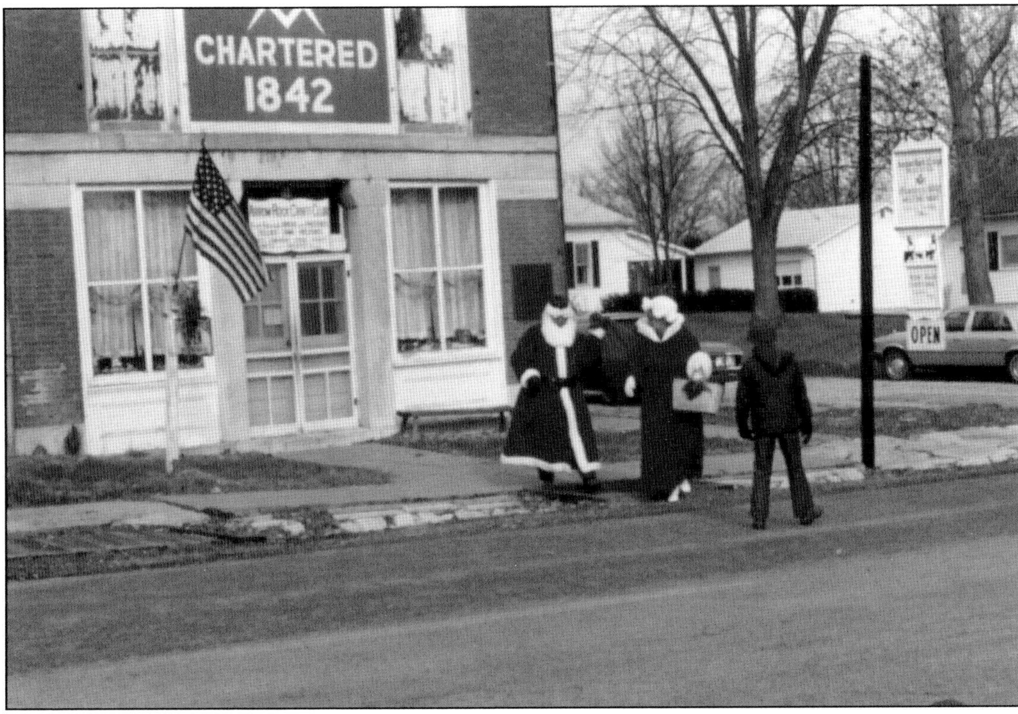

Santa and Mrs. Claus make an appearance during the annual "Hanging of the Greens" ceremony on the Saturday following Thanksgiving. The jolly couple has been brought to life by many different portrayers. In 1976, Herb Templeton and Ginny Fisher, along with their elf assistant, Lisa Smith, emerge from the Arrow Rock Craft Club and make their way down Main Street toward an anxious crowd of children on the boardwalk. Mary Ann Turley and Elmer Zimmerman had taken the reins of the sleigh (or, in Arrow Rock's case, the fire truck) by 1985. (Above, courtesy of Friends of Arrow Rock; below, courtesy of the Vinson family.)

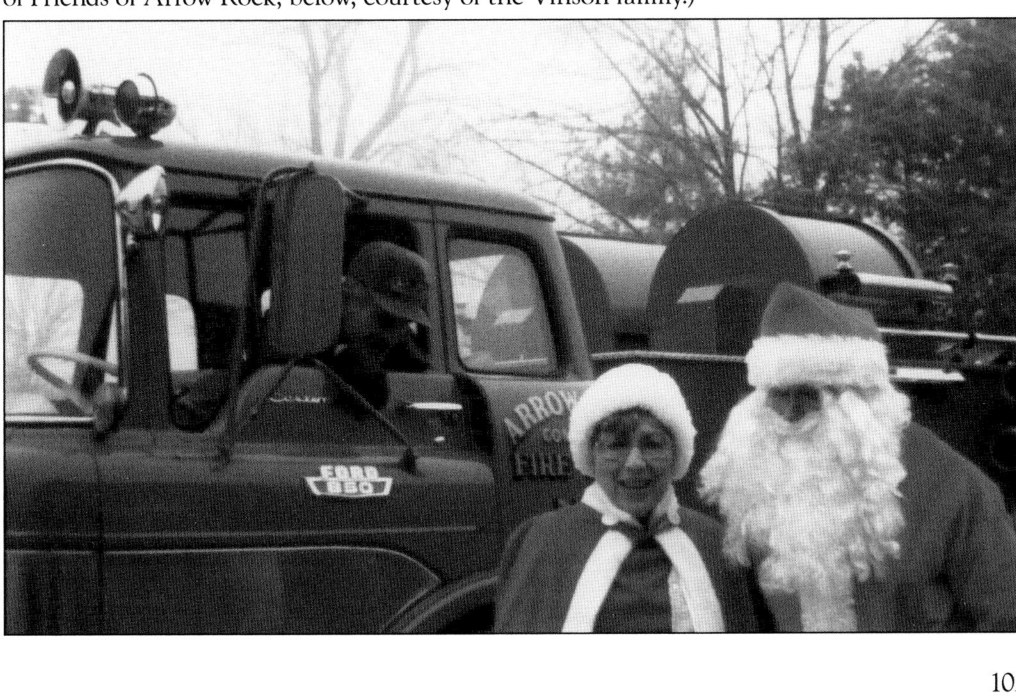

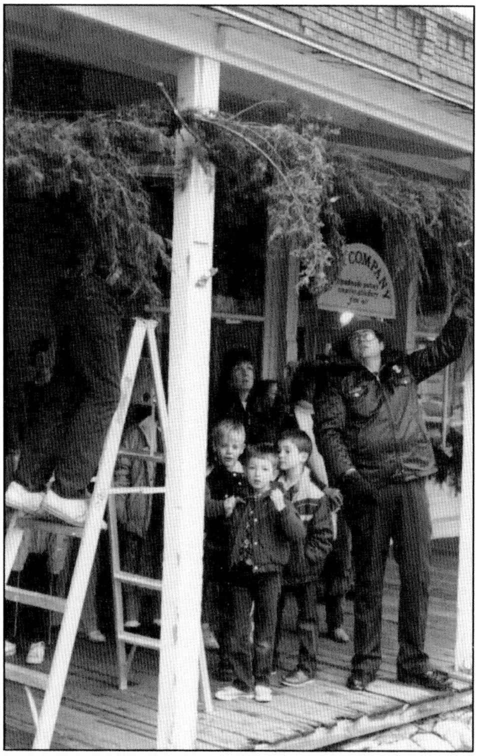

There is nothing artificial about the holiday decorations in Arrow Rock. Community members start collecting cedar boughs the weekend before Thanksgiving, which they turn into ropes of live greenery. During the annual Hanging of the Greens event on the Saturday after Thanksgiving, volunteers hang the greenery from one end of the boardwalk to the other while carolers sing songs of the season. (Courtesy of the Vinson family.)

Some of the most memorable occasions for the citizens of Arrow Rock, past and present, do not revolve around the carefully planned, tourism-building events but are found in the informal gatherings of friends and neighbors, like this congenial group of Arrow Rockers from the 1960s. (Courtesy of Friends of Arrow Rock.)

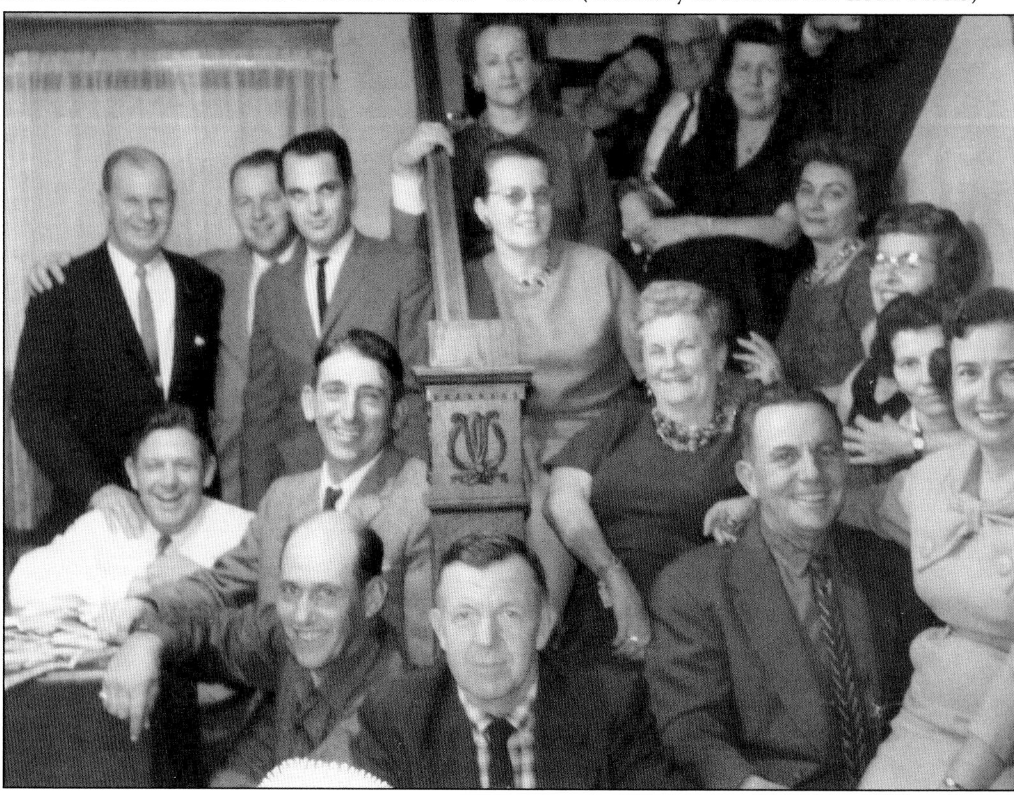

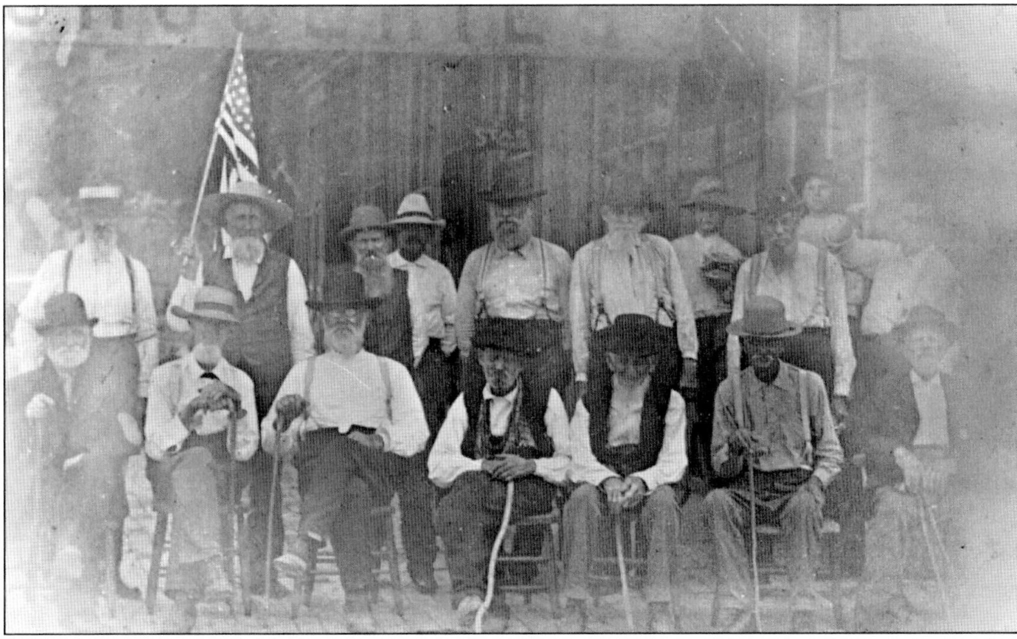

What a difference a century makes. In 1901, the senior citizens of Arrow Rock were grizzled, bearded old men. The group above gathered at the local grocery store for their moment in front of the camera. A little more than 100 years later, Arrow Rock's senior citizens are decidedly more vibrant and, in this case, more feminine. These women are actively involved in community events and organizations. The ladies who have stopped to admire the autumn decorations at the entrance to town are, from left to right, Rosemary Kelly, Mary Burge, Nadine Ozias, and Mary Kathryn Feuers. (Above, courtesy of Missouri Department of Natural Resources; below, courtesy of Mary Kathryn Feuers.)

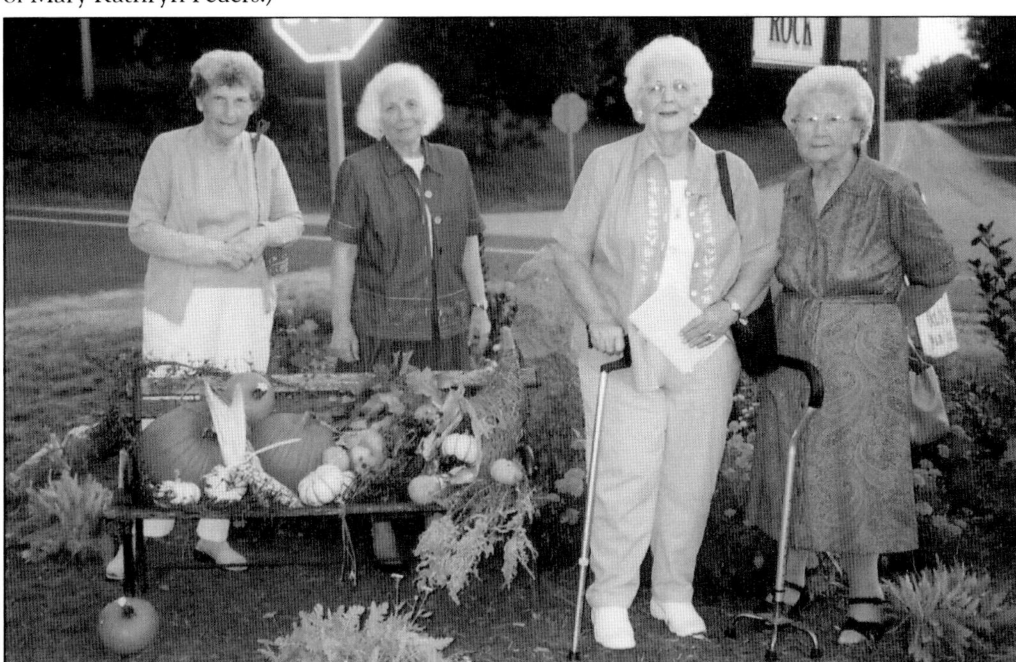

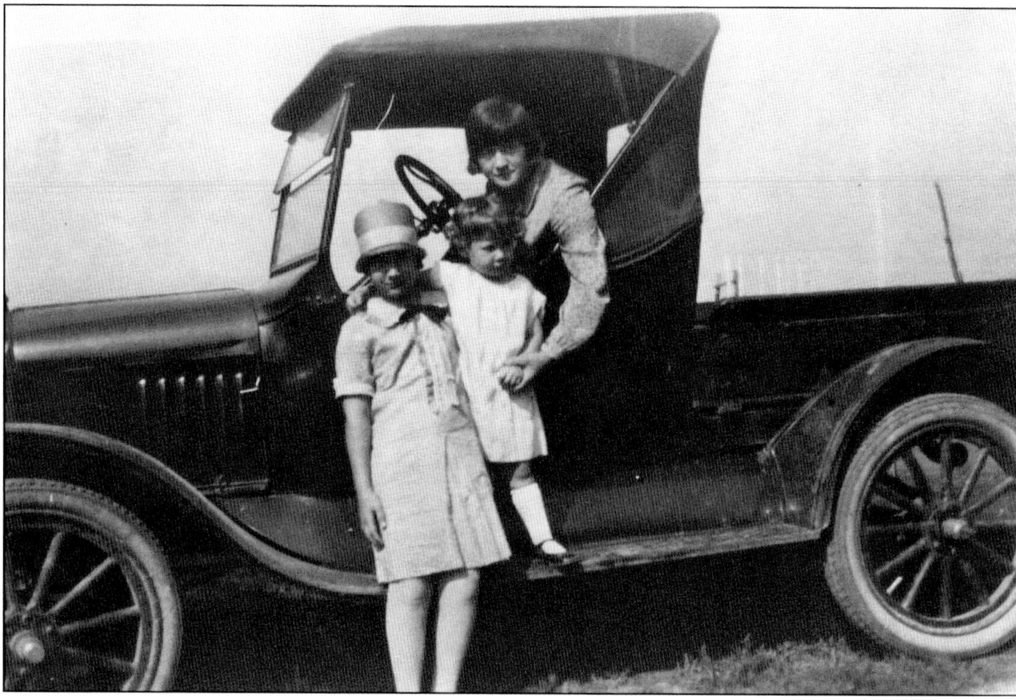

The women of the Moseley family hop on board the "dog wagon." The vehicle earned that name because it was the truck Forrest Moseley used to transport his dogs for fox hunting. The passengers are, from left to right, Dorothy, Mary Kathryn, and Virginia "Jennie" Kathryn Brockway Moseley. (Courtesy of Mary Kathryn Feuers.)

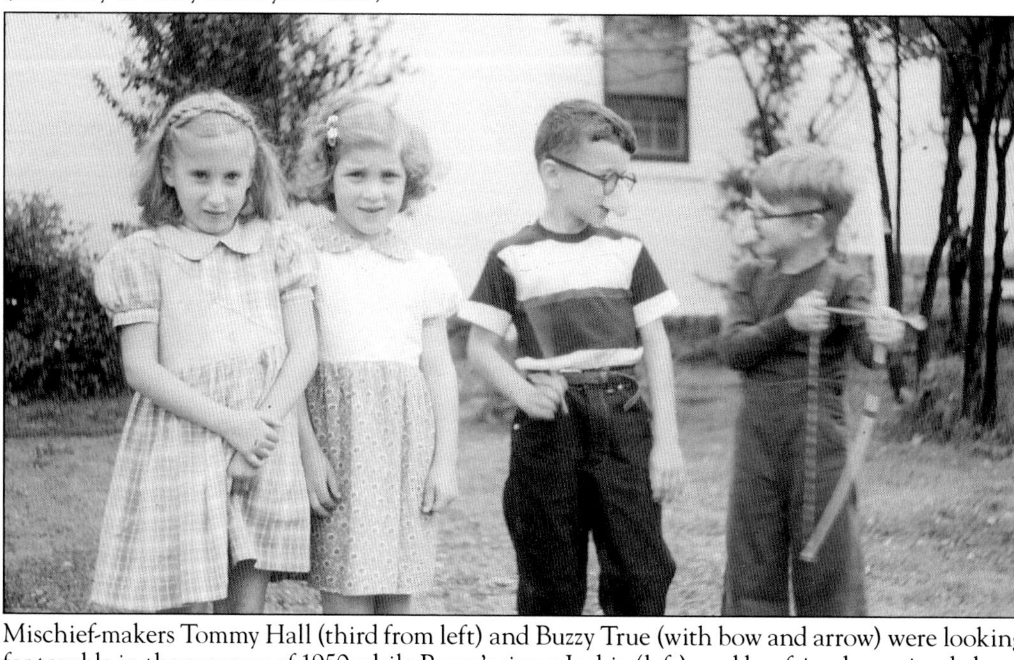

Mischief-makers Tommy Hall (third from left) and Buzzy True (with bow and arrow) were looking for trouble in the summer of 1950 while Buzzy's sister, Jackie (left), and her friend remained above it all. The boys survived their rough-and-tumble adventures and have both grown up to serve on the board of trustees of the Friends of Arrow Rock. (Courtesy of Thomas B. Hall III.)

Four friends from Marshall, Missouri, were seeking adventure in Arrow Rock in 1952. "We played all over the mostly deserted village on a Sunday afternoon," said Missy (Mullally) Backer. They are, from left to right, Ginger Kessler (now Spriggs), Backer, Jeanne Phillips, and Joyce Kramer (now Marcum). (Courtesy of Missy Backer.)

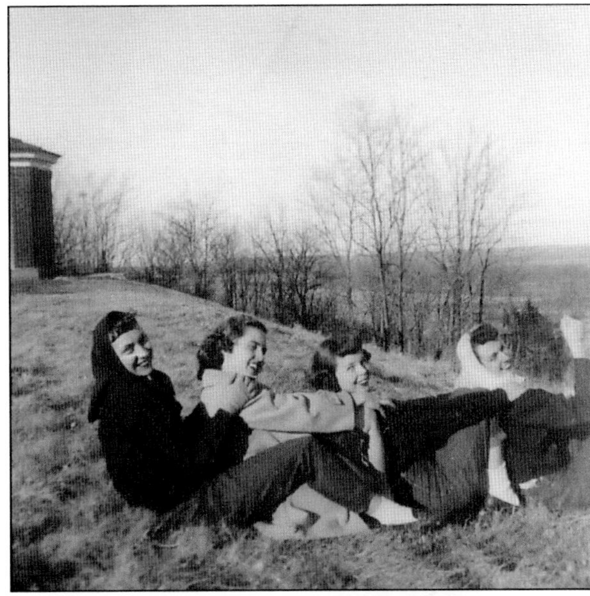

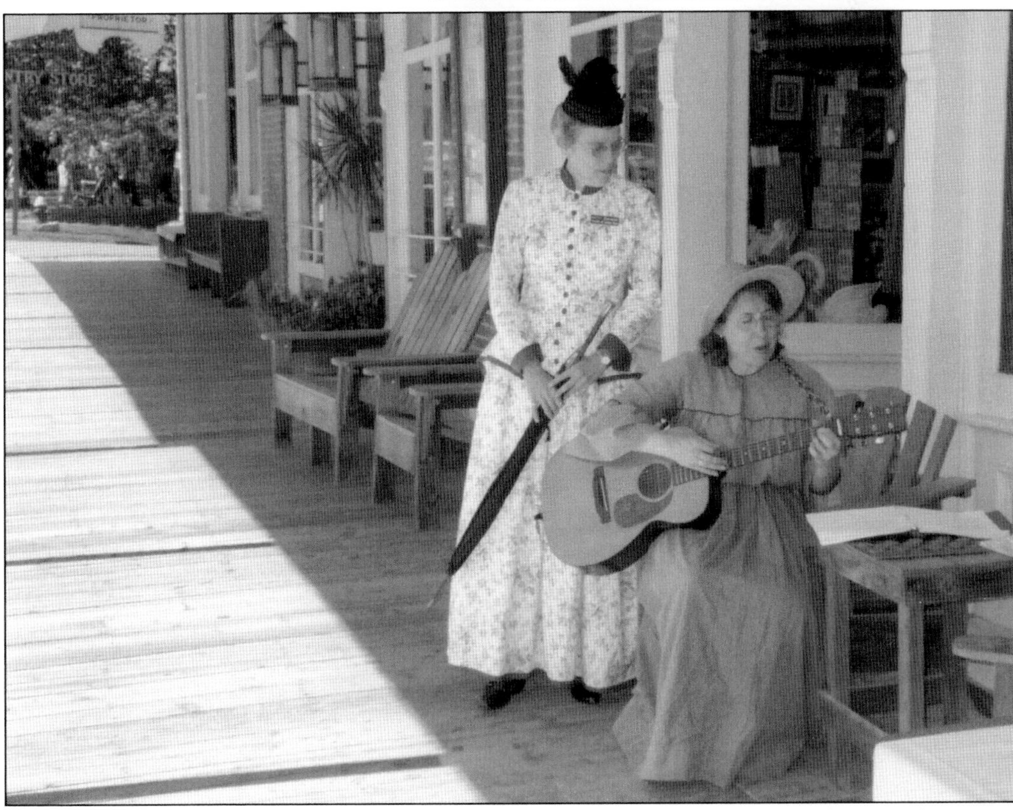

Kathy Borgman listens while Tempe McGlaughlin performs on a Heritage Craft Festival morning. Borgman and McGlaughlin are two of the most familiar faces on the boardwalk, whether they are wearing period garb for the Heritage Craft Festival or dressed for their jobs as Friends of Arrow Rock executive director and Arrow Rock postmaster, respectively. (Courtesy of Missouri Department of Natural Resources.)

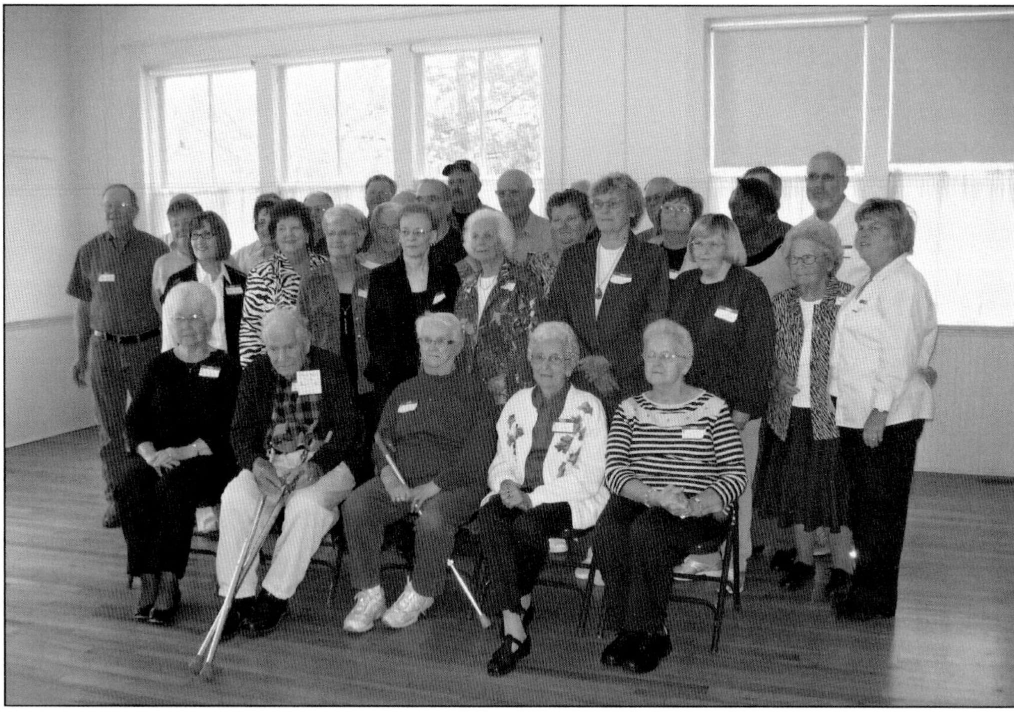

Although the Arrow Rock School closed its doors in 1968, fond memories and school spirit live on through its former students. School alumni, many of whom still live in the area, gather every five years for a reunion at the Old Schoolhouse, like this celebration in 2010. (Courtesy of Elaine Breshears.)

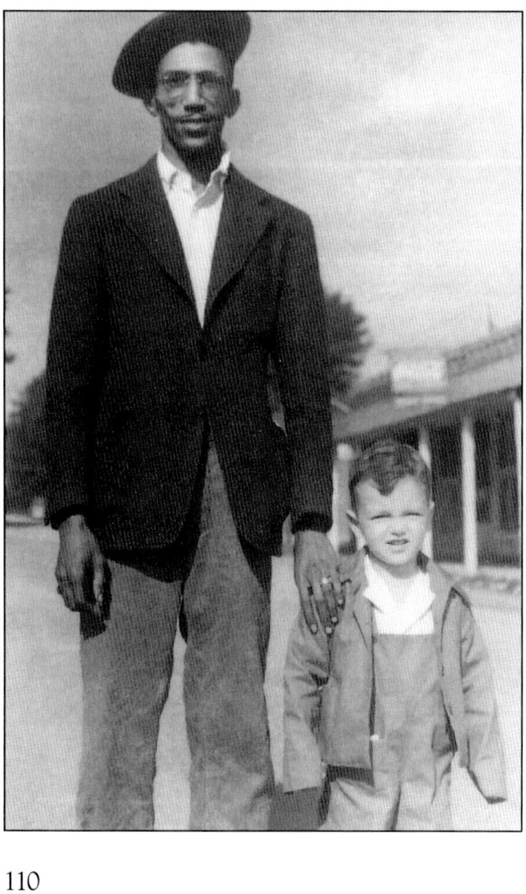

Local jack-of-all trades Preston Banks was well liked by the residents of Arrow Rock in 1946, including two-year-old Tommy Hall. Banks lived in the village until his death in 1968, and Hall grew up to become a medical doctor and the president of the Friends of Arrow Rock. (Courtesy of Thomas B. Hall III.)

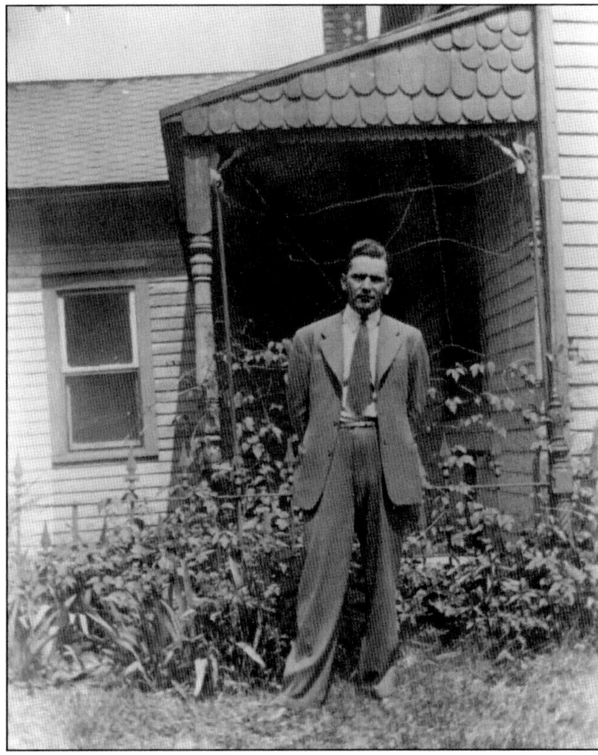

Arvel Townsend, a longtime resident with deep Arrow Rock roots, enjoyed a 38-year career as a railroad conductor. He served on the town's board of trustees, knew all the best fishing spots, and could often be found pulling up a chair at a poker game. But around Arrow Rock, he is most remembered for his prowess at the game of checkers. After his retirement from the railroad, Townsend was a regular fixture on the boardwalk, where he kept a checkers game waiting for any willing opponent. (Right, courtesy of Missouri Department of Natural Resources; below, courtesy of Friends of Arrow Rock.)

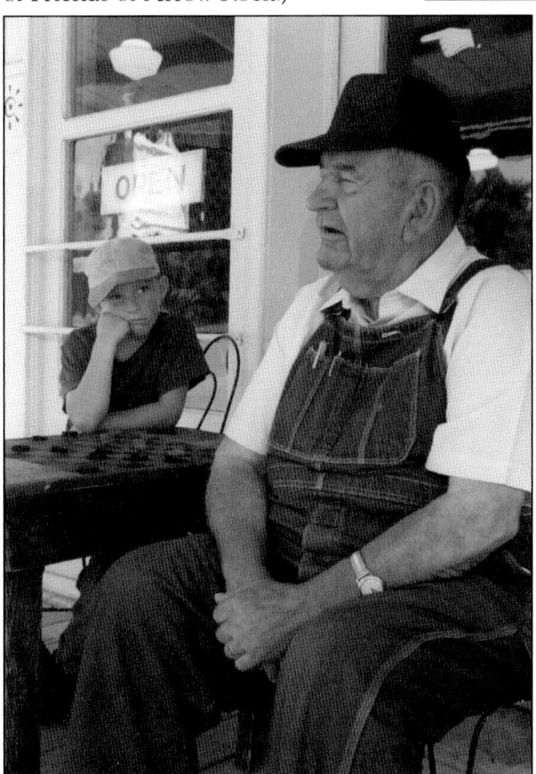

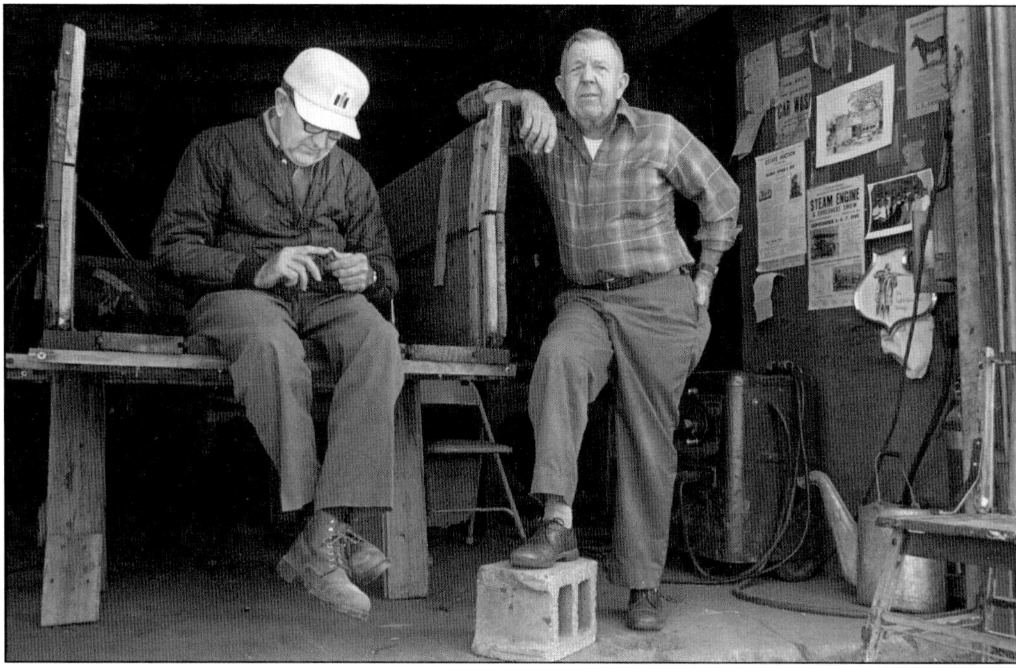

Farmer Robert Feuers (left) and retired Arrow Rock State Park superintendent Robert Stith swap stories and pass the time at Herb Templeton's blacksmith shop on the west end of Main Street. Templeton's shop was the place to go for repairs of all sorts, from broken plows to faulty radios, or to catch up on the news of the day. (Courtesy of Mary Kathryn Feuers.)

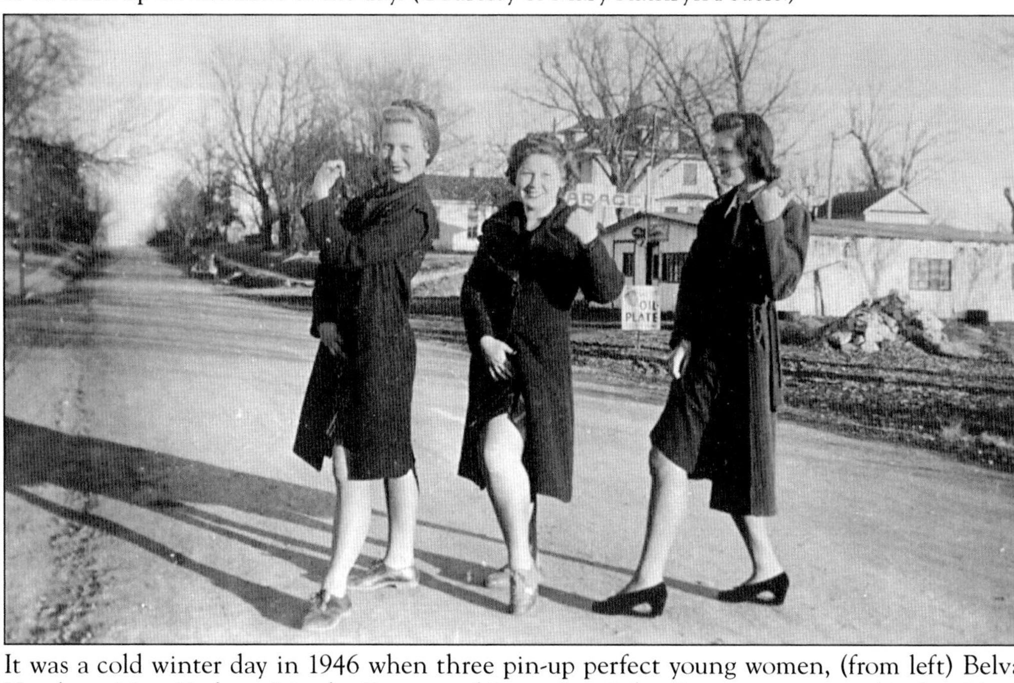

It was a cold winter day in 1946 when three pin-up perfect young women, (from left) Belva Humburg, Mary Kathryn Moseley Feuers, and Emma Lee Baker Brown, were out to hitch a ride to the other end of Arrow Rock's Main Street. Humburg and Feuers still live in the area. (Courtesy of Missouri Department of Natural Resources.)

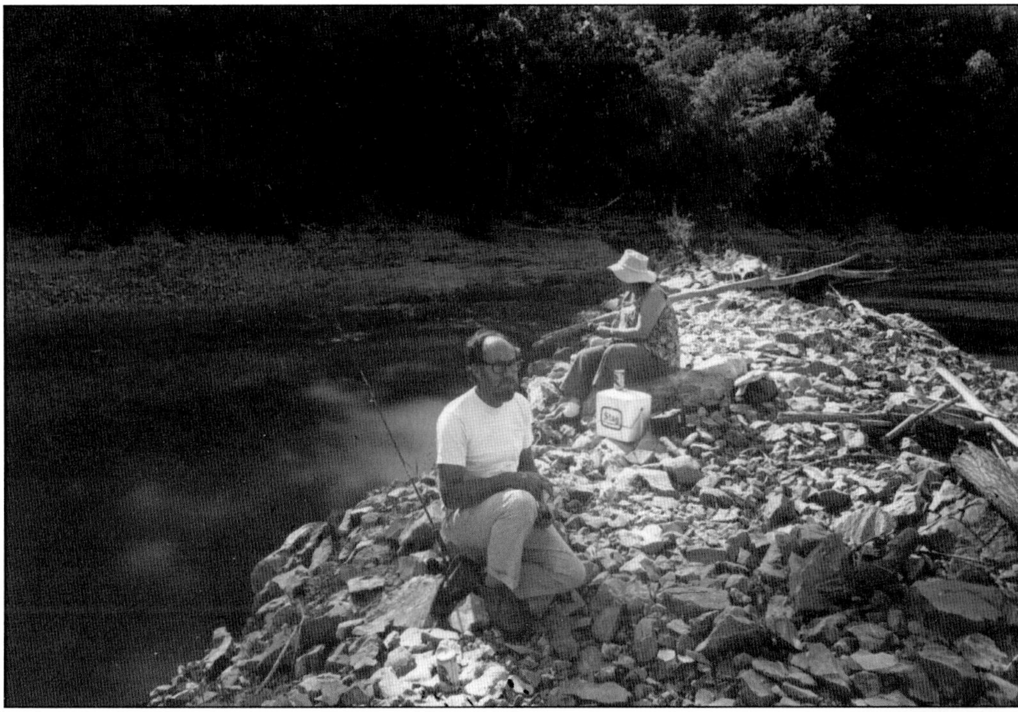

The trek from Arrow Rock to the Missouri River is considerably longer now than it was in the 1800s, but in the 1970s, Ted and Ginny Fisher found that the fishing made it worth the walk. The river yields several species of catfish and carp, plus the occasional crappie, pike or walleye, for the very lucky (or very patient) angler. (Courtesy of Anna Mae Hodge.)

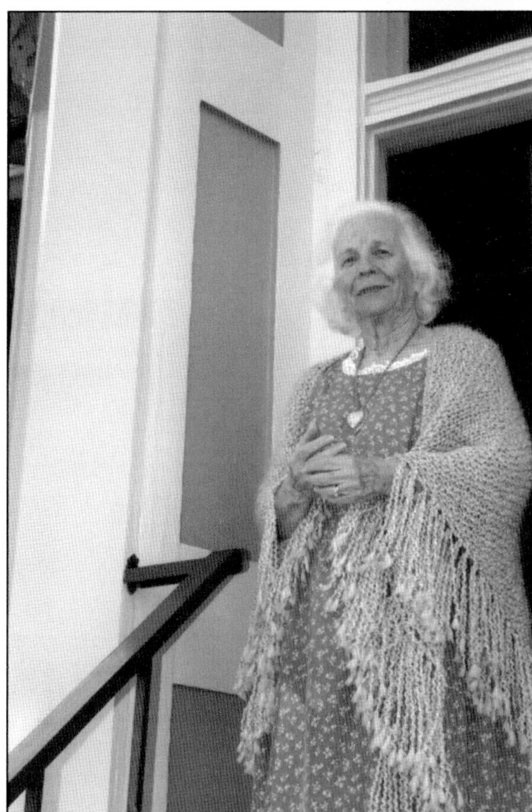

Mary Burge takes pride in her status as the oldest living citizen born in Arrow Rock. For much of her life, Burge helped her husband with farm chores, but she was born to perform. She sings in small ensembles, often appears in regional theater productions, and has worked as a movie extra. She is seen here portraying Nannie Sites, the much-adored wife of gunsmith Johnny Sites. (Courtesy of Mary Burge.)

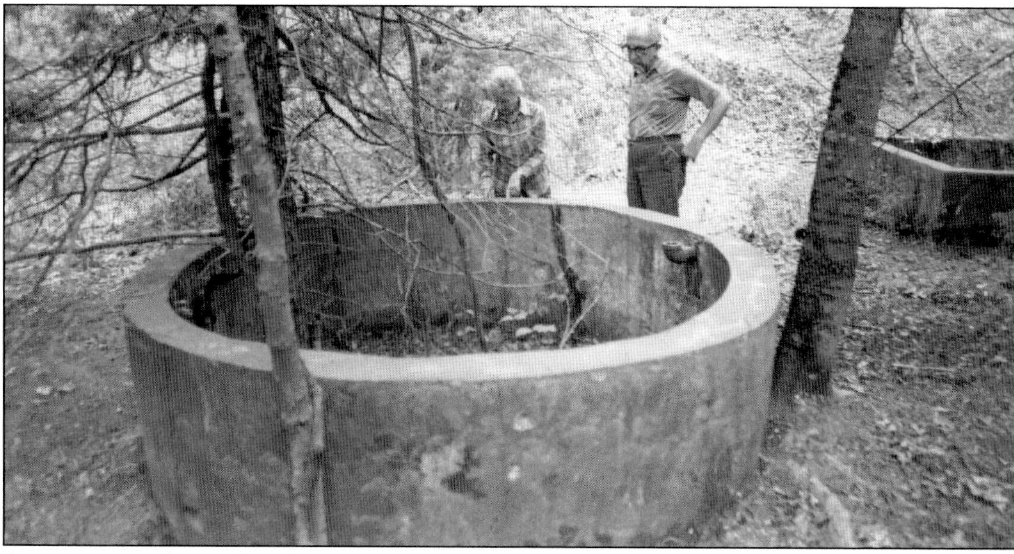

Anna Mae Hodge and Hal Sandy inspect the remnants of a Prohibition-era still discovered in the woods on the edge of Arrow Rock. During the 1920s, when the Daughters of the American Revolution were working to create a wholesome and historical tourist attraction at the Arrow Rock Tavern, bootleggers were taking a different approach to economic development in the fading town. (Courtesy of Anna Mae Hodge.)

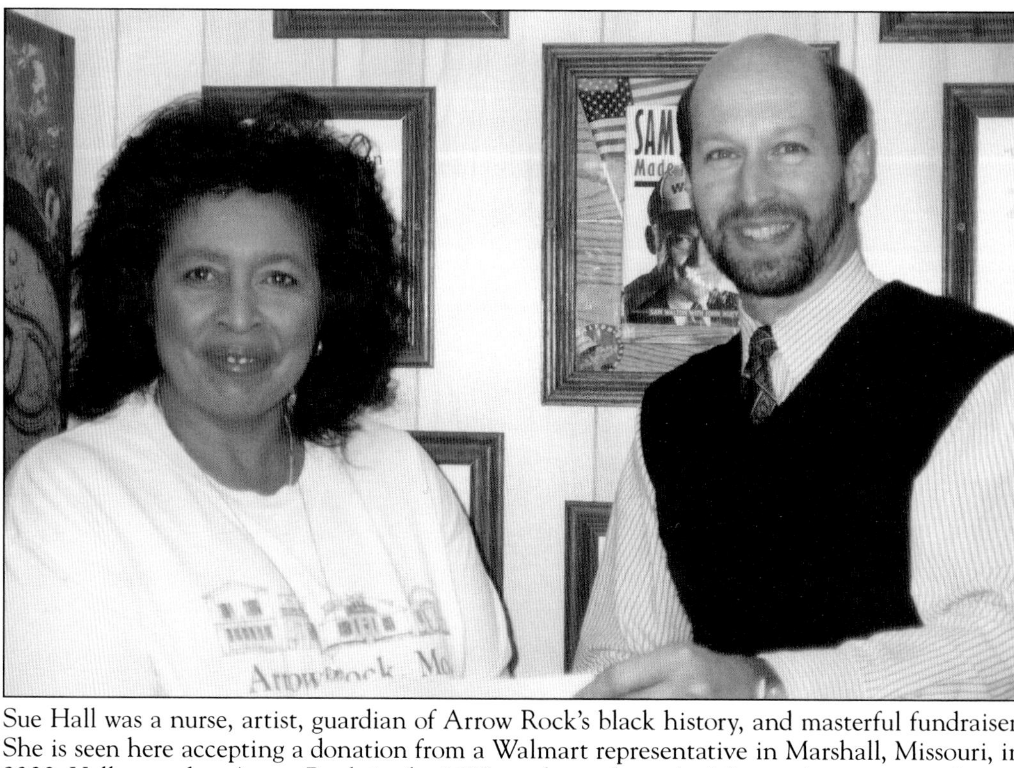

Sue Hall was a nurse, artist, guardian of Arrow Rock's black history, and masterful fundraiser. She is seen here accepting a donation from a Walmart representative in Marshall, Missouri, in 2000. Hall moved to Arrow Rock in the 1970s and was the only African American resident of Arrow Rock when she passed away in 2009. (Courtesy of Friends of Arrow Rock.)

The one-room stone jail in Arrow Rock may have housed only one prisoner during its history, but it has served as the backdrop for thousands of family photographs spanning generations of visitors. When he was eight years old, Marty Selby (left) and his brother Michael posed for a photograph when their parents traveled from their home in Columbia, Missouri, to the Arrow Rock State Park for a picnic outing. In 2005, Marty, now a full-time resident of Arrow Rock, posed for a photograph in the same place, this time with his grandsons Tate (left) and Axton. (Images courtesy of Marty Selby.)

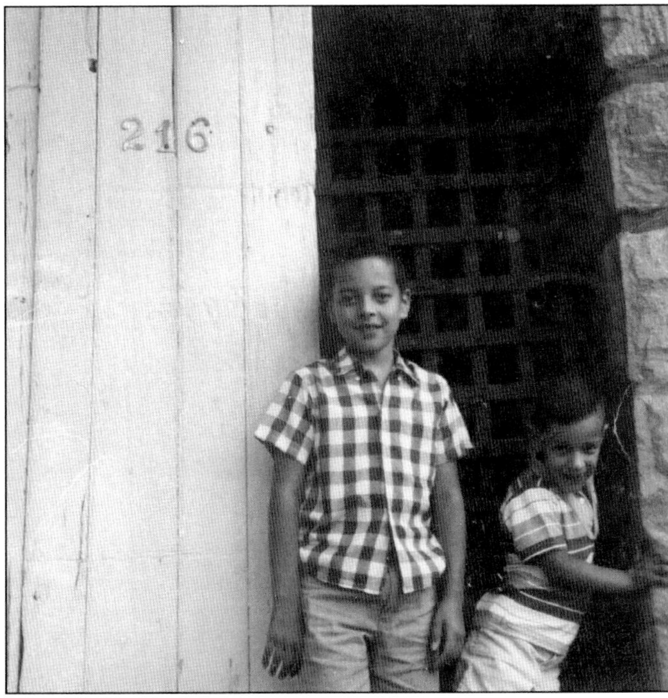

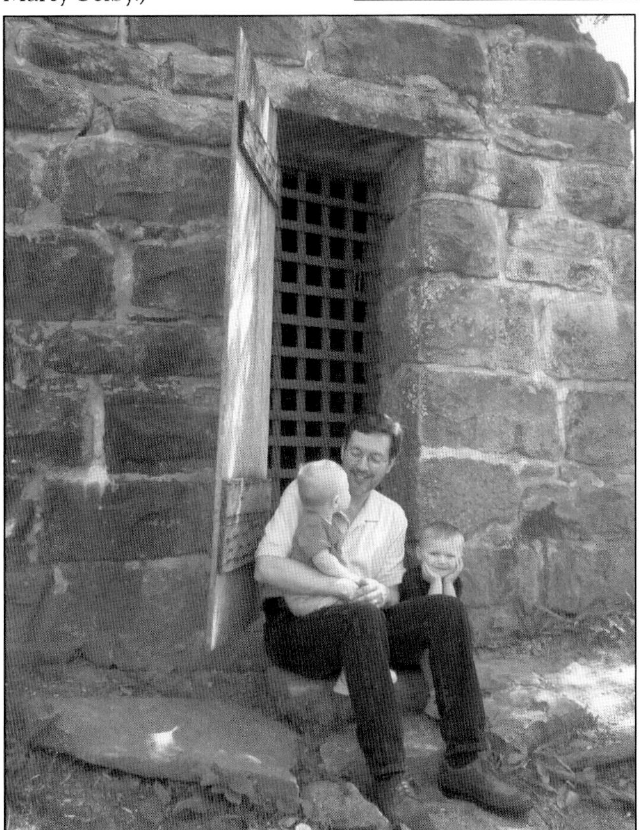

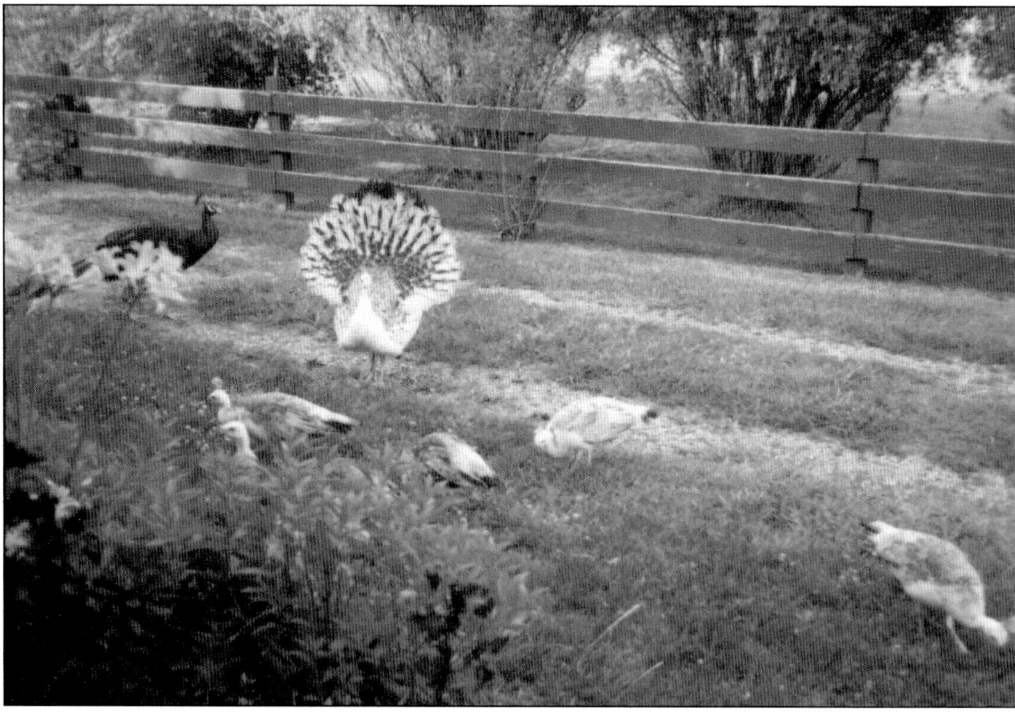

Peacocks Adam and Eve and their offspring rarely stayed in their own yard at the home of Ted and Ginny Fisher. The birds roamed the town, often stopping traffic when they decided to rest in the road and startling residents with shrill calls. Local children who grew up in the 1980s fondly recall trick-or-treating at the Fisher home and receiving gifts of peacock feathers. (Courtesy of Friends of Arrow Rock.)

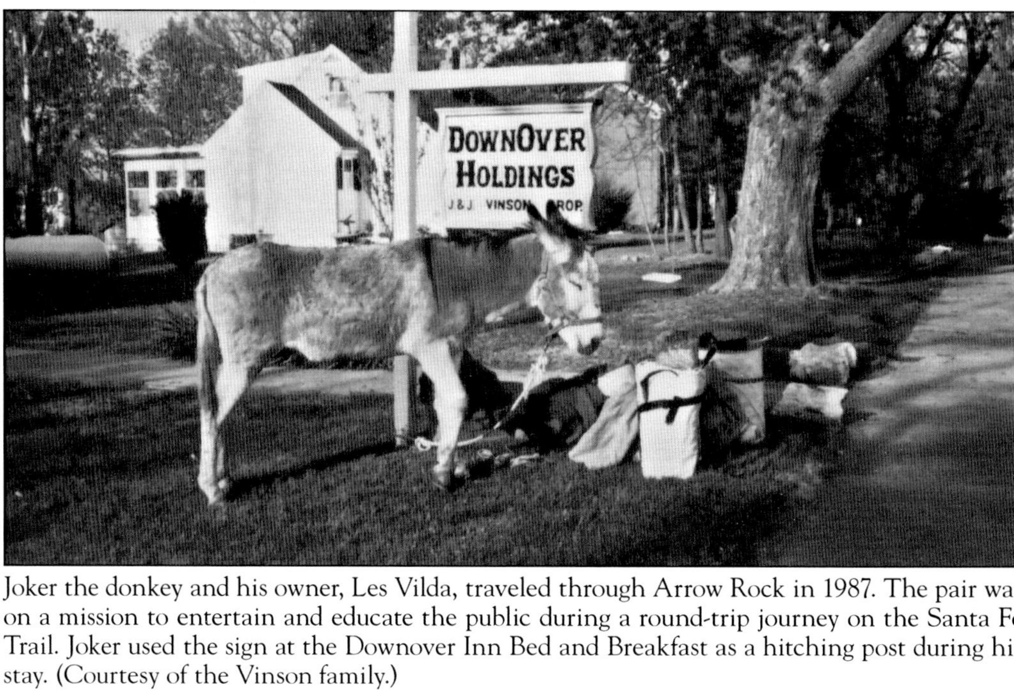

Joker the donkey and his owner, Les Vilda, traveled through Arrow Rock in 1987. The pair was on a mission to entertain and educate the public during a round-trip journey on the Santa Fe Trail. Joker used the sign at the Downover Inn Bed and Breakfast as a hitching post during his stay. (Courtesy of the Vinson family.)

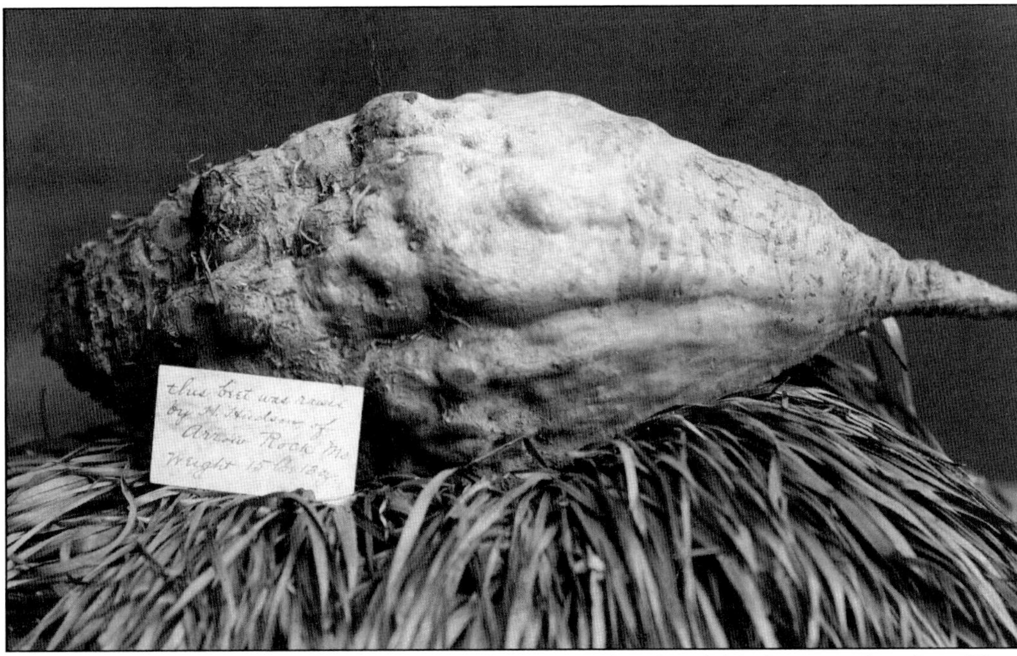

In the late 1800s, photography was both rare and expensive, but that didn't deter proud gardener Harry Hudson from preserving his 15-pound, 13-ounce beet to be admired by future generations. Surely, he would be pleased to know that the beet goes on. (Courtesy of the Friends of Arrow Rock.)

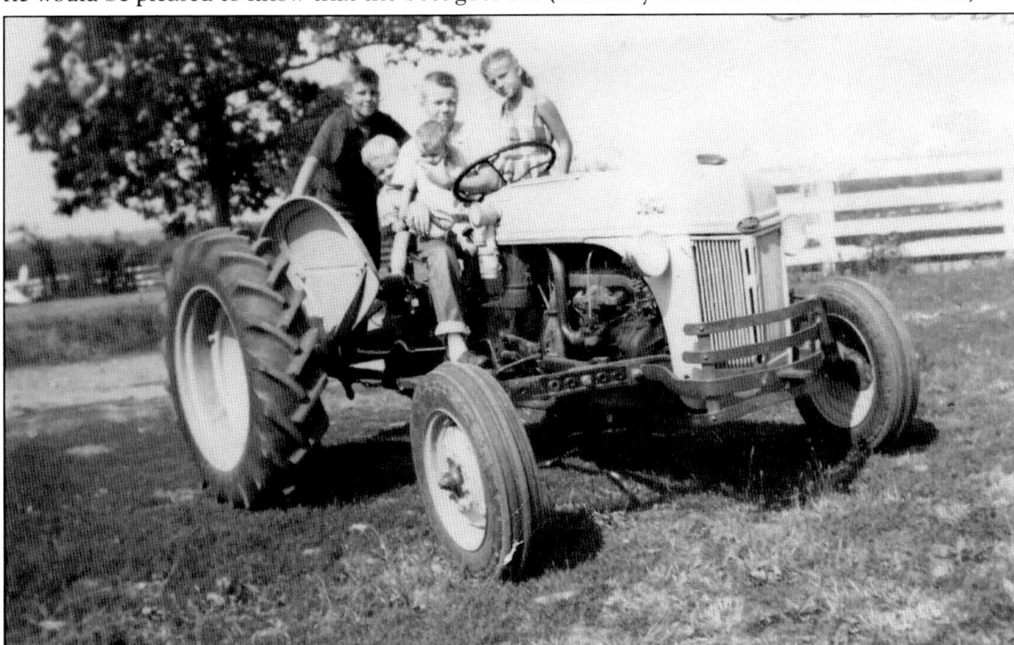

Agriculture in Arrow Rock has changed dramatically since the days when hemp and tobacco plantations fueled the local economy, but farming continues to sustain many families in the Arrow Rock vicinity. In 1952, the Stith children—Bobby, Gary, Ellen, Steve, and Elaine—climbed aboard the Ford tractor on Clem and Beulah Thompson's farm south of Arrow Rock. (Courtesy of Elaine Breshears.)

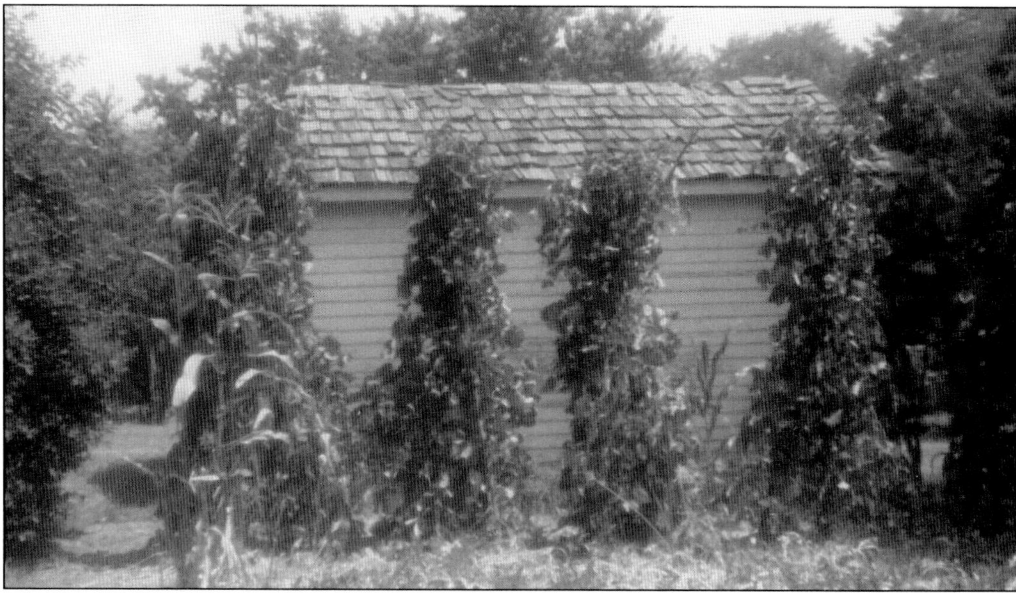

When avid gardener Corinne Jackson's ambition outgrew her small yard, she planted a vegetable garden on Arrow Rock State Historic Site property behind the Academy Boarding House. In 1983, the well-tended garden yielded a bumper crop, including buckets full of Kentucky Wonder pole beans. (Courtesy of Missouri Department of Natural Resources.)

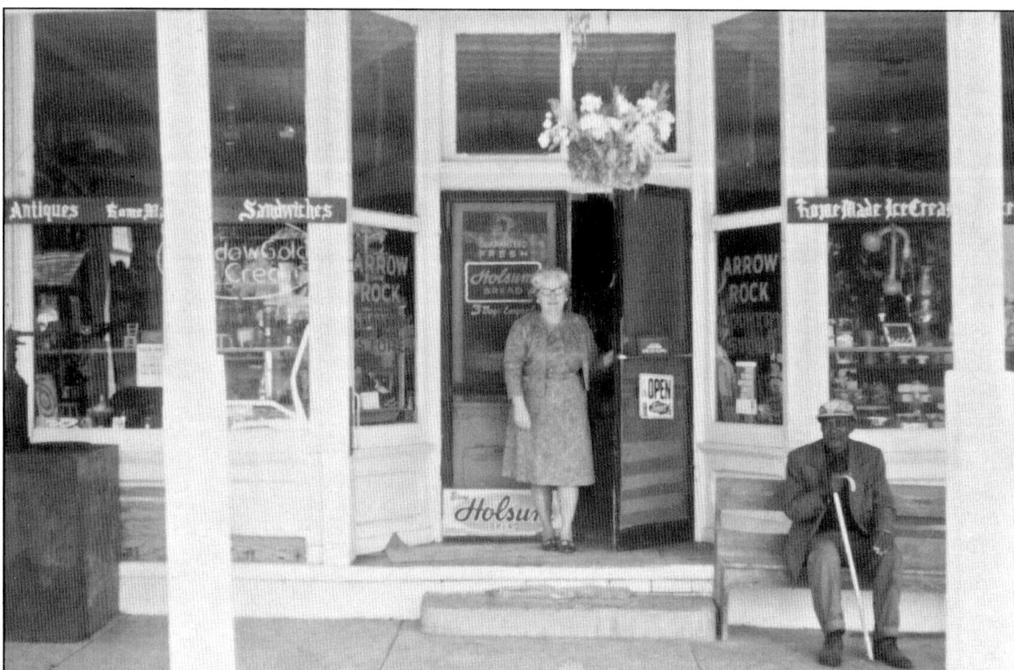

In 1965, sisters and retired schoolteachers Buena Stolberg (pictured) and Corinne Jackson bought the Country Store and the home across the street. The women, who are fondly remembered as "the sisters," ran the store until 1985. Stolberg's knack for management served her well not only in business but also in her leadership roles in local organizations. (Courtesy of Missouri Department of Natural Resources.)

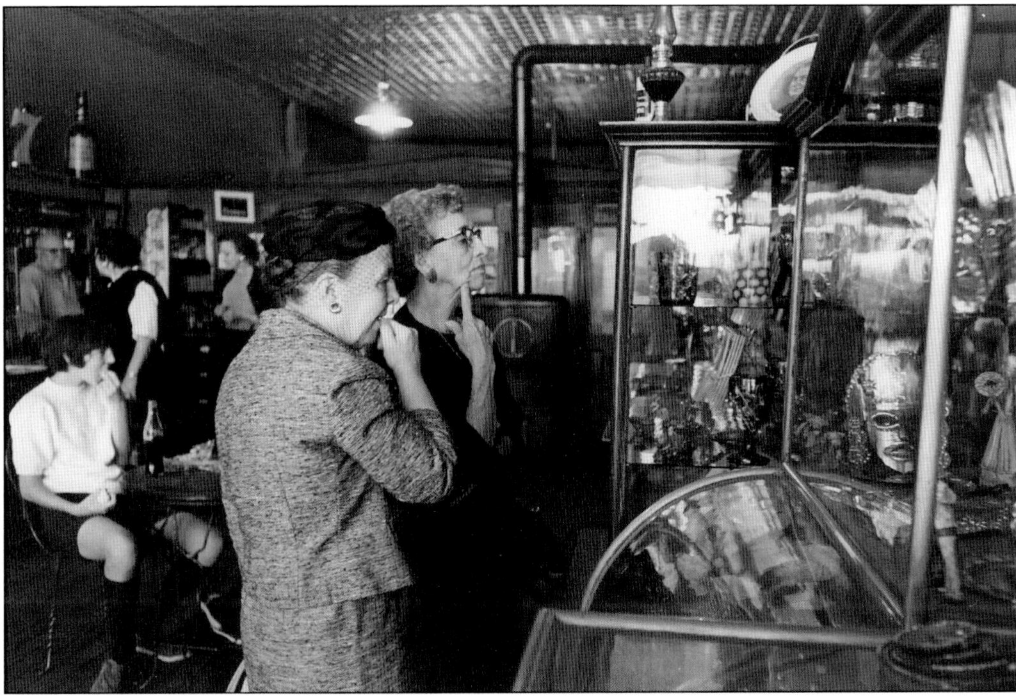

In the 1950s, Fletcher C. "Red" Argubright, seen here behind the counter, purchased the drugstore on the Arrow Rock boardwalk and added liquor to the refreshments available for sale. Argubright took an early stand for civil rights in his business, serving both white and black customers. In this image, a pair of shoppers studies some of the unusual items in the display case. (Courtesy of Friends of Arrow Rock.)

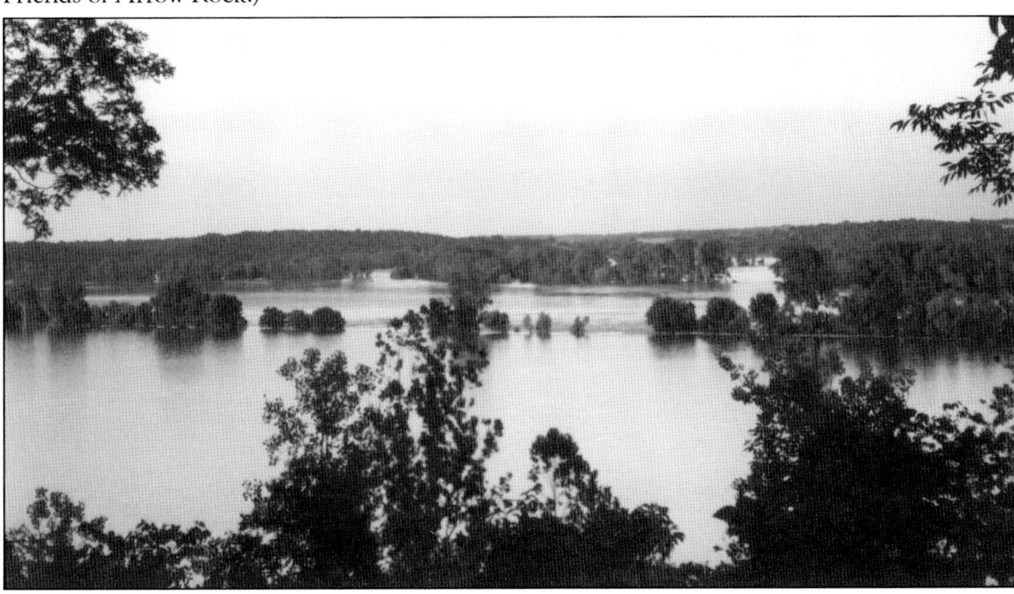

Arrow Rock's location high on a bluff over the Missouri River Valley protected it from the devastation that accompanied the Great Flood of 1993. Normally, the river is not visible from anywhere in Arrow Rock, but during that year, the river broke through levees, flooding fields and farmland. (Courtesy of Friends of Arrow Rock.)

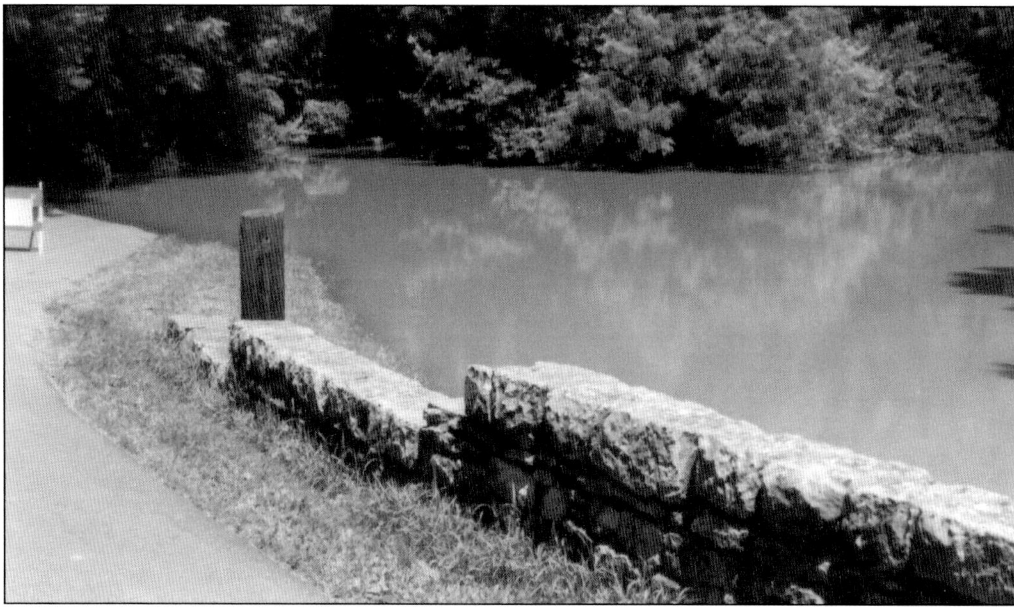

During the Great Flood of 1993, Big Spring in Arrow Rock was engulfed by a muddy pool that covered the roadway through the park area. The damage was minor compared to what other towns endured, but submerged roadways and closed bridges made travel to and from the village difficult. Tourism suffered as a result. (Courtesy of Missouri Department of Natural Resources.)

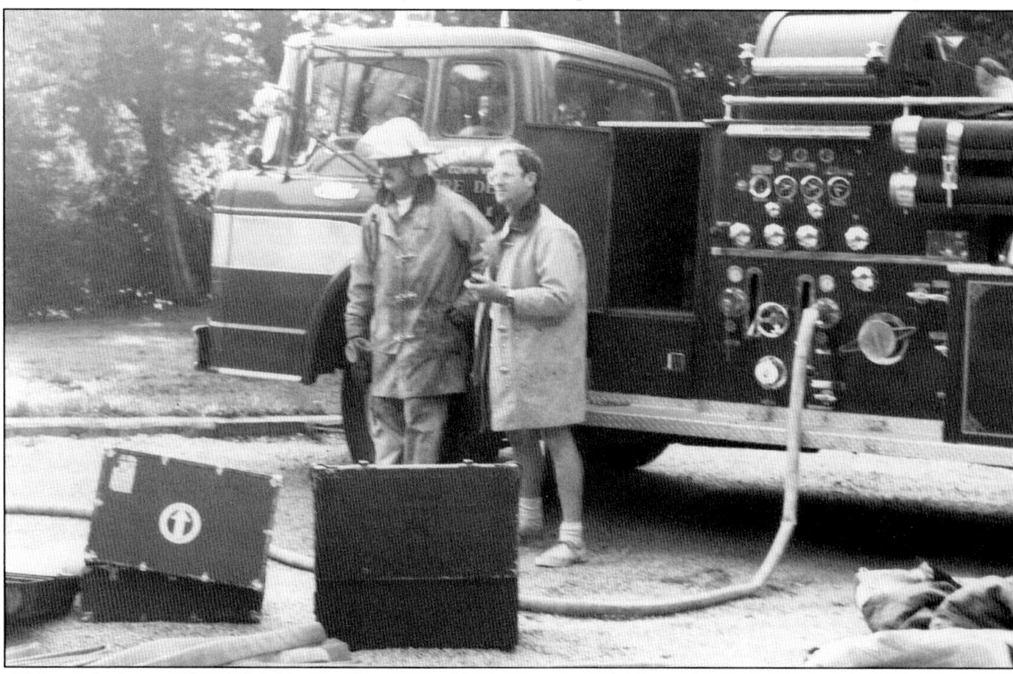

Although Arrow Rock had been devastated by two major fires in the past, it wasn't until 1972 that a group of citizens got together to form the Arrow Rock Community Volunteer Fire Department. The department serves the town and the outlying rural area. In 1996, the firefighters responded to the alarm when a washer caught fire at the Arrow Rock Tavern. (Courtesy of Missouri Department of Natural Resources.)

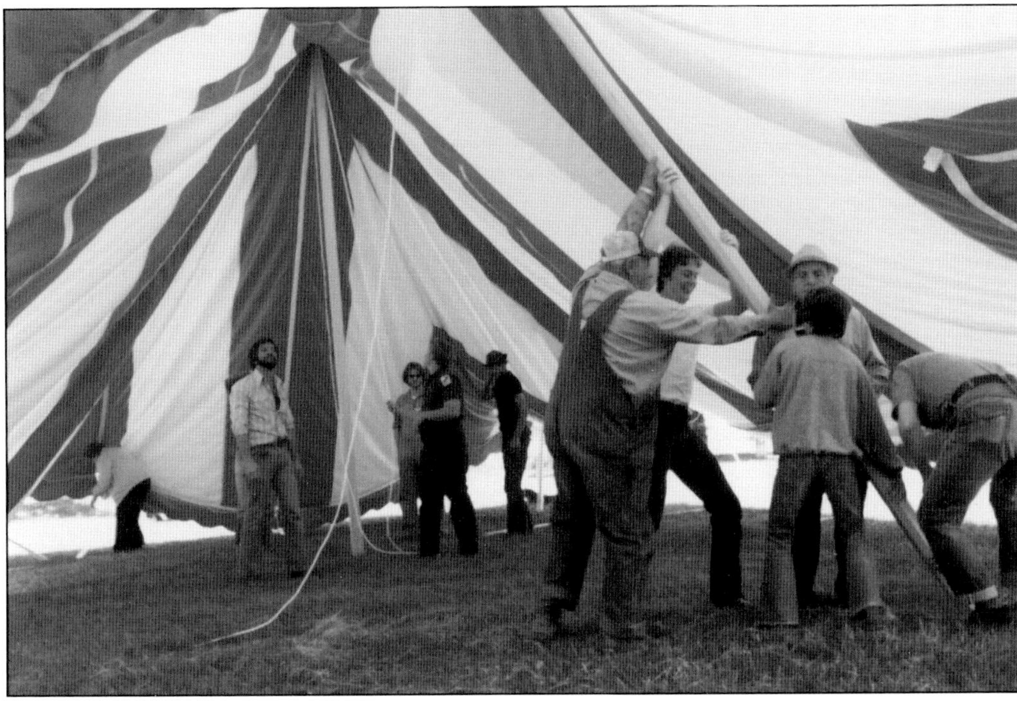

It took cooperation and a whole lot of muscle to put up the big tent for the Arrow Rock Community Volunteer Fire Department's annual Pig Supper. Clay Marsh, the bearded man on the left, supervises the effort. The fire department relies on the modest dues it collects from fire district members and fundraisers such as the Pig Supper to keep it supplied with trucks, training materials, and equipment. Below, community volunteers serve up roasted pork and all the fixings for the hungry crowds at the September event. The Pig Supper, which began in the late 1970s, was discontinued in 2010. (Images courtesy of Friends of Arrow Rock.)

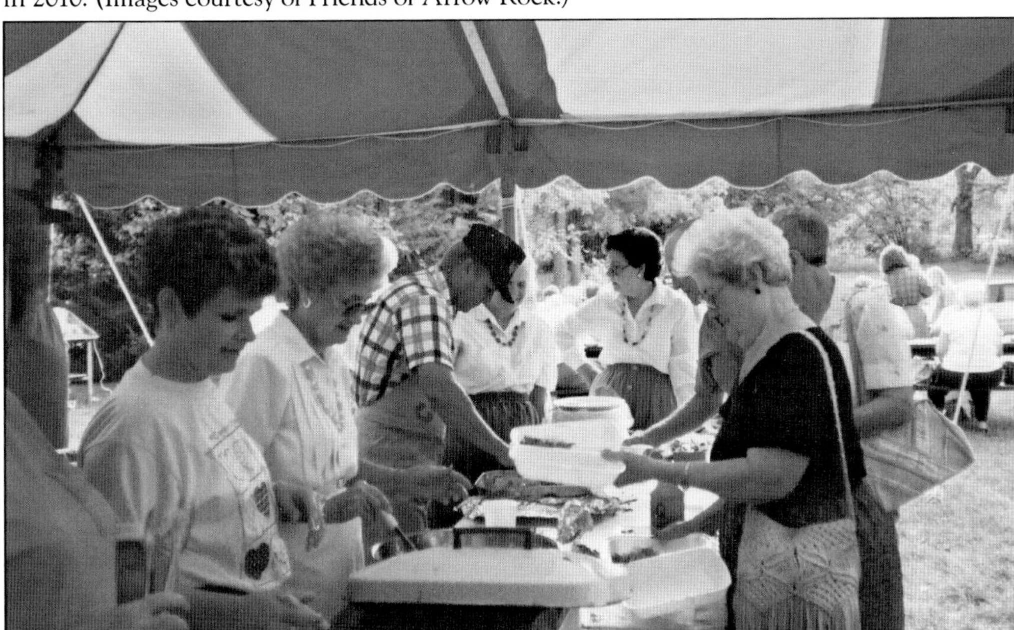

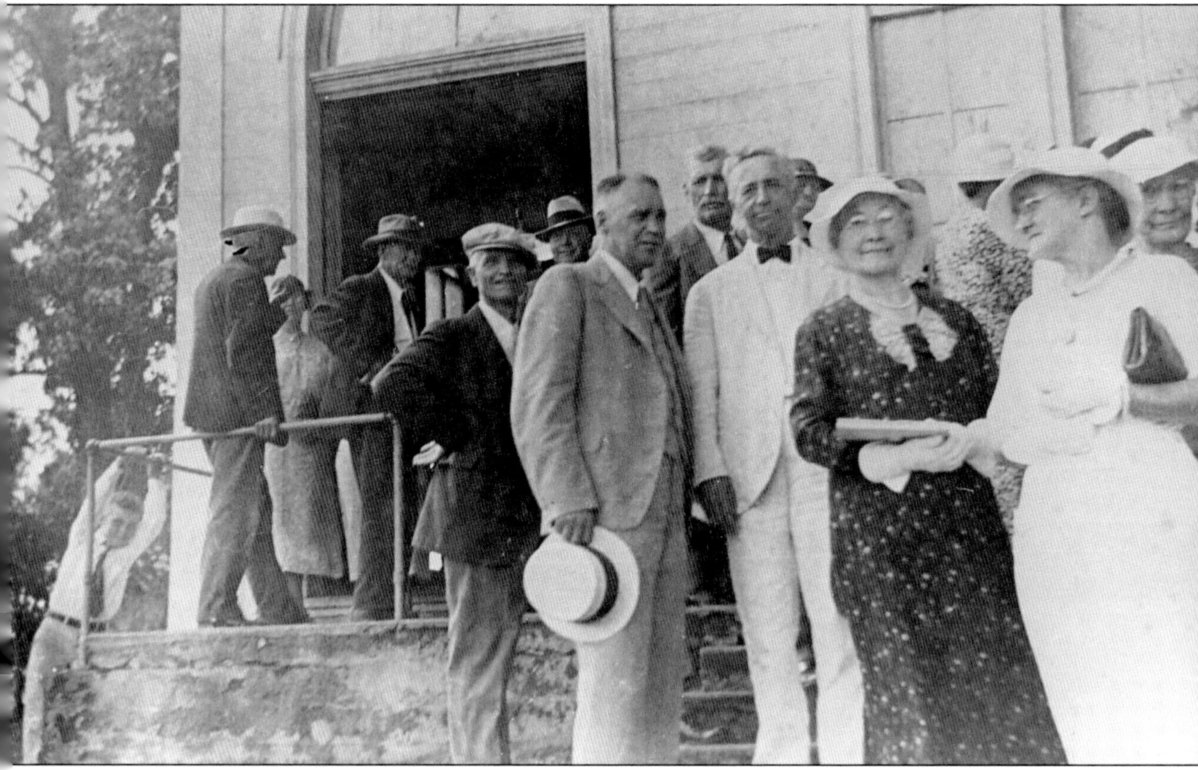

The Arrow Rock Baptist Church purchased the lot on the corner of Second and High Streets in 1853. After the first church building burned in 1872, the congregation chose a Gothic style of architecture for the replacement. In 1930, when this congregation was exiting a Sunday service and young Bill Burge was swinging from the porch railing, the church was still going strong. By mid-century, a dwindling population was taking its toll on the church rolls. For a few years, beginning in 1945, the Baptist, Methodist and Christian churches took turns holding Sunday services, but continued to toil under the burden of maintaining separate buildings. After much discussion, the three churches united in 1950 to form the Federated Church. The Baptist church building has enjoyed a robust revival as the Arrow Rock Lyceum Theatre. (Courtesy of Friends of Arrow Rock.)

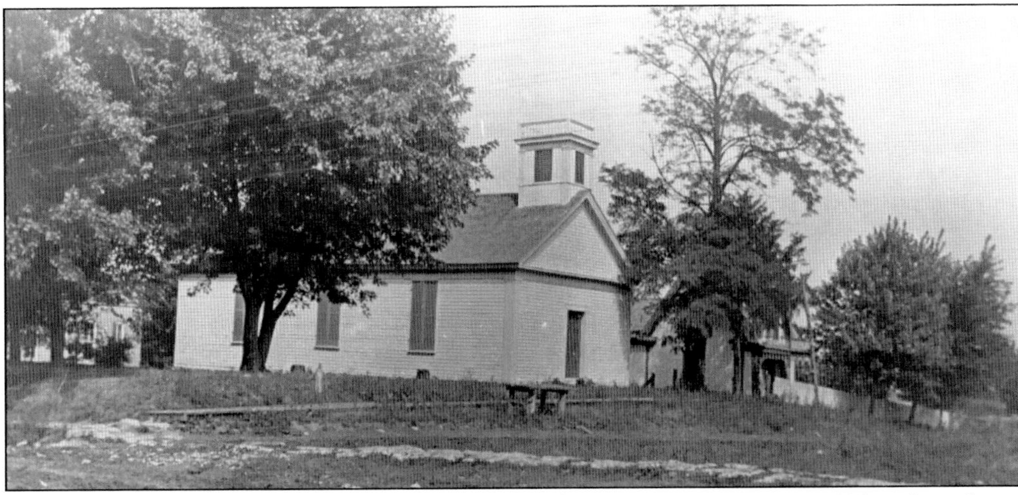

The Zion Evangelical and Reformed Church adopted its constitution in May 1899 and purchased the former Presbyterian church building on Main Street the following year. Until 1910, when an English Sunday school class was added, all services were conducted in German. The use of German was discontinued altogether in 1930, except on rare occasions to appease an older member. (Courtesy of Missouri Department of Natural Resources.)

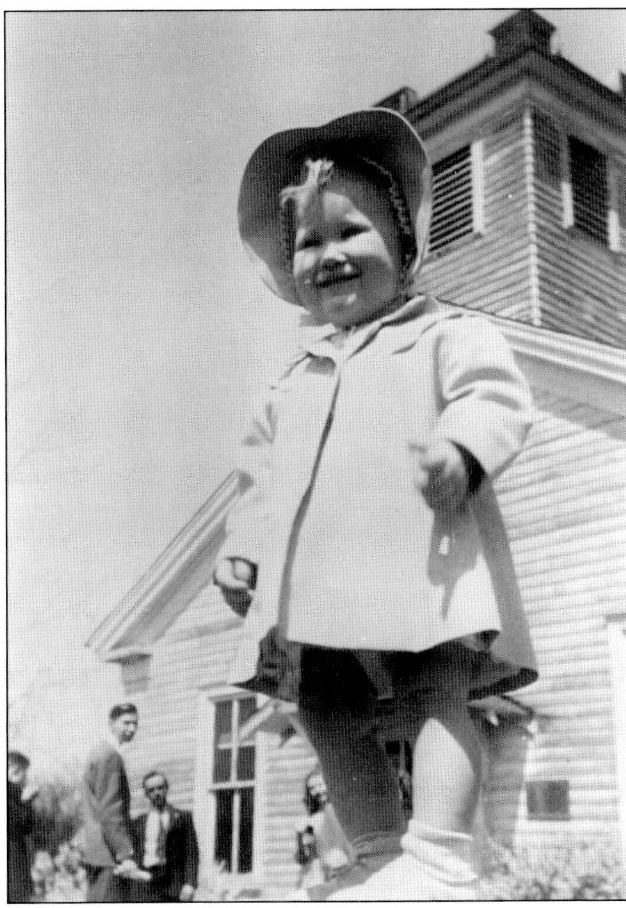

Even after three other Arrow Rock churches merged into the Federated Church, the Zion Church remained an active, independent congregation. Above, little Linda Feuers shows off brand new walking skills in front of the church in the 1950s. Zion Church celebrated its centennial in 1999 but dissolved a few years later. In 2007, the local Masonic chapter purchased the church for its lodge hall. (Courtesy of Friends of Arrow Rock.)

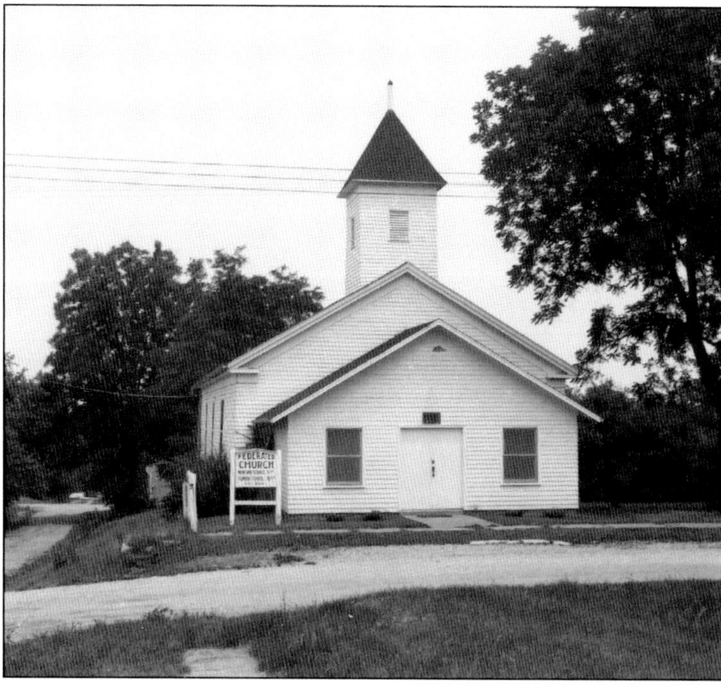

In 1950, the Arrow Rock Methodist Church building, constructed in 1843, opened its doors to the Baptist and Christian congregations. Together, the congregations would form the Arrow Rock Federated Church. Church services incorporate traditions from all three denominations. The Federated Church is the only active congregation in Arrow Rock today. (Courtesy of Friends of Arrow Rock.)

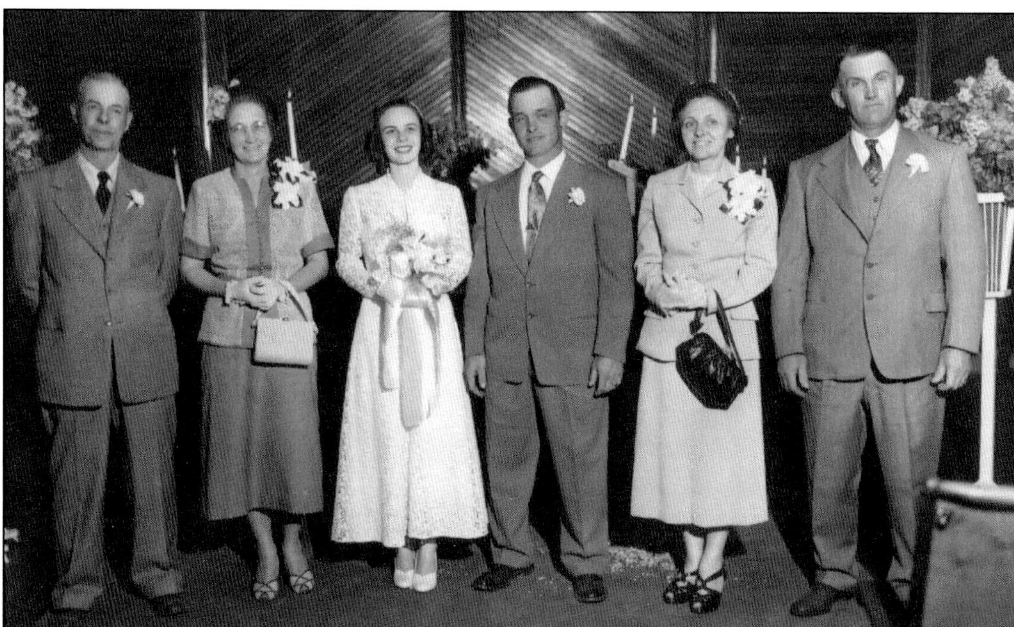

Mary Hogge learned about the concept of federated churches while studying at the University of Missouri and brought the idea home to Arrow Rock. It is appropriate then that hers was the first wedding held at the Arrow Rock Federated Church. From left to right are Albert Hogge, Mary Hogge, Mary Hogge Burge, William Burge, Ruth Burge, and Lynn Burge. (Courtesy of Mary Burge.)

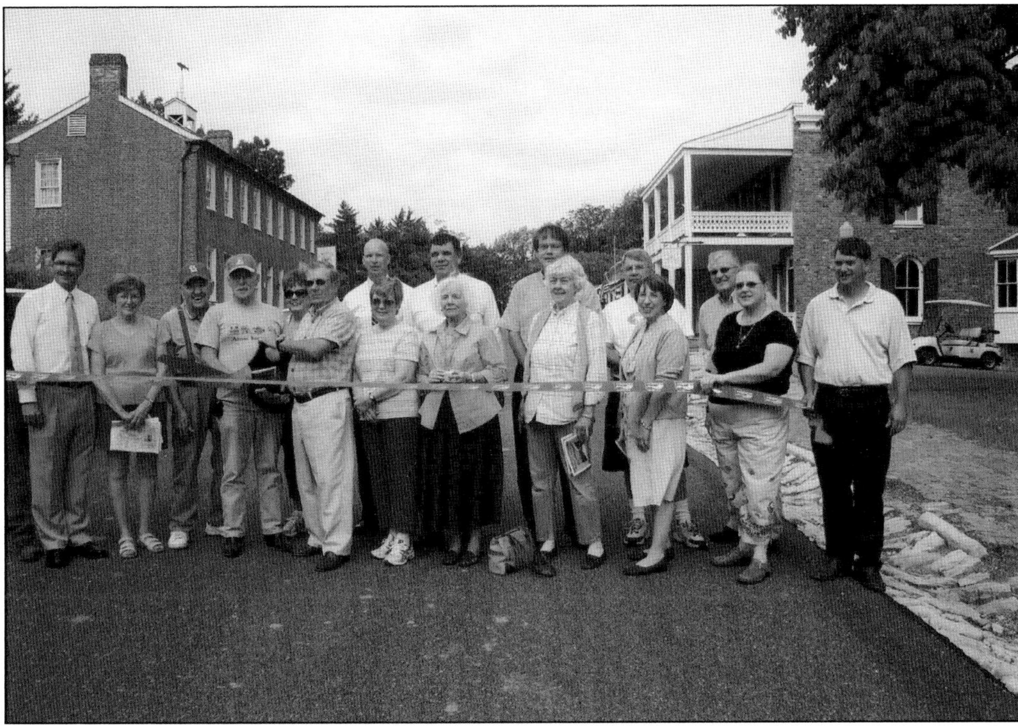

In 2007, the Missouri Department of Transportation repaved Arrow Rock's Main Street, then turned the street over to the town for future maintenance. Members of the town board, other Arrow Rock citizens, and Missouri Department of Transportation officials gathered for a ribbon-cutting ceremony to mark completion of the project. (Courtesy of Mary Burge.)

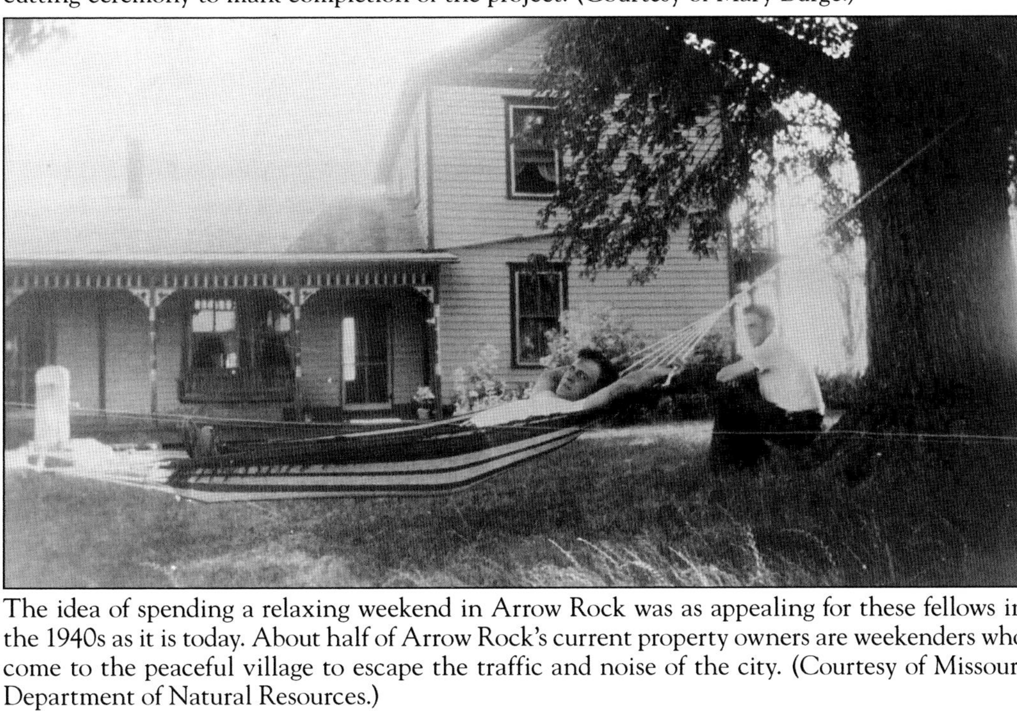

The idea of spending a relaxing weekend in Arrow Rock was as appealing for these fellows in the 1940s as it is today. About half of Arrow Rock's current property owners are weekenders who come to the peaceful village to escape the traffic and noise of the city. (Courtesy of Missouri Department of Natural Resources.)

Bibliography

Dickey, Michael. *Arrow Rock: Crossroads of the Missouri Frontier.* Arrow Rock, MO: Friends of Arrow Rock, Inc., 2004.

Fisher, Virginia Lee, et al. *Arrow Rock Places: The Architecture and Environs of Arrow Rock, Missouri, A National Historic Landmark.* Arrow Rock, MO: Historic Arrow Rock Council, 1988.

Gentzler, Lynn Wolf, ed. and Roger E. Robinson, comp. *"But I Forget That I Am A Painter and Not a Politician": The Letters of George Caleb Bingham.* Columbia, MO: State Historical Society of Missouri, 2011.

Hamilton, Jean Tyree. *Arrow Rock: Where Wheels Started West*, rev. ed. Marshall, MO: Friends of Arrow Rock, Inc., 1972.

Pheiffer, Abigail, Leah Gallo and Shane Epping. *Arrow Rock: Where the Past is the Future.* Columbia, MO: School of Journalism, University of Missouri, 2008.

Phillips, Authorene Wilson. *Arrow Rock: The Story of a Missouri Village.* Columbia, MO: University of Missouri Press, 2005.

Prouse, Marcia Joy, ed. *Arrow Rock: 20th Century Frontier Town.* Columbia, MO: School of Journalism, University of Missouri, 1981.

Rainey, T.C. *Along the Old Trail: Pioneer Sketches of Arrow Rock and Vicinity.* Marshall, MO: Marshall Chapter, Daughters of the American Revolution, 1914.

About the Friends of Arrow Rock

The mission of the Friends of Arrow Rock is to share the Missouri frontier experience with current and future generations. As stewards of its history, the Friends of Arrow Rock safeguard the memories of the village by preserving its buildings and artifacts. Through exhibits and educational programs, the Friends of Arrow Rock convey the history of the area to children and adults, grounding them in the past to prepare them for the future. Learn more at www.friendsofarrowrock.org.

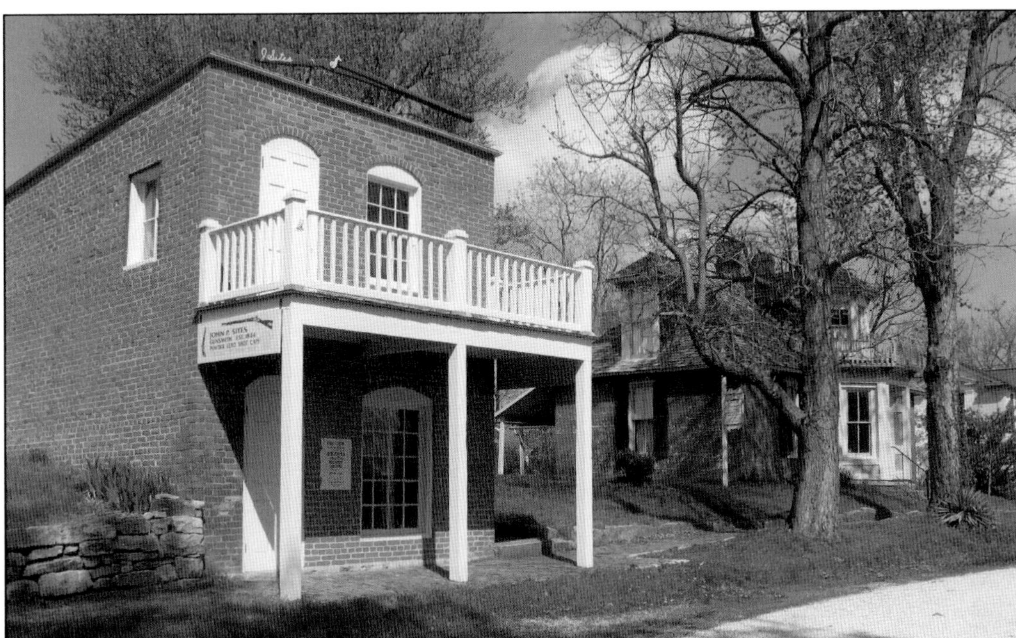

The Sites Gun Shop, on left, and the Sites House are two of the 13 properties owned and maintained by the Friends of Arrow Rock. These two historic buildings contain extensive collections of artifacts and furnishings that are authentic to the period, and are open to the public for tours and educational events. (Courtesy of Friends of Arrow Rock.)